Make College Yours

Mindsets and Methods for College Success

Development Edition

by Layli Liss

with additional contributions
by Neil Liss and Karl Meiner

Make College Yours

ISBN: 978-1-943536-58-0

Development Edition 0.9 (Fall 2019)

Special Thanks!

This textbook is being developed with a grant from John and Bobbie Clyde. Their generous gift supports the involvement of Chemeketa faculty in this project.

Chemeketa Press

Chemeketa Press is a nonprofit publishing endeavor at Chemeketa Community College. Working together with faculty, staff, and students, we develop and publish affordable and effective alternatives to commercial textbooks. All proceeds from the sale of this book will be used to develop new textbooks. For more information, please visit www.chemeketapress.org.

Publisher: David Hallett
Director: Steve Richardson
Managing Editor: Brian Mosher
Instructional Editor: Stephanie Lenox
Design Editor: Ronald Cox IV
Manuscript Development: Steve Richardson, Brian Mosher
Interior Design: Matthew Sanchez, Steve Richardson
Cover Design: Ronald Cox IV

Chemeketa First Year Experience Faculty

The development of this text and the accompanying course materials and faculty training is led by a Development Team of Michele Burke, Layli Liss, Karl Meiner, Nathan Pratt, and Colin Stapp. Layli Liss leads the team. More than twenty First Year Experience faculty also serve on a Review Team, providing direction and feedback for the development of the textbook, course design, and course materials. The First Year Experience program is directed by Denise Galey-Oldham.

Printed in the United States of America.

Contents

About Development Editions

Chemeketa Press uses a software development model to publish textbooks that are more affordable and more effective than commercial textbooks. This means that we first publish books like this textbook when they are fully functional and *mostly* finished, like an early release of a new software program. We then work with the faculty and students who are using the development edition — you, for example — to make improvements, correct errors, and thus prepare the book for its final publication in about a year. Because this is still a work in progress, we've reduced the price to you by 20 percent.

You can join Chemeketa Press in its mission to make textbooks affordable again by helping us finish this textbook. Do you have any suggestions for how we can make this book more effective for you and others? Have you found any errors within chapters? If so, let us know. You can either tell your professor, who will tell us, or you can contact us directly at collegepress@chemeketa.edu. When you find an error, turn to the back of the book and record it on the corrections page you'll find there. Your professor will collect these at the end of the course. Thanks for your help!

Make College Yours

Coming to college was a good decision on your part. You came here for a reason, and as long as you are willing to take college for what it is, you won't be disappointed.

Students come to college for a thousand different reasons, but almost all of those reasons come down to a single word—*change*. They want things to be different in some way, and they come to college to make that difference. Fortunately, every college of any kind is designed to bring change to the lives of its students.

Isn't this great? You want to change, grow, learn new ideas, develop new skills, possibly break into a profession, and here you are now in college, a place that specializes in that kind of change. The only problem, as you may have already noticed, is that college expects you to already know what's expected of you, even though you've only been there for a few days. It expects you to understand how class schedules and financial aid deadlines and everything else works, what it means by terms like "syllabus" and "final exam schedule," what to bring to class, who to talk to when you have questions—*everything*.

If you think that's ridiculous, you're right. College has no business expecting that from you as a new college student. Especially if you haven't been exposed to college before, coming to college is like coming into a foreign country. And even if you *have* been prepared for this by the examples of older siblings, for example, or a rigorous high school experience, being in college is not the same thing as hearing about being in college. There's still a lot to figure out if you're going to get the most out of the experience.

In the end, though, it is still mostly up to you to figure out how to navigate through college and make the most of this amazing opportunity. This book will help you get started so that you will have more success and less confusion right from the start.

The first two chapters begin with two things you really should know from the start—how the culture of college operates and how you can play your chosen part within that culture. After that, we'll look at how learning in college works and how to cope the discomfort of taking responsibility for your learning. We'll wrap things up by looking at how you can get the most out of learning with others while you're here and how to find opportunities for learning that take place outside the classroom.

Before we get to any of that, though, the first and most important thing for you to remember as you begin your college career is that you belong here. You can do this. Don't let anyone—including yourself—say otherwise. It's going to be frustrating sometimes, of course. When has learning new stuff ever *not* been frustrating? That doesn't matter. What matters is that you're here. You're doing this. You belong. You're ready to make college yours.

Self-assessment

Before you begin reading the chapter, answer the following questions. Don't spend too much time on your answer. Instead, respond with your first thought. The goal is to see where you are right now. We'll return to this assessment at the end of the chapter to see if or how your thinking has changed about these topics.

	Disagree	Unsure	Somewhat agree	Agree	Strongly agree
College professors assume students chose to pursue higher education and make life adjustments to prioritize college learning.	O	O	O	O	O
My typical schedule prioritizes college learning.	O	O	O	O	O
College professors expect students to attend every class, focus, participate, and take notes as needed.	O	O	O	O	O
I have the personal resources to attend every class, focus, participate, and take notes as needed.	O	O	O	O	O
College professors expect students to submit their best work by its due date and do so honestly.	O	O	O	O	O
I am committed to doing my best work honestly and by the due date.	O	O	O	O	O
College professors expect students to seek help if they are confused.	O	O	O	O	O
I recognize when I am confused and seek help from trustworthy resources.	O	O	O	O	O
College professors hold students accountable to due dates and do not typically announce or send out reminders.	O	O	O	O	O
I have a system to keep track of my activities, tasks, and responsibilities on a daily basis and do not expect someone else to remind me.	O	O	O	O	O

The more you agree with the above statements, the more prepared you are to enter the culture of college.

Chapter 1

Entering the Culture of College

As you'll find in just about any other situation that involves people—home, work, church, France—college operates according to certain unspoken rules of its own. It has expectations about how people should behave and relate to each other based on the different roles they have (like student or professor). It has its own specialized words and phrases. When you do something that doesn't fit the role you have, it has ways of bringing you back in line. If you don't figure out how to fulfill the responsibilities of your role, you can find yourself on the outs. When you put together these components of a shared understanding, you have a thing called "culture."

Entering a new culture is always at least a little jarring. Even going to a friend's house for the first time can be a big shock that requires you to figure out the culture of that household and shape your own behavior to fit in. *Great*, you think, *these people are huggers.* They use dorky words like "knucklehead" as terms of endearment. They expect you to wash my own dishes. When you called your friend's dad "sir," they all laughed at you and started calling each other "sir" as if it was the funniest thing they'd ever heard.

If that's how your friend's family culture works, and if you want to fit in, then guess what? You need to hug them back, call them knuckleheads, and wash your own dishes. You may call your own father "sir," but don't do that here. You need to follow *their* cultural rules, even if they're nothing like your own. Once you figure out how to fit into their family culture, it's fun to be there as a slightly different version of yourself.

Entering college can be jarring for the same reasons. You have tons of new systems to figure out—financial aid, the bookstore, course schedules, testing. People talk to you as if you understand what "FAFSA" means. You're expected to find your classrooms and be there on time—and bring a pencil and something to write on, apparently—without any help from anyone else. It's an enormous amount to process all at once. But, once you get the basics figured out, you'll find that it's exciting to be here and actively learning and discovering a slightly different version of yourself.

All glory comes from
daring to begin.
— Eugene F. Ware

You might notice that college is *kind of* like high school, or *kind of* like the military, or *kind of* like the place where you work. However, it's a mistake to treat college as if it has the same general culture as high school, the military, work, or any other culture you belong to. They may be similar, but they aren't the same. If you use the high school, Army, or work version of yourself in this new situation, then you're going to only *kind of* mesh with this environment. To really do well in the college situation, you must take it for what it is and create a new, college version of yourself that fits into this peculiar new culture.

We can't cover the entire culture of college in one chapter, so for now, we'll focus on the two most important rules for you to understand and follow right from the start:

» You are responsible for your own learning.

» You are responsible for everything else, too.

You Are Responsible
for Your Own Learning

As you already know, the best way for you to really learn something new is for you to explore it on your own, try it out, make mistakes, and then correct them. That's how you learned how to skateboard, play *World of Warcraft*, raise children, do your job—and just about everything else that's important to you. You taught yourself, more or less.

This process that you already understand is called "inquiry," and the entire culture of college is built around this same process of exploring something new, trying it out, doing things wrong, and correcting your mistakes. In class and after class, your professors will throw you into the deep end of the pool and invite you to teach yourself how to swim through new material.

Most professors offer some coaching as you splash around, trying not to drown, but if you do drown—that is, fail to learn the new material—that's your problem, not theirs. Their job is to provide you an opportunity to learn. Your job is to make yourself do all the work. You have to tell yourself to do the homework. You have to tell yourself to study new material and practice for exams. You have to look at the errors in your graded work and learn how to fix them. If you do that, great. If you don't, that's your business.

Figure 1. Most professors present important verbal information in class, from key due dates to material that will end up on a test. Paying close attention and taking strategic notes during class can help you do your best to receive and remember all the facts.

For most students, this is usually the one big difference between the culture of high school and the culture of college. In high school, teachers and principals tell you you're responsible for your own learning, but generally, they push you along, nagging you about homework, letting you take tests until you pass, giving you extra credit to make sure you pass a class. In college, it really is your choice to do the work or not. If you choose not to, that's the way it goes. You can always retake the class, take more responsibility for your learning, and replace the D or F with a better grade.

Alicia knew how to be a great high school student. Really great. She turned in all her assignments on time. She raised her hand in class. She smiled when teachers said something cringe-worthy that was supposed to be funny. Through her four years, she did well because she did what she was told. Alicia was a great high school student because she was happy to wait for specific instructions on what to think, what to write, how to write and when to write it, and became a superstar at giving back to her teachers exactly what they expected.

Now in college, Alicia struggles with how to be a great college student. She does not always get specific reminders from her teachers about what to turn in and when to do so. She does not always, well, ever, get detailed

Figure 2. Figuring out what college expects from you is a lot of work, and then you have to do it. Many students have to work just as hard at becoming a student as they do on their actual class work.

explanations for what to write. She is rarely told by her professors what she is supposed to think. Alicia has been a little shocked that her teachers often expect her to give them her opinions. She had never practiced this thing called "inquiry." Because she had always relied on her high school teachers' detailed instructions and schedules, Alicia had never had the opportunity to learn something on her own. Now, Alicia is starting to trust her own reactions and starting to learn what they are.

Other parts of this book will look in more detail at this process of inquiry, but this is something you should be thinking about from week one. We'll next take a quick look at the four steps in this process and how they might apply early in the term.

Step 1: Engage and Explore

When you are engaged in an activity, it means you actively participate in it rather than passively observe. Your attention and energy are focused. You've been presented with something interesting or odd, and you wonder about it. Or, you might be plain confused and want to sort it out. Of course, you could also have a lifelong dream to become a forensic accountant and catch white-collar criminals, so your accounting courses feel like a blast of cool, fresh air in your lungs. Inquiry requires this kind of engagement.

Some professors are quite showy and good at grabbing their students' attention. Some—most, really—aren't. Professors are not usually showy because they find the subject they teach gripping and necessary on its own, so there is no need for "infotainment." From their point of view, college is a choice and a commitment that students make, so being engaged at some level is a given.

Curiosity, confusion, or a personal drive to catch bad guys leads to questions. Generating your own questions is ideal. You own the process that way. Some courses encourage you to come up with your own questions right away, such as English and philosophy. Other courses identify the key questions for you. Still, those key questions won't always have obvious answers. To find out the answers, you explore a variety of resources which include taking notes from a lecture and an assigned reading, discussing ideas with a variety of people, practicing techniques in a lab, and visiting the library for additional materials. This is the beginning of inquiry.

Figure 3. The campus library provides access to a wealth of resources. Reference and instructional librarians offer one-on-one research help and teach students how to navigate a variety of information sources. They're friendly, too.

In her psychology class, Alicia was introduced to generations research and how generational attitudes form and influence people. It was interesting, so when her professor assigned a paper for the course, her mind floated over to it. Still, the instructions called for her to "discuss" the topic of her choosing. She asked her professor what he meant by that, and he said to find something interesting about it and share what she learned. So, the paper is not about what the teacher thinks about generational attitudes or what the textbook says about them. Alicia felt frustration creeping in. It was so much easier when she passively copied down information in high school. Now, Alicia must actively search for information. She feels panic over having to analyze her own thoughts and opinions for the first time.

Alicia shared her woe with her freshman seminar professor who pointed her in the direction of the writing center. Alicia dutifully made an appointment. The consultant she met with first asked Alicia questions about her

In a time of drastic change, it is the learners who inherit the future.

— Eric Hoffer

interest in generations research. Alicia mentioned she was surprised to hear how different generations viewed taking time off work. From there, the consultant asked about other areas of life that might be different between the generations. After some thinking, Alicia identified romantic relationships. The consultant guided Alicia to come up with as many questions as possible about relationships. Now, Alicia felt like she could start a discussion.

Step 2: Try It Out

You cannot know what chocolate tastes like unless you taste chocolate. You cannot know how much a one-minute *YouTube* file will weigh down your smartphone unless you follow the process for calculating the number of electrons needed to send and store the data. You cannot know about Baby Boomers' attitudes towards romantic relationships unless you ask a bunch of Baby Boomers about their attitudes towards romantic relationships, or at least look up survey information about them.

Armed with her questions, Alicia goes forth and discusses. Alicia asks her mother what she thinks about relationships. She chats up a happily married, greatest generation-looking couple strolling in the city park who laugh and smile through her questions. She talks to the kid who must be some kind of child prodigy that sits behind her in math. He was a bit embarrassed by the questions, honestly. She surveys a couple of students working in the library and the librarian. They all give her different points of view from different generations. Some of their ideas conflict, and some of their thoughts are deeply personal. Alicia listens to each, writing down as much as she can while they talk. After hearing what they have to share, she feels a throbbing sensation in her chest as she realizes that she, too, has some ideas worth sharing.

Step 3: Make Mistakes

Alicia really enjoyed her roaming discussion on relationships. She feels like she has got a bunch of useful information. Now, she can write her paper. She takes out her notes and sits at her laptop to begin.

The notes are rough. She had gotten so involved in her conversations that she did not write down much of what they actually said. Her memory alone can't get her through an entire paper. She looks back at her assignment sheet and now sees further instructions she had missed: "summarize, analyze, and synthesize." Also, there's something about using the college's research databases and APA format. *I am such a knucklehead,* Alicia thought to herself.

With any new effort, you will not get it right the first time, or maybe even the second or third time. Each time will be an improvement over the last, though, as you learn from the fumbles you have along the way.

Step 4: Correct Your Mistakes

Try again to do it better. Looking at her meager notes, Alicia recognized how important it is for her to pay attention throughout, perhaps even to ask further questions that clarify what her interviews mean. A little embarrassed and irritated, she went back to her mother, the child prodigy, and the librarian and asked if they would answer some follow-up questions. It wasn't hard to find new interviewees in the library.

Alicia wasn't able to track down the couple she met in the city park, but the librarian helped her with the database. She found an article com-

Figure 4. Help is never far away in the library. In addition to research assistance, libraries often have staff on site to help students use computer applications and to help troubleshoot online tasks. If you're not sure how to do something, just ask.

paring older Americans' views on love and marriage with those of Generation X. It lined up with what she remembered from the conversation as well as some ideas from class. She knew how to summarize and did so with her research notes. She then went back to the writing center two more times for help with analyzing, synthesizing, and APA format.

Like Alicia, when you walk into the classroom on the first day, it may seem like a work or military situation where your professor is in command and you and the other students have no choice but to do as you're told. When the professor hands out the syllabus, it's not like he's handing out a menu and asking you what new ideas you'd like to order. He's giving *you* the orders, telling you what to do in this class and when to do it. Your professor has all of the control, just like at work or in the military, so it sure looks like your professor must also be responsible for your learning. It looks like all you have to do is follow orders.

However, this is college, not work or the military. Following orders won't hurt, but it won't guarantee that you learn anything or that you hang on to what you do learn. For you to really learn something and make it a part of yourself, you have to—in your mind—thank your professor for throwing you into the deep end of the algebra, writing, or psychology pool. Then, you have to teach yourself to swim in that pool by—wait for it—engaging and exploring the new ideas, trying them out, making errors, and correcting your mistakes. If you take responsibility for your learning, you will learn. If you just follow orders, you probably won't.

You Be the Judge 1

Below are some typical students doing the work of college. At what point in the inquiry process is each student? Jot down your ideas. When you finish, turn to the end of the chapter to check them.

1. Leonel's professor assigns an analysis paper using academic journals from the library's online database. Leonel doesn't follow the professor's presentation on how to find articles appropriate to the assignment. He uses a regular Internet search engine instead of the library database of academic journals. Because he uses the wrong kind of sources and does not cite them correctly in the paper, he receives a C- on the assignment. Fortunately, he can revise it and resubmit. He walks over to the reference librarian's desk. After a one-on-one consultation with a library specialist, he finds better sources. He rewrites the paper based on his professor's criteria.

2. Marta is processing her chemistry class from earlier in the day. She has three full pages of notes. She compares them with material from her textbook. She locates the learning goals and review questions in the textbook and lines up the information. She prepares a study sheet by listing the questions on one side of the page and

the answers—as near as she can tell—on the other.

3. Shawn is the first to admit that he's an Olympic-level procrastinator. Knowing this, he plans to follow the advice of his freshman seminar professor and keep to a study schedule. He sets up reminders in his smartphone and they alert him as planned. He manages to follow through on his math homework but gets hung up in an Internet squabble about the greatest guitar players of all time when he is supposed to be outlining his English essay. He goes to English class empty-handed.

4. Denise has been casually filling notebooks with sketches of landscapes for years, but now that she is in college, she feels inspired to get more serious and signs up for an introduction to drawing course. Though nervous at first, during her first class in the studio, she puts pencil to sketch pad and draws.

You Are Responsible for Everything Else, Too

The culture of college assumes that a student's number one priority is academic study. Being a responsible student, one who takes learning and inquiry to heart, means that you are also responsible for managing all the other areas of your life to make it happen.

You're responsible for figuring out your educational goals, for example. You're responsible for planning your schedule each term so that you eventually have all the courses you need to graduate. You're responsible for registering for those courses. You're responsible for knowing and meeting application deadlines for financial aid. You're responsible for getting your books and other course materials before the term starts. You're responsible for knowing how to navigate the college's online learning system. You're responsible for your transportation. If you drive, you are responsible for knowing how to get a parking permit and where you are allowed to park.

But, wait, there's more. You are responsible for managing your finances, work commitments, and maybe even managing the lives of your children or younger siblings. You're responsible for managing your social life, which can include soothing your unhappy non-college-going friends when you can't hang out with them. You are responsible for getting a decent night's sleep, which can be tricky with all these other responsibilities. And, of course, you're responsible for studying. You're even responsible for managing your confusion. If you're confused, it's on you to figure it out.

Other chapters in this book will examine how you can handle some of these responsibilities. However, there are three important concerns for students as they begin to manage their time in college, so we'll look at those now. The first is to manage your confusion by learning how to get the help you need. The second is for you to work with integrity. The third and most important responsibility is for you to manage your time.

Taking Responsibility for Your Confusion

Every college in the world is ready to help you figure out how to manage almost all of these responsibilities. They hire advisors and counselors to help you make better decisions about what to study and when. They have tutoring centers, peer advisors, handbooks, and websites. Your professors tell

I am personally persuaded that the essence of the best thinking in the area of time management can be captured in a single phrase: organize and execute around priorities.
— Stephen Covey

Figure 5. Many college campuses have a writing center where students can make one-on-one appointments to get help with writing assignments. Make sure you know the details of your assignment to get the most out of a consultation. It's also a good idea to bring the assignment instructions with you.

you — every single day — to let them know if you have any questions. You're not alone when you come to college, but you *are* in charge. If you don't ask for their help, you won't get it.

Alicia took charge when she had questions about her psychology paper. She had never had to take this much responsibility for researching and creating information. She first approached her professor to get more direction about what she was expected to write. While he offered some help, it wasn't enough, so Alicia shared her confusion with her freshman seminar professor, who encouraged her to seek out the writing center. Alicia had thought of herself as a good writer in high school and worried that asking for help this early in college was a bad sign.

Nevertheless, Alicia accepted that she didn't know how to get started on a college-level paper. Her freshman seminar professor was so positive about the life-changing effects of the writing center, she had to give it a try. It turned out the writing center was the promised life-changing experience — Alicia went back twice.

She ran into trouble again when she realized her notes were incomplete, meaning she did not have written sources for her paper, just interviews. She relied on her own common sense and went back to the folks she had interviewed. Having chatted up the reference librarian as well, she discovered another ally who helped her get additional sources.

Her last challenge was properly formatting her paper. The writing center staff gave her a handout and a sample paper, but she felt a bit overwhelmed by all the detailed instructions. Out of curiosity, she did an Internet search for "APA format paper" and discovered a template she could download and use. She pasted her writing into the template, and it looked correct. The writing center consultant had warned Alicia to be careful with using online tools, so she double-checked to make sure the document looked like the sample paper she was given.

Figure 6. Most professors have rules against using phones or other devices in class, especially during a quiz or test. Your academic integrity begins and ends with honest, wise choices that reflect your desire to learn.

Alicia experienced confusion most of the way through this paper. Her own problem-solving abilities as well as her ability to ask for help allowed her to complete it successfully and be better prepared for the next one.

Taking Responsibility for Your Integrity

The culture of college expects you to do your own work and to be honest in your interactions with others. That's what you expect of yourself as well. However, the challenges that come with teaching yourself new ideas may tempt you—or even compel you—to compromise your ethics. You may feel tempted to invent or "bend the truth" to get an extension on a deadline. Without confidence in your ability to meet a professor's expectations, you may convince yourself to copy and paste paragraphs you find online instead of taking more time to write your own paper. Not owning up to your confusion and seeking the help that you need may tempt you to smuggle in a cheat sheet or snag a neighbor's answer on a test.

You can sometimes get away with this, too, because college generally works on the honor system. That is, it assumes you are working with honor and integrity until you prove otherwise.

Figure 7. Even students who do everything right can still make mistakes or miss details. Be straightforward with yourself and your professor about any mistakes you make.

Academic integrity means doing your own work, being truthful in your words and actions, and taking responsibility for your choices. Having academic integrity begins with the belief that learning and demonstrating what you learn honestly is a matter of personal growth and the foundation of career development. Learning is not a competition or a series of boxes to check off. The purpose of any assignment is to prove to yourself and to the school that you achieved a learning goal, not just to comply with rules or to avoid some sort of punishment. The goal isn't to impress others with your high GPA, it's to show that you've mastered the material needed for the degree. For many students, having academic integrity means having courage and faith. You need courage to tackle difficulties head-on and faith that your efforts will make a difference.

Academic integrity also means taking pride in putting forth your best work. There are many opportunities to take shortcuts and do "just enough." Often, you may be the only person who knows what kind of effort you put in. Sometimes, your best effort may seem way more than what is needed. Yet, academic integrity calls for you to be the best version of yourself as a learner, regardless of whether or not other people notice.

One way to maintain integrity is to remind yourself of why you are in college. Having a clear vision of why you are there can place a strong focus on your actions. If your goal is to lay the groundwork for a career, you can show integrity by making wise choices that will prepare you for the future. Any choice that keeps you from being better prepared, including all those temptations to "bend the truth," will get in the way of your goals. If your goal is to learn as much as you can, you can show integrity by not taking shortcuts or doing "just enough." Integrity honors your commitment to learning, despite the difficulties that may come up. Perhaps most importantly, integrity is about valuing yourself and the knowledge you gain. Learning with integrity is how you fulfill your commitment to your goals and get as much out of the college experience as possible.

Nikki enrolled in college to become a nurse. She was required to take a handful of general education courses first and her grades would determine her eligibility for the program. Needless to say, she felt intense pressure to earn As.

To help her focus on the big picture, she posted a copy of the international pledge for nurses on a keepsake board in her bedroom. It read, in part: "In the full knowledge of the obligations I am undertaking, I promise to care for the sick with all of the skill and understanding I possess . . . I will endeavor to keep my professional knowledge and skill at the highest level and to give loyal support and cooperation to all members of the health team. I will do my utmost to . . . uphold the integrity of the nurse." This became her personal oath as she tackled her coursework. Focusing on it fueled all her efforts, even when the going got tough.

Another way to maintain academic integrity is to take a "no-excuses" attitude. Making excuses is an easy way to lose your integrity. Nearly everybody will forget an assignment or fail to adequately prepare for coursework or an exam. Blaming the professor, classmates, your boss, family, or friends for such mistakes is avoiding personal responsibility. When this situation happens to you, own it and figure out how not to repeat the mistake.

In spite of Nikki's considerable focus, she misread the due date for an important assignment and arrived to her psychology class empty-handed. When the professor called for the assignment to be turned in, she was irritated. She thought, "Why didn't he say anything in the last class?" She noticed a few other students looked thrown off, too. One student did pipe up, "You never mentioned we had an assignment due." The professor replied flatly, "I didn't have to mention it. The due date is listed on the assignment sheet and the course schedule."

After class, Nikki spoke with the professor, confessed her mistake, and shared how annoyed she was with herself. She said that she understood it may not be possible, but she still asked for a single day's extension to complete it. The professor appreciated Nikki's honesty. He recognized that Nikki had been consistently responsible up until that point, so he gave her the extension.

Taking Responsibility for Your Time

Consider, once again, Alicia. In high school, she was a great student in part because other people helped her manage her time. Actually, other people completely controlled her time. Her teachers told her how much time to spend on each assignment. Her mother checked in to make sure she was doing her homework. Her boss told her when to show up for work. Her dog told her when he needed to be walked. She was great, really great, at following other people's schedules. Now in college, she has to create and follow her own. How does anybody learn to do that?

An exciting thing about college is that, for the most part, you have some freedom to arrange your days and weeks as you please. Hopefully, it's clear by now that while you have that freedom, you also have responsibilities. You have to figure out how much time to devote to each assignment in each course. You have to determine what time of day and under what conditions you study best. You must plan for your meals, your work, your workout, your time with friends or with your dog (who still needs walking, by the way), or even time alone. You have to find time to sleep, too, without a curfew or lights-out rule.

As a student new to college, you do not yet know the true measure of those responsibilities in terms of the hours, days, and weeks you must dedicate to meet them. But you are still responsible for learning it—and quickly. Look at your syllabus and locate any discussion of late work or missing deadlines. You will see something like this:

> All assignments are due at the beginning of the class period. Communication is the first key to our willingness to accept late work. If the student does not communicate that an assignment will be late *before* its due date, the acceptance and points awarded will be left to the professor's discretion.

This means that you have to know *ahead* of time that you will have trouble meeting a deadline. Ahead of time does not mean 11:59 p.m. on the night before it's due, by the way. To succeed, you have to raise your awareness of the time demands of college and then learn to keep track of your tasks, prioritize certain tasks over others, and create routines so that you follow through.

As you transition to a new routine, take stock of your current one and evaluate how you use your time. If you already follow a fairly consistent schedule of waking, eating, working, recreating, and sleeping, you will not experience a big shift in how you manage your time. If you have little to no routine with ample flexibility in your day, switching to a study-centered weekly schedule will be bumpy, but doable, if you keep your goals for college front and center.

Figure 8. Use a planner, calendar, or schedule to help you keep track of all the new things you need to remember. Find the tool that's right for you and, most importantly, remember to *use* it.

Taking responsibility for their own time often causes students their first big freak-out of their college career. You may keep a complete and elegant record of your weekly tasks, but then only follow through on a third of it. Following through is, of course, the bigger battle. Later chapters will discuss ways to get better at following through. Chapter 3 will give you some specific tools to help you manage your time and avoid some of the common pitfalls of time management. In the meantime, remember that the way you manage your time should connect with your growing sense of integrity and your goals for bettering yourself. Being mindful about how you use your time reflects that freedom to choose your life's path.

Final Thoughts

Having explored this first chapter, you now know you are responsible for getting unconfused, for having integrity in your actions, and for managing your time. You also know that you are responsible for everything else, too. And knowing is half the battle, right? Now you need to engage with all the focus and energy you can muster and make it so. The rest involves trying it out, making mistakes, and making corrections.

Learning how to adapt to any new culture involves trial and error. It will happen in all your courses as you take responsibility for your learning, and it will happen in college in general as you take responsibility for everything else.

Mistakes will be made—by you, by others—and that's okay. Don't let them discourage you. They're part of learning, so that means you're getting somewhere. Don't let the fear of mistakes keep you locked into what's comfortable, either. You won't learn anything if you protect yourself like that. You can't learn to swim without getting into the water and splashing about. Those little failures along the way are the key to your success, so just keep going. You will learn to float, paddle, and start to move forward in this new situation.

You Be the Judge 2

How well are these students demonstrating personal responsibility within the culture of college? If they aren't doing so well, what could they do differently? Jot down your ideas. When you finish, turn to the end of the chapter to check them.

1. Marina has a five-year-old daughter and works while taking a full course load. With careful planning, regular correspondence with her professors, and the help of study partners, she is generally able to keep up with her assignments. Three weeks into winter term, however, Marina catches a nasty cold. She has no choice but to take a couple days off work and miss a few classes. She emails all her professors notifying them of her situation. She offers to submit what work she can online and via email. Marina loses some participation points in one class, but by the next week, she is sitting in her classes, blowing her nose, and sipping hot tea with lemon.

2. Seamus is supporting himself while he goes to college. He works an afternoon shift at his job, so he scheduled early classes for the term. He has his own car, but it needs heaps of repairs to keep it functional, so Seamus takes every opportunity he can get for overtime. By the middle of the term, his work schedule has worn on him and he begins arriving late to most of his courses. He is physically present, but not so much mentally. When Seamus bombs a biology midterm, he asks for extra credit. To his surprise, his professor looks at him funny, shakes his head, and says no. "This professor is ridiculous," Seamus tells his friends. "Anyone who is going to school and working full-time needs makeup work now and then."

3. Luis has skipped a week of his college algebra class. As a college student in his first term, he is overwhelmed by the sheer volume of homework assigned in every class. Completely stressed out, he retreats to his bedroom where he watches movies for a couple of days until he starts to relax again. In an honest email to his math professor, he tells his story. The two set up a time to meet before the next class meeting, and later, with the help of the college tutoring center, Luis catches up with the algebra homework and finishes the term with a B-.

Reflect on Your Self-Assessment

You took a few moments at the beginning of this chapter to establish a sort of baseline for how ready you are to enter the culture of college. The higher your score, the more prepared you are for this new environment. If your scores are a little low, that's okay—this is likely a new experience. Now you know a bit more about what to expect. The following DIY and upcoming chapters will give you some suggestions and tools to help you become the successful, college version of you.

Do It Yourself

Here are some practical things that you can do to help get used to the culture of college:

1. Write a mission statement explaining why you have chosen to pursue a college education. First, identify what life goals you have that a college education will help you meet. Then, write a statement that states how you will take responsibility for your own learning, your confusion, your time, and your integrity.

2. Read your syllabi carefully. Compare them with each other to get a sense of what your different professors expect. Make notes about their expectations and policies. If anything isn't clear, take responsibility for your confusion and talk it over with the professor. If you recognize you will have some trouble with any elements of the class, identify the resources you can use to help.

3. Seek out your professors and introduce yourself as soon as possible. Visit during their office hours (listed on the syllabus) or make an appointment to meet outside of those hours. If your schedule makes this difficult, send an introductory email or see if they offer video conferencing. Tell them a little bit about yourself and your goals. Ask them why they teach and what they find most interesting about their subject area. Then, ask questions about resources they recommend and strategies that successful students have used.

4. Begin to manage your time. Using the course schedule which is typically included with the syllabus, identify all your major assignments, quizzes,

and exams and record their due dates in a term calendar. List any other important events as well.

5. Get organized. If you are not already in the habit of organizing your materials, figure out a system that will get you started. Get a 1-1/2 inch three-ring binder for each class you are taking, along with some dividers and loose-leaf paper. If multiple binders are too much to keep track of, then use one big one. Plan to use a little time each day to organize hand-outs, notes, work completed and work-in-progress in your binder.

You Be the Judge 1 Ideas

1. Leonel is correcting his mistake of using inappropriate reference materials. When students take the opportunity to improve on a first effort, it brings a warm smile to many a professor's face.

2. Marta is engaging with the ideas of her chemistry class and developing the key questions they answer. Her chemistry professor would be impressed.

3. Shawn is screwing up his first attempts at a time-management system. This is to be expected. If something doesn't work at first, figure out why and try something else. Shawn's freshman seminar professor is still proud of him for trying and not quite getting it right the first time.

4. Denise is giving the formal study of drawing a try. She will be operating under new expectations. To maintain her love of art, she will want to think about the new expectations as an opportunity to grow in her skills.

You Be the Judge 2 Ideas

1. Marina's academic forecast appears bright. She has a significant load to carry as she manages her courses, and, understandably, even something as normal as a common cold can temporarily knock her off track. These things happen and dealing with them in the moment rather than wallowing is a key skill. By communicating honestly and promptly with her professors, Marina makes the most of a difficult situation.

2. Seamus's attempt to balance a challenging workload with his academics deserves respect. Many students in college must work to support themselves. However, if Seamus can't find the time and energy to learn, he is wasting his tuition dollars. A professor can't reduce or change course requirements for some students due to difficult life circumstances while maintaining higher expectations for others. It is unfair to both. By deciding to go to college, Seamus must accept the responsibility of meeting expectations. He would be better served by honestly evaluating how much time he must commit to college and if it is enough to succeed. He might also want to evaluate his finances to see how he could limit his need for overtime.

3. Luis is not alone. People in college often feel like screaming into the abyss over their workload. His turnaround is no easy feat. It takes powerful self-awareness and motivation to pull oneself out of an academic tailspin, but it is possible. By being truthful with himself and accepting help, people can find the strength to change self-defeating habits. Luis will most likely avoid a similar problem the next time he begins to feel challenged by his workload.

Self-assessment

Before you begin reading the chapter, answer the following questions. Don't spend too much time on your answer. Instead, respond with your first thought. The goal is to see where you are right now. We'll return to this assessment at the end of the chapter to see if or how your thinking has changed about these topics.

	Disagree	Unsure	Somewhat agree	Agree	Strongly agree
I am aware that my college offers enrichment activities beyond the classroom, including performances and opportunities to connect with different cultures and backgrounds.	O	O	O	O	O
I am aware that my college offers free academic support services that can help me succeed in my coursework.	O	O	O	O	O
I am aware that my college partners with community organizations, including local businesses, to provide students with community-based educational experiences.	O	O	O	O	O
I am aware that my college gives students a voice in how the college operates through student government.	O	O	O	O	O
I am aware that my college offers career counseling and coaching to help me find meaningful employment.	O	O	O	O	O
I will plan to use academic support services when I need assistance with my coursework.	O	O	O	O	O
I will plan to participate in community-based educational opportunities.	O	O	O	O	O
I will plan to learn about my chosen career path as soon as possible, or I will plan to use my college's career counseling service to identify a career path as soon as possible.	O	O	O	O	O
I will learn about student government at my college and participate according to my ability.	O	O	O	O	O

The more you agree with the above statements, the more connected you will feel to your college community. Making connections to the college community supports your motivation to stick it out.

Chapter 2

Making Connections

In high school, Reda moved silently through her days like a drifting cloud. She had solid attendance. She enjoyed math a great deal but rarely spoke in class. At the time, it simply wasn't in her nature to be a participator. After taking a number of years away from the classroom, she decided college would be different. She wanted more than memories of balancing home-work and her evening shift at the Nike outlet.

Her first week on campus was frenzied, and between work and class, she wasn't sure exactly where or how to connect with others on campus. All of that changed when she saw robots in the main quad. Students were racing these complex machines they'd created, and a small crowd had gathered to watch. She'd never taken a particular interest in mechanical engineering of any sort before, but the happy energy of the students in the club was infectious. She was hooked. Suddenly, she had a new reason to get to campus each day.

Reda's story is a common one—except perhaps for the robot part. On any college campus, you'll find a broad range of activities and opportunities outside the classroom. The beauty of these opportunities is that many of them will be unfamiliar to you. They'll offer you a chance to explore and discover and expand what you know and what you enjoy. All you have to do is look around a bit and find something new that engages you.

You can think of your college community as a training ground. Class-rooms present academic challenges designed to fine-tune your critical thinking to solve increasingly more complex problems. Similarly, on-campus organizations allow you to work together with other students and professors in pursuit of a common goal. Off-campus opportunities give you a way to learn from professionals in a variety of businesses and governmental organi-zations.

This chapter offers you some general directions for places to explore outside the classroom. Some of these opportunities will help you inside the classroom as you add them to your support network. However, many will lead you away from school and into your community and profession—the places where you'll spend most of your time after college. It may take some time and effort to feel comfortable finding and establishing these new con-nections, but you will find that it is energy well spent.

Figure 1. Students can be involved in activity at their college in so many ways. Most student resources and services have offices on campus, so finding ways to connect is just a few steps away.

Making Campus Connections

Building relationships on a college campus takes initiative. As this book points out in nearly every chapter, you're responsible for your learning and just about everything else. When it comes to making connections on campus, you're responsible for making those, too. Fortunately, there are plenty of people on campus who also want to connect with you, so even a little bit of initiative will go a long way. Once you begin to connect to the people, resources, and opportunities on campus, it gets easier to keep making connections.

Academic Resources

The first connections that every student should start to make are with the college's academic resources. Academic resources include general tutoring for most subjects and the college library. There are also more specialized places like the campus writing center and math learning center. These resources offer excellent help from successful students and often actual professors.

Your professors and advisor will certainly help you to find these resources, but don't forget that the information is also posted on your college's website—just start surfing it a bit. Most schools have a "student services" section or something similar on their site. You'll be amazed at all the academic support that's available. You'll also be amazed at the cost for this support—nothing. In almost all cases, it's already been paid for by your tuition and the support of taxpayers. All you have to do is use it.

If you haven't found what you're looking for on the website or from your professors, you can get help finding what you're looking for from living human people, too. You'll find them in the library at the reference desk and in the campus information centers, which are usually located near other student services like the business office or the counseling center.

> The greatness of a community is most accurately measured by the compassionate actions of its members.
> — Coretta Scott King

Student Organizations

On any college campus, student organizations provide many opportunities for you to explore new topics and activities. Some of these organizations are clubs that focus on a common interest. Some are service organizations that pursue a common mission.

In the first few weeks of the school year, many student organizations showcase what they have to offer through club fairs and information sessions. Try to take time between or after your classes to see what opportunities are out there. All of these clubs present unique opportunities, but they have something in common—they allow you to build positive, meaningful relationships with others in the college community. These relationships help form another layer of support. They give you a place to learn from others who will encourage and support you, just as you will encourage and support them.

After the first few weeks of the college year, you can still explore all the student organization options by visiting the student life section of the college website. This is your one-stop superstore for finding student clubs that engage you.

Most student clubs are more topical than competitive. Some are narrowly focused, like a science fiction club. Others are cultural in nature, and some focus on contemporary social issues like mental health. You'll find clubs that explore the arts: dance, theater, or ceramics. Some may involve more unconventional activities like knitting sweaters for trees—yes, it's a real thing—quidditch, or bungee jumping. More than anything, these groups bring together people who share some common interests.

An important student group that often leads to valuable connections, not just on campus but in the professional world, is your school's honor society. Groups like Phi Theta Kappa accept members who achieve and maintain a

Figure 2. Student government is a great way to get involved with issues around your campus. Help lead the way to a better experience for future students by engaging with the student associations on your campus that impact students' well-being.

certain GPA. Being able to include your membership in an organization like this can improve your résumé, too.

Your campus' multicultural center is another student-focused gateway to the world. This group provides multicultural education to the campus community through student engagement. You will find events throughout the year, such as movie nights and conversation tables, that support the diverse cultures making up your college and the surrounding community.

What if you don't find the club you are looking for? Maybe you wanted to find a club for cooking Italian food or doing origami. The good news is that most colleges have a well-defined process for forming clubs —which often includes some initial funding. There is paperwork involved and hoops to jump through, of course, just as you'll find in any organization. However, most colleges keep the process fairly straightforward when it comes to student organizations. Your college's website can help point you to someone who can help you start or reactivate a club, usually through student services.

Student Government

Student government is a campus group that plays an important role in the college. In this organization, students work together to ensure that student voices are considered in matters that affect the college. This includes issues like courses and curriculum, work in promoting diversity, campus events, and promoting student well-being throughout the college experience.

Student government is intentionally organized to include as many campus voices as possible. Most student governments have specific representatives for a variety of student groups. There are veteran, athletic, multicultural, international, and disability services representatives. These reps try to provide a voice for a broad spectrum of student needs.

Karl learned a great deal about leadership by participating in student government. For two years, he worked with a wide range of students in matters that impacted all college community members. During his first year in student government, he helped organize a Halloween dance where the proceeds went towards enhancing the student recreation center. He also sat in on a couple of meetings with the Board of Education where student fees were being decided for the next academic year.

During his second year, he took on a leadership role. In becoming a student government secretary, he learned about organizing meetings and leading team-building exercises. He also learned how to manage his time to the nanosecond. Between taking a full course load, working part-time at an auto shop, and fulfilling his student government duties, his plate was full.

Karl's student government experience made him a much more confident person. He wasn't exactly shy before he became involved, but he didn't like to put himself out there. By interacting with others at board meetings and student forums, however, he learned that it wasn't that big of a deal—and that it was kind of fun, sometimes, to be seen and respected. He even learned how to apply the skills he learned in his writing course by writing several proposals for the college's Board of Education. Likewise, he used his experience in student government meetings to facilitate group work in his academic courses.

Student government is a great place for people who want to help make the college experience a supportive, enriching experience for students of all ages and cultural backgrounds.

You Be the Judge 1

Based on the following questions, what are some possible connections you could make to build positive relationships on campus? Jot down your ideas. When you finish, turn to the end of the chapter to check them.

1. Do you enjoy friendly, athletic competition? Are you a fan of running until you can't breathe or training until your muscles contract into a throbbing painful mass? Are you a fan of practicing with a team in anticipation of an upcoming match?

2. Is there some form of art that you enjoy or want to learn more about? Are you interested in having your work displayed in a gallery? Would you like to have a short story, essay, or poem published?

3. Do you love music so much that it consumes you? Is there a guitarist, rapper, or dancer that you think is an under-appreciated genius?

4. Is your homework piling up around your shoulders? Are you so busy that you want to scream into the void?

A true community is not just about being geographically close to someone or part of the same social web network. It's about feeling connected and responsible for what happens. Humanity is our ultimate community, and everyone plays a crucial role.

— Yehuda Berg

Making Community Connections

As a valuable hub and resource in its community, your college has connections that extend beyond the borders of its campus or campuses. Most colleges provide students with many opportunities to build relationships with governmental agencies, cultural and religious organizations, businesses, and nonprofit organizations. It's worth your time to take advantage of these opportunities—as practical applications to what you're learning in the classroom, as resources to add to your support system, and as new pathways to explore.

Student Support

Adilah was coming back to school after a decade in the workplace. With a daughter now entering preschool, she decided it was time to advance her education to elevate her employment opportunities. However, going to college meant taking a financial hit. She couldn't go to school, take care of her daughter, and work the same hours she had been working before.

Fortunately, a student in Adilah's biology class told her about the college life center on campus. This department had information about and connections to many governmental and government-supported agencies. Being a student often involves making sacrifices. This means that there will be times when you, like Adilah, could use some help. The college life center on your campus can link you to an extensive network of off-campus resources that may have just the support you need.

Because some of these associations help people with children, Adilah was able to find a new car seat for her daughter. That meant Adilah had just a little more money than she'd expected, so she was able to buy the lab kit that she would otherwise have had to postpone. She also got help finding housing assistance and more affordable insurance so that her budget had wiggle room in it for her family.

Volunteer Opportunities

The help that Adilah received from off-campus organizations really made a difference for her return to school. As a result, she decided that she wanted to help others to make it through their own challenges. College had given her plenty of experience with time management, so when she began her second year of school, she was able to carve out a few hours on the weekend to volunteer some time. She helped work the phones at the child service agency that she connected with at the start of school. Adilah loved the chance to give back to the community that had supported her.

There is no shortage of places to volunteer your time when you can spare it. Doing so not only rewards you in the material sense of building a better résumé, but it is also personally fulfilling. Your college life center can help you connect with these opportunities to serve others in the same way it helps you connect with them to receive support.

You have unique skills and abilities. Do you have a knack with tools? You could volunteer some time with groups that do repair work around the community. Do you have valuable textbooks for courses you've already taken? The college lending library can help you put them into the hands of other students. Do you love to garden? The local food bank may have a place for you to help take care of their community garden. Talk to your college's outreach faculty and staff to get suggestions for places that might benefit from your talents.

Figure 3. Many student life organizations offer food pantry services to students in need. This service provides food resources and directs students toward additional information about need-based resources in their community.

Cultural and Religious Organizations

Cultural events happen all around us throughout the school year. Your campus multicultural center has access to dates, times, and locations for many of them. Participating in these events not only enriches you by providing insight and access to the traditions of many cultures, but there are also side benefits. You can experience different types of music, delicious new foods, and learn history from multiple perspectives.

Many students enjoy participating in faith-related activities. If you are interested in learning about different religious or cultural traditions, your campus ministry services and student groups can connect you with new opportunities to explore and learn. You may find that sharing holiday activities and participating in religious or cultural ceremonies can provide a spiritual and emotional boost, too, as you wrestle with academic challenges.

These spiritual connections also provide new volunteer opportunities.

Figure 4. Multicultural centers host events, study groups, and conversation tables throughout the year. This hub of activity for cultural learning provides all students with opportunities to learn from and about their diverse fellow students.

You Be the Judge 2

Consider the following students' interests and needs. What off-campus connections would you direct them towards? Jot down your ideas. When you finish, turn to the end of the chapter to check them.

1. Gus juggles a full course load and works part-time at a service station near his apartment. He and his roommates split the cost of utilities in addition to the rent, but the costs really add up. Their landlord is threatening to evict them if they don't start paying some new maintenance fees that he's added to their monthly rent. Gus and his roommate aren't sure if this is legal.

2. Malika is a music fiend. She gets immeasurable pleasure from discovering new rhythms and beats. Her favorite activity is seeing live music. As a student, her cash flow is limited.

3. Portia is an aspiring artist. She is taking introductory courses on campus, and she enjoys learning about different artistic genres. While she has found terrific outlets on campus, she is always seeking more art to admire and study.

4. Jesse has decided his guitar skills have matured to a point where he'd like to play music in public. He doesn't have the time to devote to being in a band of any sort, but he really wants to play for others.

Many faith-related organizations support their community in a number of ways. They organize food drives, they accept donations for people in need, and they run child-centered activities. You can become an asset to your community by lending your time and talents to these endeavors.

Your college likely has access to some arts organizations in the community, as well. Libraries, theaters, community centers, and museums provide many opportunities for interested students. Many arts organizations offer student discounts. Check with your college life center to see if there are theaters or museums in town that offer reduced rates for students. These resources can support your academic development and provide you with enriching cultural development.

Making Professional Connections

It is an excellent use of your time to build connections with businesses and professional organizations, and your college can help you do that. Participating in mentorships, job shadows, and professional organizations will give your future career opportunities a significant boost.

Just as your on-campus coursework helps you develop valuable critical thinking skills, off-campus professional and career relationships help you build skills for the workplace. Learning from people working in the community is also a good way to explore what facets of the professional, working world you are more likely to enjoy.

Job Shadows

A job shadow provides students opportunities to peek behind the curtain of a profession that interests them. Students spend a day or part of a day watching first-hand as someone goes through their work routine. Job shadows won't earn you any money or build much experience for your résumé, but they do offer an informed perspective on future career choices.

You may have an interest in working with animals, for example. The career placement center on your campus can help you explore different occupations that focus on animals. Somewhere not too far away, there's probably a farm that needs people to help run it or a shelter that needs someone to cuddle the kittens. The career center may also have connections to a local veterinarian's office that periodically accepts interns or people to shadow the professionals as they work.

Success is no accident. It is hard work, perseverance, learning, studying, sacrifice and most of all, love of what you are doing or learning to do.
— Pelé

Figure 5. Career centers help students find the resources they need. They can make interoffice referrals to other programs or even show students how to access community resources that aren't connected to campus.

Jayme loved animals as far back as she could remember. Her trips to the beach were never about jumping into the crashing waves. Instead, she hunted for starfish and hoped for a sea lion sighting. As she worked her way through her early prerequisite courses, she began to wonder about careers that involved animal life. At the campus career center, she learned that a nearby veterinarian office sometimes accepted students to shadow portions of an employee's day. Delighted, she followed the directions for arranging a job shadow. Jayme counted the days before her shadow in anticipation.

On the day of the job shadow, Jayme introduced herself at the reception desk and waited a few minutes until the veterinarian's assistant could meet her. For the four hours that followed, she was introduced to what a day in the office looked like. She observed the process of intake for a dog who had eaten a sock. Towards the end of her day, she was briefly allowed to quietly watch in the observation room as an adopted cat was given some booster shots.

Watching the needle made her a tad queasy, but Jayme was sold. She loved her time with the vet's assistant. Back on campus, she later took the initiative to meet with a counselor who laid out possible course pathways to accommodate her new career interest. Two terms later, Jayme was introduced to the possibility of a job internship.

Cooperative Work Experience

Many colleges offer a cooperative work experience by pairing you with a local employer. These partnerships give students an opportunity for both paid and unpaid internships. During an internship, students make a long-term commitment to an employer as they gain valuable real-world experience and build useful professional relationships.

Here's how it works: your college partners with an employer. Often, seminars are offered where students share and reflect upon their completed internship experience. Upon completion, the employer will also generally

Figure 6. The Cooperative Work Experience office puts students in contact with local businesses. These connections can become internships, job trainings, or job shadows. This work experience is good for applying for jobs other places, or even at the business where you were trained.

provide an evaluation of student development in the professional environment. If you get chosen for an internship, paid or not, the position requires a fair amount of responsibility. Paid internships tend to be competitive, so a positive, proven classroom persona is a must (you'll learn all about personas in Chapter 3).

Three terms after her job shadow, Jayme was able to arrange an unpaid internship at the same veterinarian's office. For most of the next term, she took a course seminar where she met regularly with a faculty member who helped her plan out how her professional work could fit with her course studies. Between schoolwork and her duties at the internship, Jayme had to make good use of her time management skills.

Although she wasn't paid, Jayme gained tremendous experience with hands-on training in a professional environment. Those skills distinguished her as someone who can step into an actual working position due to her familiarity with the demands of the profession. And aside from the college credit she earned by participating in the internship, she built professional relationships. Those contacts proved to be excellent resources for references when Jayme began seeking a full-time job.

Student Employment

If you'd prefer not to stray too far from campus while you're studying, your campus career center or human resource center can link you to positions that either pay you in cash or offer tuition waivers. These career centers can sometimes connect you to alumni who have connections to positions off campus as well.

Many students are also able to earn some extra cash while helping their fellow students as tutors in the campus tutoring center. If you have a particular academic specialty, you may be able to use that skill to help others and gain valuable work experience at the same time.

Noah was in Jayme's writing class. While he was interested in hearing about her internship experience, he didn't yet have the time for that sort of commitment. His course load was already packed as he worked hard to fulfill all his general education requirements to transfer to a four-year university. He also needed a constant flow of cash for gas and weekend fun.

At the campus career center, he learned about a part-time library clerk position. It paid minimum wage for him to shelve library materials and

You Be the Judge 3

Consider the following students. What professional connections make sense for each of them? Jot down your ideas. When you finish, turn to the end of the chapter to check them.

1. Moises earns As and Bs in all his writing courses. He doesn't freak out like some of his classmates when assigned larger term papers. Instead, he finds himself enjoying the process. During his second year of course work, Moises is strapped for cash. He doesn't have a car, so he needs employment near campus.

2. As she inches towards her final two terms of school, Ivanna finds herself interested in careers in both the legal system and in law enforcement. The courses she took in the history of law and criminology fascinated her. But, on her own, she just isn't sure which type of career to pursue.

3. Franklin is just plain broke. He knows he wants to stay in school, but his bills are piling up. By midterms, Franklin is contemplating dropping out because he is having no luck in his job search, and his course work demands a tremendous amount of time and energy.

4. Carleen is having the time of her life taking horticulture courses. At first, she simply enjoyed biology courses. But this soon led to classwork in the campus agricultural center. Carleen is thriving in these classes and learning from the faculty, but she feels she might be ready to take the next step and experience the day-to-day routine of a horticulture-related profession.

use his computer skills to input information into the library database. As a bonus, he gained a practical understanding of how to make the library's many resources work for him in his courses. An added benefit was the quiet atmosphere of the library helped him relax after a hard day of classes.

After two terms in that position, Noah was offered another, more advanced position at the library. There were GPA requirements he had to maintain, but this opportunity paid more and meant more responsibility. He worked the circulation desk and assisted faculty and staff with the use of equipment and technology.

Noah wasn't quite sure that he'd ever have a career that directly related to this experience. Still, he was building a strong résumé, learning valuable professional skills, honing his time management, and he developed outstanding relationships with professionals who would serve as references for future employment.

> Passion is what gives meaning to our lives. It's what allows us to achieve success beyond our wildest imagination. Try to find a career path that you have a passion for.
> — Henry Samueli

Final Thoughts

College is more than the sum of its classrooms. It is a place where you can lay the groundwork for the future version of yourself by engaging actively in the present. The classroom is at the heart of the experience, of course, but by making other connections, you're able to enrich your engagement and explore the community and profession that college is preparing you for.

Making connections on and beyond campus helps you to build support systems for your studies. It brings new people into your life — and you into theirs. It gives you new experiences. These connections can help you explore possible professions, earn a little money, and develop a résumé for when you're ready to find regular employment.

Making the most of your college experience depends on your willingness to take a bold step forward into the unknown and the uncomfortable. Working with people in a group can be challenging, even when that group is focused on a personal interest of yours. However, building these relationships and exploring these new pathways will change your life.

You'll be amazed at what you learn from these connections. All you have to do is be willing to take a few steps forward.

Success is not final, failure is not fatal: it is the courage to continue that counts.
— Winston Churchill

Reflect on Your Self-Assessment

At the beginning of this chapter, you took a personal inventory of your current lifestyle, interests, and needs. Now, take some time to look over your answers, and do a bit of surfing through your college's website. Make a list of those that can support you academically, professionally, and socially and start making those connections. Consider some of the DIYs that follow.

Do It Yourself

Here are some practical things you can do on your own to start making connections on campus—and beyond:

1. Locate and visit your college's academic support services such as the tutoring center, the writing center, and the library. Visualize yourself there, getting work done. Chat with a representative to learn more about what services they offer and how you can access them.

2. Locate and visit your college career or employment services and chat with a representative about what services they offer and how you can access them.

3. Locate and visit your student life office to learn about student clubs and other extracurricular opportunities. If you schedule allows, challenge yourself to attend at least one meeting of a group that interests you early in the term. Or, identify a college-sponsored service project to support.

4. Locate your college's events calendar and identify enrichment activities such as sport competitions, guest speakers, art exhibits, dramatic and musical performances to attend during the term.

5. Locate and talk to your student government representatives to learn about how to make a difference to the campus community through student government. Go to a student government meeting when it is an option. Find out what opportunities for participating in student government exist.

You Be the Judge 1 Ideas

1. Your college likely not only has competitive athletic teams, but also a few club sports. Students participate in running clubs, aerobics groups, and ultimate frisbee teams. Building relationships with people who share a common fitness interest is a positive way to develop your engagement in college life. Having other people to motivate you is a good way to stay fit.

2. Your college has student publications and student galleries waiting for your work. There may be courses you have to take to get published or to have your work displayed. But there are also book groups, ceramics clubs, and ballroom dance groups where only your attendance is necessary to participate. The college website is your friend. Use it to find the artistic outlet you crave.

3. It wouldn't be college if there wasn't music somewhere. Keep an eye out for student talent shows. What music courses are available on your campus for students? Maybe you should form a club that listens to and discusses the virtues of progressive electronic rock.

4. Your academic resources are waiting for you. At the writing center, you will get expert direction on composing your research paper. In the math learning center, you'll find someone who can give you one-on-one attention in figuring out how to use a new formula. Resources like this can help lessen the academic weight you feel pressing down on you.

You Be the Judge 2 Ideas

1. Gus will find that his campus life department will likely have connections to outside agencies that can provide free legal advice. In addition, they can provide direction to resources that highlight local statutes on tenant rights. Most of this information is publicly available online but navigating government websites can be as frustrating as a Rubik's Cube. The legal aid groups that your college has knowledge of and connections to can help you navigate these sites.

2. The multicultural center on campus would be a great resource for Malika. The people there have access to a calendar of cultural events that will expose her to a range of new musical experiences. Moreover, she could check with student life and the art department to see if there are local theaters that offer student discounts.

3. Portia's art professors will be all too happy to point her towards museums nearby that house interesting exhibits. These places likely have student discounts as well. The public library and local community center are good places to connect with for artistic direction also.

4. Jesse is about to build his résumé by doing what he loves. His campus life center offers a number of avenues to volunteer time. Jesse could play for kids at the local library, for the general public at a community center, or at a holiday event for a local faith organization.

You Be the Judge 3 Ideas

1. Moises would benefit from talking to the career center or looking on the college website for tutoring opportunities. Students clamor every term for tutor support in their writing courses. For some students, it is incredibly hard work. Finding a paid tutoring position may require some guidance, so it would be a good idea to get to know campus life and career center faculty, staff, and student representatives.

2. Ivanna needs to go on at least one job shadow. It is perfectly normal to have many interests while in college. Ivanna should contact campus life or the career center to see what partnerships the college might have with local law enforcement. The centers may also advise Ivanna to send emails or make phone calls to nearby legal firms to inquire about job shadow possibilities. Witnessing someone in a professional environment first-hand can help Ivanna decide whether or not it's the job for her.

3. An on-campus job would be ideal for Franklin. There are positions all over campus that need filling. It is a matter of personal initiative. Franklin should apply online and meet in person with the human resources and career center offices for guidance. He may not get his first choice, but he needs to get his foot in the door if he wants to find a job he really likes.

4. An internship would be perfect for Carleen. She should talk to her professors and schedule time with a guidance counselor for information on what types of internships are available for her. Some colleges have partnerships with local farms and other agriculture sites. Others have access to wineries in need of people with horticultural skills.

Self-assessment

Before you begin reading the chapter, answer the following questions. Don't spend too much time on your answer. Instead, respond with your first thought. The goal is to see where you are right now. We'll return to this assessment at the end of the chapter to see if or how your thinking has changed about these topics.

	Disagree	Unsure	Somewhat agree	Agree	Strongly agree
I am aware that different social situations may require different ways of interacting with others.	O	O	O	O	O
Adjusting how you behave in different social situations is important to workplace and college success.	O	O	O	O	O
I want to make a good first impression when I meet new people.	O	O	O	O	O
I recognize that my preferred ways of interacting with others might not serve me well in unfamiliar situations.	O	O	O	O	O
I can move in and out of different social situations without difficulty or discomfort.	O	O	O	O	O
I expect to feel uncomfortable in new situations, but recognize this feeling passes with more experience.	O	O	O	O	O
I understand professors' expectations for preparation and participation in the college classroom.	O	O	O	O	O
I know how to meet professors' expectations for preparation and participation.	O	O	O	O	O
I understand professors' expectations for online communication and participation.	O	O	O	O	O
I know how to meet the expectations for online communication and participation.	O	O	O	O	O

The more you agree with the above statements, the more likely you can develop a successful college persona.

Chapter 3

Developing Your College Persona

To succeed in college, it helps to have an effective college persona. The word "persona" simply means the way you present yourself to the world — the clothes you wear, the words you choose and how you say them, the way you walk down a crowded hall, and your habit of smiling while quietly complaining under your breath. As you navigate through college, having an effective college persona means presenting yourself in a way that meets the expectations of the college culture.

Bobby decided that the way to succeed in college was to impress everyone by having something to say about everything. For every question, he waved his arm like those wiggly tube men at car dealerships. When others spoke, he added his own comments to what they said, sometimes cutting them off before they were done. As the class went on, Bobby's voice rose like a DJ preparing to drop the bass. By the end of class, his persona had annoyed or offended everyone in the classroom and gotten in the way of his success — and the success of others.

Don't be that guy.

Instead, build the persona your professors expect within the culture of college. This will be a persona that makes a good impression by getting the most out of every class and working well with others.

Meeting the expectations of college may mean trying on a set of new behaviors that result in a new version of you. These will probably be different from the at-home version of you, the at-work version of you, or the hanging-out-with-friends-late-at-night version of you. Don't worry about that—it's still you. Just as you have learned to automatically adjust your persona to fit the home situation, the work situation, and the hanging-out-with-friends situation, you will soon learn to adjust your persona to better fit the college situation.

In this chapter, we'll first talk about how personas work in general. Then, we'll look at what goes into a successful college persona.

> For every one of us that succeeds, it's because there's somebody there to show you the way out. The light doesn't always necessarily have to be in your family; for me it was teachers and school.
>
> — Oprah Winfrey

Personas and Emotional Intelligence

A persona is the set of behaviors you choose to present to others. It consists of the information and actions that you think are appropriate for a given situation.

If you're having dinner with your grandparents, for example, you only give them information that you think interests them. You love them, and you know what they love to hear about your life. You tell them how school is going. You tell them how hard you are working at your job. You filter out the information about your ticket for going fifty-five in a school zone or all the trouble you're having with your ex. Likewise, you probably wear nicer clothes to dinner. You speak loud enough so they can hear you. You avoid swear words—and even normal, modern terms that your friends would understand but not your grandparents. In this situation, you become the dinner-with-grandparents version of yourself.

The next morning when you show up for work, the dinner-with-grandparents version of you is long gone. Now, you're wearing clean slacks and a nice shirt because customers will trust you more, especially if you're in the business of selling shirts. You never stop smiling. When you talk with customers, you keep all information about yourself to yourself. You only talk about how awesome the shirt is that the customer just picked up—although this other shirt, for just a little more, is even more awesome. In the work situation, this is the work version of you.

You're probably a master of personas like this. Although you have a core identity that you can think of as the essential you, nobody ever sees that full, unedited version of yourself. From situation to situation, you filter out the parts of you that don't fit. As much as possible, you dress, speak, and act as the situation calls for. From home to work to friends to church to shopping to Disneyland to—*wherever*—it's always you who shows up, but you're always presenting a slightly different persona.

Persona is one way you express your emotional intelligence. Emotional intelligence is a powerful concept that can explain a person's success (or failure) better than standard intelligence. Emotional intelligence includes the awareness and regulation of your emotions. It is the ability to recognize your emotional state and manage it according to your wants and needs. When you self-regulate, you don't do anything regrettable, such as complaining

Figure 1. Always treat the people you meet with respect. Each positive interaction contributes to the overall health and happiness of your college community. Your respect for others also helps you to build new relationships within the college.

to a customer about your lame boss who scheduled you to work when your favorite band, Wax Accident, is in town.

Emotional intelligence also involves social awareness and relationship management, which you'll learn more about in Chapter 7. You can recognize, understand, and influence the emotions of others. That's why you wait until your boss is in a good mood and get him to reminisce about his favorite Grateful Dead concert before asking him to change your shift so you can see Wax Accident at the end of the month. Switching from one persona to another is being emotionally intelligent. You are using your social awareness to "read the room" and adapting to achieve your goals.

This involves self-regulation, presenting the parts of you—along with the suitable appearance, actions, and language—that fit that situation and create positive relationships in the process. Some might look at this and say that you're being "two-faced" by shifting from one persona to another. You may even think that about yourself. However, that's not usually a fair judgment. You're only being "two-faced" when you're trying to deceive someone with a phony persona so that they will not notice if you are late for work or maybe loan you the keys to their car.

Most of the time, adjusting your persona to fit the situation is a good thing. It helps the others in that situation to be comfortable, and it helps you to get along with them. Within any situation, there are unwritten, cultural rules about what's appropriate and what isn't. If you follow the rules for dinner-with-grandparents when you are out with your friends, they will make fun of you for being such a weirdo. If you follow the rules for out-late-with-friends while having dinner with your grandparents, they will fall over dead from shock. That's why you use different personas for different situations. You are simply following those unwritten rules so you can be yourself within that situation.

To be clear, building a new persona is not about doing away with any of your other effective personas. It is also not about placing one persona above all others as the "best." It's about knowing which behaviors are most fitting for the circumstances and using them. It's about recognizing that new situations may require new behaviors. It's about growing your emotional intelligence.

Think about how this works for your history professor. She is a human, just like you, so she also has twenty-seven personas for the twenty-seven situations she faces on a regular basis. When she enters the classroom situation, she doesn't show you her at-home persona. She knows that she can't wear her oversized Hello Kitty T-shirt and soccer shorts to class. She can't swear at you the way she swears at the television during the news. She knows it's not appropriate for her to share her love poems with you, too, and thank goodness for that. All those parts of her identity are truly who she is, but soccer shorts and love poems would distract from the work of teaching you the lessons of history.

In the classroom, she instead shows you her professor persona. She will wear her workplace casual wrap dress subtly decorated with language from Elizabeth Cady Stanton's *Declaration of Sentiments and Resolutions*. She speaks with a polished, professional voice that can be heard clearly by everyone in the room but is not too loud for people who may be sensitive to loud noises. She brings you her in-depth knowledge of US history instead of reciting the sonnet that compares her beloved to a cornstalk. This is the persona that fits the classroom. It's focused on the lesson plan, and it ensures you stay engaged. If she presented her at-home persona, it would distract you from learning about the causes of the Civil War or that women were not considered citizens until a hundred years ago.

Julisa is sitting in that same US history classroom, but she's there as a student. At home, Julisa is never without headphones. She enjoys listening to music—loud music—whether she's doing homework, working out, or walking the dog. Her parents tell her to turn it down all the time, and she does for a few minutes, but as soon they leave the room, she turns the volume back up to jackhammer-level decibels. Her parents are annoyed with this behavior, but they've come to accept this from Julisa, and she knows she can get away with it.

When she enters her classroom, however, Julisa puts on her classroom persona. She puts her headphones away. For the duration of the class, she takes notes, joins in the class discussion, reads her paper to her editing group, and responds to the papers her peers have written—all without her beloved beats. Her student persona helps her to stay engaged. Even during exams, when she feels her stomach twisting into knots, she resists the urge to pull out her headphones and sink into the comforting embrace of music. She knows that it would distract her and those around her.

Chapter 1 introduced three essential expectations, or rules, that shape the college situation. The first expectation is inquiry. College expects you to grow through investigation, trial and error, and correction. The second expectation is that you are personally engaged in your work. The third is that you take responsibility for yourself and your work. In the next two sections, we'll look at how to build an engaged and responsible college persona.

You Be the Judge 1

Consider the following scenarios. Which personas are appropriate to the college situation? Jot down your ideas. When you finish, turn to the end of the chapter to check them.

1. Omar has not read the short story assigned for today's literature class meeting. He takes the first five minutes of his discussion group's time to explain the disastrous events that prevented him from reading the assignment.

2. Crystal is generally a loud, cheerful person who is known among her friends for interrupting people to make jokes. In her college courses, Crystal tends to listen actively and participates when she has questions about assignments.

3. Eliseo dislikes math more than any other subject. In his college algebra class, he thanks the professor after each day's lesson, hoping that, by being friendly, he might get an extra point or two from his professor if his final grade isn't quite passing.

4. Stephyn hates her manager at work with the white-hot intensity of a thousand burning suns. However, she smiles politely and speaks respectfully to her manager.

An Effective College Persona

Taking responsibility for yourself and your work translates outwardly to managing your time and other responsibilities such that your college work is not sidelined. College expects you to be personally engaged as you grow through investigation, trial and error, and correction. This means, outwardly, an effective college persona is one that actively and respectfully participates in the course activities.

Setting Goals

You've made the decision to attend college, which likely means you have some goals for yourself. They might not be crystallized—in fact, they may be a bit murky. At minimum, you have a goal to learn—to improve your knowledge. For many students, they have the goal of a degree and a career, a better job with better security. Whatever your long-term goals might be, you will need to set some smaller goals, some benchmarks along the way to reach them. Chapter 8 of this book will give you some practical approaches to setting goals that can help. In the meantime, it's important to always remember why you're here, why you decided to come to school. This can help you stay focused and help you pick yourself up when you fall down.

Managing Your Time

Rebecca has two children in elementary school and one of them has special needs. She learned how to juggle meal prep, laundry, family fun, house cleaning, and medical appointments around her job as a part-time clerk at the local garden supply store. She relied heavily on friends and family members to help. Once her kids started attending school most of the day and her daughter with special needs had a good after-school program, she decided to pursue her long-held dream of managing a nursery. She enrolled in college.

Before the term began, she worked with an advisor to create a course schedule that fits around her family. After the first week, she tallied up her reading assignments, math problems, and upcoming quizzes and got a bit dizzy. Then, she got organized. She drew up a weekly schedule. It dawned on her that she might not be able to work as much and still do well in school. She called a family meeting and shared her schedule of "mom's study time."

She talked with her family about reducing her work hours. She asked for their support, too. She knew that she would not be able to pull this off if she didn't have her family's help.

Nearly everyone underestimates the time demands of college. The student without the weekly structure of a job or the hectic demands of parenting feels like he has plenty of time for everything, until he doesn't. The younger student who has had his time managed for him by parents and high school teachers up until now is in for a bit of a shock. On the other hand, a student with both employment and parenting responsibilities might misjudge how much time it takes to get everything done. A working parent like Rebecca may have an advantage here, though. Experience has taught her to manage her time, as well as her children's. Her mom persona transfers well to the persona needed for college. But, she, like all new college students, needs a few pointers.

1. Attend Class

This is one of those rules that is actually written down and accepted as common sense, but many students struggle to follow it. The behaviors of a workplace persona apply here. At work, if you do not show up, you do not get paid, and you might get fired. If you are not in class, you will miss course content that matters, and you may fail.

Imagine not showing up for work for a few days with no notice. What would happen? Work does not get done, and it becomes a problem for your boss. Believe it or not, the same thing happens in college. You don't get the information (and, *yes*, you *did miss* important course content) and now you're expecting someone else to teach you the information outside of class. You have now turned your attendance problem into someone else's problem. You may even find yourself failing the course. In fact, if you miss more than three classes, you probably will. That F grade now stands for "fired." You didn't get the job done because you didn't show up.

With a traditional course, show up on time and do not leave until the last announcement is made and you've written it down. If you miss class due to illness, a changing work schedule, or a similarly serious matter, visit your professor outside of class to get caught up. For an online course, log in at least twice a week (more if the schedule requires it) to complete your online tasks and read any announcements, schedule changes, or issues that come up.

Figure 2. Your persona at home might be different than your persona at school, but the knowledge you've gained outside of school can help you to develop an effective persona as a college student.

When Rebecca's daughter was too sick to go to school, Rebecca had to miss class. She reviewed the syllabi for her courses to see what resources she could use. Most had a website with course materials posted. While her daughter slept, she read through the materials, took notes, and wrote down questions she had. She read her textbooks and did what she could to make sense of the day's topics. She contacted her professors and set up appointments to meet them later that week to go over what she missed.

2. Take Class Seriously

Remember why you made the decision to come to college. Many things will interfere with your college routine, so you may need to set expectations and establish boundaries to make the best use of your time. That means, if your sister always looks to you to babysit your little nephew when others could be doing it, you need to have a conversation with her about your goals and priorities. If your friends are always distracting you, set boundaries with them, too. Saying "yes" to school almost certainly means saying "no" to others once in a while.

It also means understanding that your new environment will not be the same as high school. Although you will take general education courses similar to those in high school, the college versions are more challenging. The courses cover more material at a faster pace. You have heard this before, but it can't be overstated: assume you will need to dedicate more time than you first expect. Don't assume your professors will regularly remind you about class assignments, accept late work, or offer extra credit to make up for missed assignments or low scores. Professors also don't look kindly on end-of-term pleas to "bump" a grade, either. Taking class seriously means understanding and meeting the professor's expectations as laid out in their syllabus.

The grades you earn in your general education courses have the same impact on your transcript as the ones for your major. In many professional fields, a recent college graduate seeking an entry level position can impress a potential employer with a better-than-average GPA. It may seem unfair, but employers will assume that your work ethic in college will be the same as your work ethic on the job. Also, many times, that assumption is correct. Your overall GPA will reflect that ethic. So, set yourself up for professional success by taking all your courses seriously.

3. No Excuses

A "no excuses" mindset will go a long way to helping you develop the discipline you need for college work, especially if you often procrastinate. Even though you might legitimately feel overwhelmed at times, justifying a missed or sloppy assignment by blaming someone or something else will set you back further. Know that professors marvel at the students like Rebecca who manage to complete their work on time and according to expectations in spite of caring for small children at home, working part-time, and taking a full-time credit load. There are always several such students on every class roster (maybe you are one of them). While professors would prefer such students did not have it so hard, the example these students set makes it difficult to listen to excuses from younger, single, childless students who complain that "professors expect too much." Take a "no excuses" mindset, and professors will marvel at you, too.

4. Stick to the Plan

For every hour in class, assume you have at least two hours of homework each week. Fun fact: this is the actual rule used to decide how much time is needed to earn a college credit by the federal government. This means if you are taking a four-credit course, you have four hours of class instruction and eight hours of homework each week.

If you are taking the recommended full-time load of fifteen credit hours, that means fifteen hours of class instruction and up to thirty hours of homework in a week. Yes, that's forty-five hours—more than a full-time job. Not all professors follow this guideline, and not all courses require that much homework. Some courses, such as anatomy and physiology, may require even more time. Even so, use this rule of thumb to set up a weekly routine with appointments set for studying.

Rebecca's advisor had mentioned this in their first meeting. She doubted it, and her first study schedule did not book that much time for homework. During the third week of the term, Rebecca had two back-to-back late nights, an argument with her husband, and a couple of guilt trips for not spending more time with her kids. She added a "days to winter break count-down" in the corner of her weekly agenda and then revised her schedule.

At a minimum, you will need to set up a term calendar and keep a weekly agenda of appointments and assignments. List all the major assignments and tests for all your courses in the term calendar. It should also include any significant events, such as your best friend's birthday, your cousin's wedding, and the Civil War football game. The term calendar is your starting point. From there, you can schedule in deadlines for key pieces of a multistep project and plan for extra study sessions to get ready for exams. Include time in your schedule to meet with tutors or visit the writing center. Look at your course calendar and see what assignments you are most likely going to need help with, when they're due, and make those appointments ahead of time when you can.

The weekly agenda can take any form — from a physical book designed to be a weekly agenda to an online calendar application to a spiral note-book where you write down the upcoming week and the tasks you need to do. There are smartphone and online applications that work nicely for this. Some of them even give you points and virtual stickers for hitting a daily target. A digital calendar is a great tool because you can build in reminders that squeak, vibrate, or flash at you. A paper or whiteboard calendar posted in a public location works, too, if you like writing your schedule down by hand. Choose what works best for you. The important thing is that you take time to write down everything that you have to do *before* you have to do it in a place that you will look at every day. And, if you find that it isn't working, take a step back and see how you need to adjust it.

5. Expect the Unexpected

Okay, this sounds ridiculous, right? How do you plan for something before you know it's going to happen? Well, you've lived long enough to know that stuff happens when you least expect it and when you have the least time to handle it. So, don't skip class just because you feel like it. Save that absence for when you get the flu or have a flat tire and can't make it to class. Give yourself extra time to get to class, especially on exam days, because you never know when parking will stink or when you will get stuck behind an elementary school bus. Those cute little pigtails and Spiderman backpacks slowly bouncing onto the bus aren't so cute when that bright yellow beast with the flashing red stop sign is keeping you from getting to campus for your test that starts in ten minutes.

Stephen Covey, a well-known author and educator, spent much of his career teaching people how to be positive and successful. The online tool kit for this book offers one of Covey's methods for auditing your time that can help you best determine how to prioritize. It also offers a tip sheet with some tricks for conquering procrastination. Chapter 4 will give you more information on avoiding procrastination as well, and for good reason. Let's face it — the dark force of the Procrastinator is strong.

Being an Active Learner

Lectures, small group work, and other classroom activities all require you to engage directly with new ideas and start to put them into practice. Whether these classroom activities take place in physical or online classrooms, you are expected to be personally engaged and responsible for yourself so that everyone gets the most out of the experience.

If you use your "with-friends" persona for classroom activities, the classroom may look like a social arena where you should act as you do with your

You Be the Judge 2

Below are some ineffective college personas. What could you do differently to be more effective? Jot down your ideas. When you finish, turn to the end of the chapter to check them.

1. You just finished a grueling eight-hour shift at the cannery, and now you have to study for a quiz in anatomy that you have tomorrow. Instead of studying, you decide to skip the exam and make up for it somehow later in the term.

2. During a class session, your sociology professor explains a particularly challenging idea that has something to do with mob behavior, but it makes no sense at all. Everyone else seems to understand it, so you nod your head thoughtfully as if you understood it, too, rather than raising your hand and asking for help.

3. You skip class after a solid streak of attending five in a row because you feel like you deserve a break. You arrive a few minutes early to the next class meeting to visit with the professor while he is setting up for class. You say, "I wasn't in class on Tuesday. Did I miss anything?"

4. You have to drive your little brother to school every morning, so you're always fifteen minutes late to class, and after two weeks of this, it has become extremely difficult to keep up with all the missed material. You decide that you will probably fail the course and have to take it again.

friends — as the leader, the clown, the quiet one, the critic, and so on. If you use your "with-strangers" persona, then the classroom may look like a public space where you should act like you do in public by being quiet or comic or loud—whatever feels comfortable in that situation.

The problem is that even though a classroom has a social dimension to it, it's not primarily a social situation. It's a learning situation that's designed to teach you new ideas and skills. Your college persona has to respond to a classroom activity by accepting it as another opportunity to investigate new ideas and make them your own. That often requires you to set aside your social personas and do things that would otherwise make you uncomfortable.

The first time that Eliseo took college algebra, he treated the classroom like it was a bus that he had to take but didn't enjoy. He sat in the back of the class and texted with friends. When he had to show his work to someone else, he did so without comment. When he had to read someone else's work and respond, he only glanced at it and smiled and said it looked great. He wasn't personally engaged, and he wasn't being honest with his classmates. He got nothing out of the class.

The second time he took college algebra, he tried to at least look like an engaged student so that it would make a nice impression on his professor. He came to class on time. He sat near the front. He took notes about new ideas. When the professor told students to work together to solve problems, he still didn't want to do it because he didn't feel confident with math, but he tried. To his astonishment, he actually started to notice errors in the work of others that he knew how to fix. By accepting the classroom for what it was, Eliseo was able to make a good impression on his professor—but more importantly, he actually got something out of it.

Leaving Ineffective Personas Behind

Developing an effective college persona probably means stepping beyond your current personas and creating a new one that fits the college situation. You may already possess ninja-level skills at adapting yourself to your situations, but usually that process happens without you noticing. Adaptation takes place over longer periods of time—sometimes years.

The social personas you have developed so far that allow you to flourish within your cultural community, your family, and with your friends will stay intact. You use them as you need them. Most personas are useful and productive. They are part of your relationship management tool kit.

You do need an effective college persona today, so that means you'll have to be more thoughtful about what you're doing. You'll have to force yourself into new behaviors that fit the college situation, even if that makes you uncomfortable. Remember, this is about developing your emotional intelligence. In order to grow that intelligence, you have to investigate the situation, try something out, probably mess up a bit, and then make a correction. With practice, your new persona becomes a more comfortable way of presenting yourself to others.

A special comment needs to be made about the reality of trauma in some students' lives. Some personas arise from highly negative, frightening situations. Conflict and insecurity can spawn personas to protect and defend a person from violence or neglect. Staying as silent, submissive, and invisible as possible, for example, protects a child from a violent parent. Being self-reliant is a survival skill in a household where a parent is chronically absent or negligent. Aggressive behavior is a sure defense in a neighborhood of bullies. Always being in control is necessary if you grew up in a household with no rules and too much chaos.

Developing new behaviors with this kind of background is hard, extremely hard. If this is you and you are in college now, it means you want to leave these circumstances behind. Hang on tight to your goals and rely on the survival spirit that got you through the tough times. Trust that you are equipped to make the changes necessary.

Being Uncomfortable

It feels good to be comfortable, and that's one reason new college students will try to use comfortable old personas in the college situation. You know how to act at work. You know how to act in public. You know how to act with friends or at home or in high school or in a library. Because college kind of looks like those other situations, it feels comfortable — at first — so use those other personas and see how it goes.

However, the whole purpose of college is to change you, expand your ideas and skills, and give you new ways of working with others and looking at the world. You've had moments of change in the past, and if you recall, most of them were uncomfortable. It wasn't comfortable to go to middle school, to learn how to run the deep fryer on your first job, to get through boot camp, to have your first child, or to move away from home. Circum-

Figure 3. Asking for help may not be your first choice. If you're confused or unsure, consider the actual risks you take and rewards you get when you seek guidance. More often than not, the rewards are worth the risk.

stances forced you to stretch and leave some old ways behind. That was probably uncomfortable until you got used to being an expanded version of yourself.

In your cultural situation, for example, it may be expected that younger people must be more considerate when talking with their elders. Whether you're younger or older, you're comfortable with that. In the college classroom, however, everyone has an equal voice. Whether a student is still a teen or enjoying the rewards of middle age, everyone's ideas are invited and welcome. If you are young, you may have to force yourself to speak up around older students. If you are older, you may have to force yourself to listen more closely to younger students.

Dmitri was a first-generation college student whose family had only been in the United States for eight years. He'd been taught that if you want something in life, you have to grab it on your own, that no one hands you anything. Consequently, he grew up thinking that asking for help was the same thing as giving up. While self-reliance is certainly an admirable and useful characteristic, college culture often expects students to work together. The college culture usually expects students to take responsibility for their own confusion—that is, ask for help when they aren't sure what to do.

Like Dmitri, many people find it difficult to admit that they need help. Because of his at-home persona, Dmitri had to work hard to ask anyone, even his professors, for help with his school work. In the end, Dmitri was faced with the choice of accepting lower grades or asking for a little help. He chose to change his college persona by asking for and accepting help.

All her life, Marissa was known for her quick temper. She had plenty of triggers, and she could get set off at the slightest hassle. This affected her friends, but because they learned to tiptoe around her triggers, it didn't have a huge impact. All that changed in college. During one biology lab, Marissa was paired with a partner who worked much slower than she did. Within the first twenty minutes of working together, Marissa lost her cool. She shouted at her partner for working at such an infuriating pace. Her partner, not surprisingly, responded with some unflattering words of her own. This resulted in a blow-up that distracted them from their work, and they didn't get any credit for their lab.

Recognizing that she couldn't succeed in college with a hair-trigger temper, Marissa took the brave step to change this facet of her persona. She watched *YouTube* videos on relaxation and deep breathing exercises. They didn't work at first, but nevertheless, she kept trying. Over time, Marissa developed coping strategies by channeling her negative emotions through exercise. As a result, her college courses became more engaging and rewarding—and she got into great shape—a far more pleasant experience for her.

Being Disciplined

Developing an effective college persona is like developing the habit of exercise. The goal of being fit is a great goal that you wholeheartedly believe in. The thought of working out at the gym, going for a run, or even taking a healthy walk is appealing, too. You're ready for it. You know you need it. However, it's now up to you to actually make the effort to work out, run, or walk. That part is challenging. It's uncomfortable.

It's easier to sit on the couch and binge-watch every episode of *The Walking Dead* while gorging on chips and guacamole. It's easier to hit the snooze button. It's easier to fold laundry or wash the dishes or do almost anything than go outside for a run. If you're going to develop the habit of exercise, though, you have to do the work, and you have to push yourself to keep doing it day after day until it becomes a habit.

It's the same with developing an effective college persona. You want to succeed in college—no question about that. You like the idea of going to class, doing the homework, doing well on exams, bragging about your grades. However, it's hard to get up early and make it on time to your morning class, so maybe you hit the snooze button instead and finish your recurring monkey dream. It's embarrassing to ask for clarification from a professor or classmate, so maybe you just ignore a confusing homework assignment and wait for the next one. It's less fun to work on your homework than it is to play *Call of Duty* until your eyes burn, so *Call of Duty* it is, maybe. Unless you really push yourself to meet the expectations of college, day by day, your college persona may not be effective.

Many students struggle with procrastination when it comes to practicing

Figure 4. Dedication and discipline will take you far in college. Remember that doing difficult things is part of the process, and that it's okay to not get it right on your first attempt.

their new college persona. In many situations, procrastination has little impact on their lives, so that makes sense. Parker, for example, was a self-described "slacker" who claimed he would even put off going to the restroom because he was too lazy to get up. At home, that was no big deal. At college, it became a serious problem. Parker routinely put off homework until the last minute. As a result, he did poor work. His grades suffered, of course, but the more serious problem was that he wasn't learning much in his classes. All that tuition money, for what?

Realizing that his at-home persona wasn't working in college, Parker began to build a more engaged college persona. His first change was to use a weekly planner for the first time in his life. The simple act of writing things down helped him begin to prioritize his school work over more tempting activities like playing soccer with his friends. He made an appointment with himself to do his dreaded English assignment in the library. Once there, he noticed how as long as he just started the assignment by giving it two minutes of his attention, the friction he felt melted away, and he was off and running. He discovered the oddly satisfying pleasure of crossing a task off a list. Over time, with practice, these new habits took hold, his classes became much more rewarding, and his grades improved.

If this practice takes time, that's okay. If you work on it for a while and then give up and binge on chips and *The Walking Dead*, don't beat yourself up about it. One of the best ways to learn something new is to learn from your mistakes. So, make your mistakes, learn from them, and move on. Did you miss an assignment deadline because you didn't schedule enough time for it? Alright then. You missed the deadline. Ask your professor if you can turn it in late, and next time, schedule enough time for the homework. Did you fail a midterm because you didn't understand how to multiply square roots? Okay. You failed the midterm. Ask for help with square roots so you don't fail the next exam.

Academic integrity is another important part of practicing your new college persona. As the pressures of homework and time management rise, it becomes tempting to start cutting corners with homework. In your writing class, you might be tempted to turn in a paper you wrote for a different course or in high school. You might even be tempted to turn in a paper that you more or less copied from three or four different websites and say it's your own. You can see how that would relieve some pressure as you learn how to manage the duties of work, school, and family.

However, solving your discomfort without integrity comes with new stress of its own. You've presented something as new work of your own when it

You Be the Judge 3

What advice would you offer the following students in modifying their personas in order to achieve their potential in college? Jot down your ideas. When you finish, turn to the end of the chapter to check them.

1. Gray has been home-schooled his entire life up until college. He is accustomed to working at his own pace, free of deadlines and due dates, and that's always worked for him. Now that he has to keep to the schedule his professors assign, he enjoys doing his homework less because he doesn't feel like he's in control of his learning, and he is beginning to fall behind on his assignments.

2. Maggie begins college twenty-five years after graduating from high school. She never felt confident as a high school student, so college makes her nervous. However, she has raised three children by herself and finds it easy to talk to the younger students in the class like she does with her own children, by telling them what to do when working in small groups. This makes her feel less nervous about college.

3. Lucy is an only child, and she has always been extraordinarily shy. Part of the requirements for her writing class is that she has to read rough drafts of her essays to a small group of other students. She hates doing this. Even worse, she has to listen to the essays of other students and tell them how to make their essays better. She's not a writing teacher. She has no idea what to say. Even the thought of these peer reviews makes her want to throw up. She begins skipping class to avoid the situation entirely.

4. Damian has a hard time sitting still, but that's not how he sees himself. The true Damian, in his mind, is always on the move — running, skateboarding, snowboarding, hiking, climbing, and more. He can't bear to sit down to do homework for more than twenty minutes at a time. Reading long chapters in a textbook is out of the question. During his classes, he stares unceasingly at the clock and finds that he bounces his left leg until the people next to him ask him to stop it. He's starting to think he just doesn't belong in college and should be looking for something else to do, perhaps something more active.

either isn't new or isn't your own. That academic dishonesty becomes a barrier between you and your professor in the same way that personal dishonesty becomes a barrier in any other relationship. At a practical level, a dishonest action like this keeps you from actually learning new skills and growing from the experience. Even if it's frustrating, it's better to try and fail at an assignment so that at least you have the opportunity to learn from your mistakes.

An Effective Digital Persona

Your digital persona is how you represent yourself through your words, icons, and images in any electronic outlet. Just as you already have a digital persona with friends and family through texting and social media, you will need to develop a digital college persona to communicate with professors and class-mates through email, online classrooms, texting, and other digital media.

It won't be surprising that your relaxed, friends-and-family digital persona is not likely an effective one for college. You have to build a new digital persona that satisfies the expectations of college culture. Those expectations come down to three main qualities:

» **Purposeful:** Your communication with others always has a job to do. That job should be clearly stated in your writing.

» **Precise:** Because you can't rely on body language or facial expressions to clarify what you mean, you have to make sure that your words alone explain exactly what you mean. This also means using the correct spelling for words.

» **Professional:** The words you use to explain your thinking needs to be more formal and respectful than you would use in personal communication. This also means using grammatical sentences to explain your ideas.

Email is the main form of digital communication that you use with your professors, the financial aid department, and other officials in college. While many classes now incorporate social media and video, the main way to communicate online with other students is still through messages in an online classroom. Those messages tend to have the same characteristics of email.

To illustrate how a digital persona works, let's compare two similar emails—an effective email and an ineffective email—so you can see the impression created by those two digital personas. We'll start with the inef-

Figure 5. Think before you send an email to your professor. Write in complete sentences. Don't just fire off a quick message like you would to a friend, and be especially careful if you're writing because you're angry or frustrated about something. Use a professional digital persona in any communication with them.

fective email, which was sent from the student's private account, pup-pypup856@gmail.com.

> *Subject:* spamlet
> *Message:*
> hey prof: 2B or not 2B writing about hamlet's madness for the essay, curious maybe about what horatio thinks, hope that works cuz I'm getting pretty sick of spamlet, honestly. Didn't think this was going to be a spamlet class, thought it was going to be a writing class.

This email might seem a little extreme, but it does happen with students who are new to college and think that the digital persona they use with their friends is appropriate for their professors. Let's take a look at it point by point.

One problem is that the purpose of the message isn't clear. Is the student asking a question about an essay assignment? Is the student writing to complain about having to write about *Hamlet*? The subject line suggests that this is a message about the play *Hamlet*, but even then, by making a joke, that's not entirely clear. The message isn't precise, either. It doesn't use correct spelling for some words, and it doesn't use grammatical sentence structure for any of the sentences. The professor can tell that this has something to do with the essay assignment he's given students in his WR121 class. He can tell from the use of "spamlet" for *Hamlet* that the student isn't happy with the topic he's assigned. With no clear purpose or message, the professor will have a hard time responding.

Another problem is that this casual writing style isn't appropriate for the more formal working relationship that the student has with the professor. The professor may be friendly, but he isn't puppypup856's actual friend. They have a working relationship, not a social relationship, so the language in the message needs to be more professional. Assuming this level of familiarity within a working relationship suggests that you don't really understand the situation, and the many spelling and grammatical errors suggest that either the writer doesn't care about these things or hasn't learned them.

This message was sent from a personal rather than a school email account, which creates one final problem. The professor doesn't know who wrote this email. There isn't a puppypup856 on any of his course rosters. He might reply to the email and ask for clarification about the purpose of the email and the identity of the writer, but he certainly doesn't have to. The writer has failed to take the situation seriously enough, so no response has been earned.

Messages like this in online classrooms have a similar effect with other students. Within a class, students also have working relationships with each other. There might be more informality to that relationship than there is between students and professors, but the situation is still one where students have a particular job to do, and the communication needs to be about that. Sloppy, informal, and imprecise writing tends to get ignored, and students tend not to take the writers of those messages seriously.

Now let's take a look at more effective email and the digital persona that goes with it. This one was sent from the student's college email account, and by the way, it was sent one full week before the third essay's deadline. See what you think:

> *Subject:* WR121 10:30 - Essay 3 Question
> *Message:*
> Professor Trabue:
>
>   For Essay 3, I would like to focus on whether or not Horatio thinks that Hamlet is mad. Hamlet tells Horatio that he isn't mad, but Horatio doesn't seem to trust Hamlet's judgment. He keeps

trying to direct Hamlet to do things differently.

My question is whether you think there is enough debate about this for me to develop an argument in response to it. I am beginning to understand how argument works, but I still have a hard time figuring out whether a question is truly debatable or not.

Thank you for helping me with this.

Gabriel Schmidt

In this message, the purpose is clear. The subject line of the message tells the professor that this will be a question about the essay assignment in his WR121 class. In the body of the message, Gabriel then introduces the topic and asks his question about it—without getting off-track to complain about *Hamlet*, a play that he is also getting tired of. The message is written precisely. The words are all correct and specific. The sentences are grammatical. There's no confusion about what Gabriel wants to find out from Professor Trabue.

You'll also notice that while it's not particularly formal, the attitude of the writer is respectful. That's the sort of tone that's appropriate for a working relationship. It doesn't assume that he and the professor are buddies. It doesn't make jokes. It sticks to the topic. This creates a more serious and thoughtful digital persona for the professor to see. The message shows the professor that Gabriel is working hard on the essay and is concerned about what he's learning. It also shows the professor that Gabriel takes their working relationship seriously. The professor is now much more likely to respond with the same level of seriousness and help Gabriel with the paper.

In online communication to other students, it's okay to relax the style of your writing a little for your peers, but you don't want to stray from the task or write like you text. Even if your word choice in those messages is closer to how you talk, you want to show them that you take the class work seriously by staying focused on the work and explaining yourself clearly.

Let's end with two general suggestions that will help you to develop and maintain an effective digital persona. First, don't type angry. Keep control of your emotions when you're writing emails or class messages or even using social media within the college situation. It's a good idea not to post anything when you are angry, stressed out, or generally in a lousy mood. You're likely to come across as less intelligent or meaner than you actually are, and once it's out there, it's out there. You can't take it back.

Second, be polite. You can never be too polite. Stay away from insults or rude comments or even teasing. Even if you intend those comments in a joking way, they rarely come across as jokes. Make requests rather than demands. Say "please" and "thank you." Apologize when you discover that you've offended someone. By being positive in this way, you create a little social buffer for yourself that will help smooth over those other — rare — times when you are careless or even insensitive and write something that you later regret. In general, don't say anything online that you would not say in person.

You Be the Judge 4

Consider the following situations. What could you do differently to create a more effective digital persona? Jot down your ideas. When you finish, turn to the end of the chapter to check them.

1. It is almost midnight, and you have a psychology paper due the next day. You can't find your assignment sheet, and you can't remember what the paper is supposed to be about. You've texted your friends from the class, but they aren't responding. In a panic, you email your professor and demand an answer right away so that you can get the paper done in time. To mask your identity, you email your professor from your private email account, puppypup856@gmail.com.

2. A classmate has been annoying you for weeks in your biology course. She's always so right about everything that it feels like showing off to you. However, when the class is assigned to read and respond to each other's final project in the online classroom, she goes too far. She posts a critical — though accurate — critique of your project and rudely mentions that it "has a lot of potential," which everyone knows really means it's terrible. You reply in the online classroom by writing, "Thanks for your BRILLIANT freaking insights." But that's not enough. Then you call her out by name on your Twitter account and make fun of her perfect hair and perfect complexion and perfect shoes.

3. Because you've had the same math professor for two terms, you feel that you and she have built a strong rapport. She often smiles at your jokes. When you miss a class and need to ask which homework problems were assigned, you decide it's okay to be less formal about it. You ask her using nothing but math-related emojis and a poop emoji that suggests you will be in serious trouble if she doesn't respond quickly.

Final Thoughts

In college, it is important to take on a persona that will help you and your fellow students get the most out of your college experience. College is just different enough from other situations in your life that this will be something new and probably awkward at first.

Don't let this stress you out. Whenever you try new things, it's normal and reasonable to feel awkward. It means you're getting somewhere and that you're growing. Give yourself time. Don't beat yourself up. You're not the same person that you were a year ago, and you're not the person that you will be in a year. You're in motion, and that will make anyone queasy from time to time.

Finally, remember that everyone around you is feeling about the same, no matter how cool they look. Soon, you will get this new situation figured out and develop a persona that allows you to meet its challenges. Once you get there, be sure to give others a helping hand. To paraphrase the poet John Donne, no one is an island. We're all in this together.

Reflect on Your Self-Assessment

As you began this chapter, you answered questions related to your current persona and some of your beliefs about what is expected from a college student. The higher your score, the more likely you have an effective college persona. Now that you've learned about this subject, consider whether you might rate any of the statements in the assessment differently. If you need to build a more successful college persona or would just like to exercise yours to keep it strong, consider some of the following DIYs.

Do It Yourself

Here are some practical things that you can do to help develop an effective college persona:

1. Analyze your current personae (yup, that's the plural of persona). Think about the different social roles you play (sibling, friend, employee, band-member, doggie day care owner, etc.). Identify what behaviors you adopt that make you successful in each of these roles. Then, think about your student persona. Determine if your current behavior as a student will

work within the culture of college. If not, identify what behaviors you want to develop to be more successful.

2. Complete a time audit. Carefully track how you used your time over a period of 3-5 days. List what you did, when you did it and how long you did it. Then, code each entry with "productive" or "not productive." "Productive" means you were working towards something meaningful whereas "not productive" means you were doing something meaningless, given your college goals. Draw a conclusion about how well you use your time.

3. If, after your time audit, you learn that you have more time on your hands than you realized and you're sort of slacking off as a result, create more structure by increasing your activity. Revisit the previous "Making Connections" chapter and challenge yourself to make yourself a bit busier. If, after your time audit, you learn that you have overextended yourself, focus on the information in "Building Personal Agency" to make decisions about setting boundaries and reducing your load.

4. Prepare a weekly plan that includes enough (two hours for every one hour in class) hours to study for each course you are taking as well as time for your other responsibilities and meaningful activities. Use a physical academic planner or an online calendar, depending on your preference. If you are using an online calendar tool, set up reminders or alerts to help you stay on track.

5. Send an email to a professor following the guidance provided in the chapter. Be amazed at the positive response you receive in return.

You Be the Judge 1 Ideas

1. Omar may need sympathy for his spate of tough luck, but his excuse-making will not be welcomed.

2. Crystal is modifying her persona to succeed in the classroom. While it may be against the grain for her to rein in her personality, it is a valid effort to adapt to classroom culture.

3. On the surface, Eliseo's attempts to impress his professor may appear a bit phony. However, as long as Eliseo is putting in a legitimate effort in his math class, thanking his professor is a useful behavior to adopt.

4. Everybody is going to work for somebody who they dislike at one point or another in their life. Stephyn has implemented a fundamentally sound strategy to maintain and advance her position.

You Be the Judge 2 Ideas

1. It can be difficult to stay focused, but you can bring your course materials to work and study on your breaks. You should also review your syllabus at the beginning of the course and note where you see potential conflicts between work and school. That way you can get more studying done earlier. Finally, even if you haven't studied enough, it's better to take the exam to see where you need to study more in the future.

2. If you get nervous in face-to-face interactions, it's a good idea to email your professors if you have questions. If you prefer not to speak in front of your classmates, you can meet with your professor during office hours. In most colleges, students can also go to a tutoring center to get help from other students who have already been successful in any given class.

3. While we need to celebrate the smallest of successes, skipping class is not really a reward for attending those few classes in a row. Also, do not ever do this. Your professor is not going to set aside time at the beginning of class to personally catch you up.

4. The best option is to look ahead and schedule courses that don't conflict with other responsibilities. Unfortunately, sometimes a course is just scheduled at the wrong time and you will simply have to wait for another term to take the class. In this case, it may be better to drop the course and try again later. However, before you do that, it is a good idea to talk with your professor to see if you have other options.

You Be the Judge 3 Ideas

1. Gray could use his cell phone's calendar app not only to schedule his due dates but sound alarms at regular intervals to remind him of impending deadlines. He could also enlist the aid of his friends and family to offer him gentle, or not so gentle, reminders that he has to get his work done on time. It would also be good for him to step back from his studies for a moment and remember that although he hasn't chosen the homework schedule, he has chosen to take these courses and is thus still in control of his education.

2. In some situations, students are receptive to having an older student direct them. It may even be comforting. However, Maggie needs to be careful only to take charge when the rest of the group is okay with that. She also needs to learn how to be more comfortable being partners with other students and letting others take charge.

3. The first thing Lucy should do is speak with her professor and be candid about her discomfort. Sometimes professors can make accommodations that will make it easier for students to share their work. Most schools also have counseling resources that can help students with particular emotional challenges like Lucy's. Although it won't help this term with her writing class, interpersonal communications courses are an excellent way to get used to sharing ideas and listening to others. Eventually, Lucy will have to work with other people, so it's important for her to find help now and develop this part of her college persona.

4. In long, lecture-style courses, Damian can choose a seat towards the back and ask his professor if it is okay for him to stand occasionally. He should become a master note-taker to draw his attention away from the clock and onto his professor. He can stand at a counter and complete homework. He can also get a stabilizing ball chair to sit on if he studies at home, but he probably shouldn't study at home because it's too distracting. It's okay to take breaks when studying. If twenty minutes is his maximum, a five-minute break to do push-ups, pull-ups, or a handstand is a good idea. However, he needs to be disciplined enough to get back at it for another twenty minutes.

You Be the Judge 4 Ideas

1. This situation arose because of poor time management and a lack of organization. Start there. If you are in dire straits concerning an assignment, do not expect a professor to reply outside of regular work hours, which are weekdays, between 8 a.m. and 5 p.m. While some may be more generous with their availability, most will draw the line at responding at a certain time regardless of how much help you need. Start writing a politely worded request for an extension and specifically state when you will complete the assignment within the next twenty-four to forty-eight hours.

2. We all get short-tempered with others at some point. But social media posts spread in unintended ways. It may feel good in the moment, but a better idea is to write your frustrations down in a private journal. You are entitled to your emotions, but social media is a dangerous place to let off steam.

3. Regardless of how comfortable you feel with anyone on a college campus, maintain a neutral, academic persona in all forms of communication. Your school is a place of business. Use polite, clear, and formal language with everyone in the institution, regardless of how long you have known them.

Self-assessment

Before you begin reading the chapter, answer the following questions. Don't spend too much time on your answer. Instead, respond with your first thought. The goal is to see where you are right now. We'll return to this assessment at the end of the chapter to see if or how your thinking has changed about these topics.

	Disagree	Unsure	Somewhat agree	Agree	Strongly agree
I feel that I have a control over what I do and when I do it, generally.	○	○	○	○	○
I am aware of the choices I make and why I make them, generally.	○	○	○	○	○
I am aware of who or what influences the choices I make, generally.	○	○	○	○	○
I am aware of how self-doubt, anxiety, and other negative emotions can influence the choices I make.	○	○	○	○	○
If it is important to me, I know how to overcome negative emotions to follow through on a choice I have made.	○	○	○	○	○
When making important decisions, I try to gather as much information as possible from trustworthy sources.	○	○	○	○	○
When making important decisions, I think about what I value most.	○	○	○	○	○
When making important decisions, I identify as many options as possible.	○	○	○	○	○
When making important decisions, I identify the likely outcomes of those options.	○	○	○	○	○
I understand why I procrastinate and take steps to deal with it.	○	○	○	○	○
It is my choice to overcome difficulties with procrastination.	○	○	○	○	○

The more you agree with the above statements, the more sense of personal agency you have. With a healthy sense of personal agency, you are more likely to seek solutions to any difficulties you encounter. With a healthy sense of personal agency, the more confident you are about decisions you make for yourself.

Chapter 4

Building Personal Agency

Miriam was confused. All during class, her psychology professor referred to the handout about the final project. However, nothing on Miriam's handout matched what her professor was talking about. She had no idea what she was required to do or how her project was going to be graded because nothing on her handout covered any of those details. As the end of class neared, the professor reminded the students that they now had all the information needed to do well on a project that would be worth a third of the final grade. He asked if there were any questions because, after today, the students were on their own.

Miriam looked around at her classmates. None of them raised a hand. No one said anything. As the final minutes of class wound down, Miriam had to make a decision. Should she risk telling her professor that his handout had none of the information she needed? Should she keep quiet and hope that her professor or some braver student would see the problem and do something?

This is a dilemma of personal agency. "Personal agency" is the belief that you can take some control of the situations you face, that your actions can affect the outcomes. Miriam wasn't sure that she could do anything—even raise her hand to ask about the project—or that it would make any difference.

This chapter will take a closer look at how your sense of personal agency influences the choices you make. We'll also look at some tools you can use to exercise your personal agency and take control over unhelpful behaviors that you know can derail your progress in college.

Understanding Personal Agency

A sense of personal agency is the awareness that you can do things to achieve the outcomes you want. You're able to set priorities and goals for yourself. You can identify the people and resources that can help you accomplish your goals. You can recognize the problems and obstacles that might keep you from succeeding and then navigate around them.

Figure 1. When you make decisions for yourself, you gain more freedom and control over what happens in your life. Registering for classes on the first available day is one way to take control over getting the schedule you want.

In any given situation, all students have *some* personal agency. Even when they stop going to class because they don't think there's anything they can do to succeed, these students are acting on their own behalf, and those actions do affect the outcomes. By building a greater sense of personal agency, however, students develop higher levels of freedom and control, and that usually helps them to become more successful in college.

When students exercise more personal agency, they take control of a situation and responsibility for their own actions. That means they develop the judgment to understand the situation more clearly. It also means they become intentional and purposeful about what they do in response to a situation. However, before any of that can happen, students must have three important underlying beliefs in place—a growth mindset, an internal locus of control, and self-efficacy. The next sections will explain these beliefs in more detail.

Growth Mindset

The growth mindset is something you will learn more about in Chapter 5, so we won't spend much time on that now. In short, with a growth mindset, you believe that your skills, knowledge, and intelligence can grow with practice. With effort, you can become more than you are now.

Locus of Control

This concept was originally developed by psychologist Julian Rotter in the 1950s. The term "locus" is simply a fancy word for "location," so with an "internal locus of control," you believe your own actions control what happens in your life. The control of those results is located within you and what you do. With an "external locus of control," you believe the main control of outcomes is in external forces—God, fate, luck, or powerful people or institutions.

Figure 2. Discernment means looking at the options in front of you and thoughtfully evaluating your different options.

Just about everyone believes they have *some* power over events in their lives. They also believe there are *some* parts of their lives over which they have little or no control, such as the deadline for financial aid applications and whether or not it will rain on game day. Having an internal locus of control doesn't mean that you think you have godlike powers over your entire situation. It means that you believe you are mostly in control of your life and that the results are primarily determined by what you do.

In Western culture and the culture of college, it's generally considered a good thing to have an internal locus of control. That's why the college culture expects so much from you. It expects you to get the results you want by achieving them for yourself. However, that's not the whole story.

In many situations, such as the culture of your family, church, or community, your success depends on recognizing external forces. Participating successfully in many situations often means yielding your own control to others who command the situation. It might mean following the teachings or ideas that define that community. For example, different religions have specific requirements for getting married, and if you would like your marriage to be recognized by those communities, you must follow those rules.

Figure 3. Asking questions is an important way to gather the information you need to understand a situation. Make sure you always have enough knowledge about what you're supposed to be doing so you can complete the work.

Even in the culture of college, where you are usually expected to figure things out on your own, there are still many times where you must accept and yield to external forces. You simply can't take control of most of the deadlines in this situation, for example. Your professors also hold most of the control over your courses. You can take the initiative to negotiate changes to assignments with your professor, but you can't simply take control over the assignment instructions or deadlines and expect happy results.

Choosing when to take control and when to yield is an important part of learning to be successful, not only in college but in life. However, before you can make that decision, you must first not only believe it's possible for you to take control, but also know when it's appropriate. That's why this idea of internal locus of control is so important to the concept of personal agency.

Self-Efficacy

The third underlying belief that allows you to fully access a sense of personal agency is self-efficacy. "Self-efficacy" is the belief that the actions you take will actually work to get you the outcome you want. It is different from the growth mindset in that self-efficacy is how you judge your present skills and knowledge. A growth mindset is a forecast of what your skills can become in the future.

Your self-efficacy changes depending on what you're asked to do. If you have been athletic most of your life, you likely have high self-efficacy when it comes to sports. If you're a lifelong book lover, you likely have high self-efficacy when it comes to reading. The more self-efficacy you have, the more you are going to access a sense of personal agency. You know what to do and how to do it, so it's easier to act on your own behalf. Without much self-efficacy, you can feel helpless and possibly anxious. Taking action is harder to do with low self-efficacy.

All three of these underlying beliefs interact with each other to produce a sense of personal agency. You believe you have control throughout your life through the choices you make, that you can make good choices, and that those good choices will result in personal growth. To further access this powerful trio of beliefs, you must develop habits of mind, such as using judgment and being purposeful.

What lies behind us and what lies before us are tiny matters compared to what lies within us.
— Oliver Wendell Holmes

Developing Judgment

"Judgment" is the process you go through to figure out what to do in the situations you face. It's also known as "critical thinking" or "thinking for yourself." When you're making a judgment, it means that you are looking at all the various factors that apply to the situation — the information about what's going on and how much you can trust that information, your guiding values, the options in front of you, and the potential consequences for the different options. You then decide what to do.

When you're exercising personal agency, judgment also looks at how much control is realistically available to you in a given situation. You look at where circumstances limit your control and accept those limitations but without yielding all your agency in the situation. Letting go of things outside of your control helps build your personal agency because it allows you the chance to map out the actual boundaries of control. You don't have control over your professor's syllabus, for example. You might be able to negotiate a deadline or assignment with the professor, but you can't simply choose to follow your own internal set of deadlines and have success.

With the limitations of your control more clearly understood, there's less guesswork involved about what you can do, and that means you're better

It is not true that life is one damn thing after another—it's one damn thing over and over.
— Edna St. Vincent Millay

able to act within those boundaries. You judge when it benefits you to let your professor or the college system guide your path. Through judgment, you can understand these external forces and align your own actions with them, mostly for your own sake.

You also use judgment to gauge your sense of self-efficacy. If you're feeling generally calm and collected, that could be a signal of high self-efficacy. Feeling overwhelmed or confused are signals that your self-efficacy is low and you would benefit from some help by others with more experience.

As you consider the situation, you examine the advantages and disadvantages of different decisions. Your choice about what to do is wise when you make an effort to understand these consequences and then act upon that understanding. You may not always be correct in this analysis, and often things turn out differently than you've imagined simply because life is so complicated. Don't worry about that. Judgment is doing the best you can with what you know. The more you exercise it, the better you'll get at assessing the pros and cons of different decisions through trial and error. It's another example of having a growth mindset.

For Miriam, the dilemma of what to do about her confusion over the final project required judgment. She had to look at the situation and think about what it meant for her to be a student who is responsible for her own learning. She also had to consider the role that her professor played in the classroom as her guide through this learning experience. She understood that she had no control over the assignment instructions or deadline, but she also understood that her confusion was something she did have some control over. All she needed to do was raise her hand and ask for help.

Thinking for herself required Miriam to overcome two negative habits she has been wrestling with. The first is her tendency to automatically doubt herself and to think that the misunderstanding is her problem. She also tends to look for evidence that fits the conclusion she wants to reach. In this case, she wanted to believe that she understood the assignment, even though she was confused, so part of her thinking at first was telling herself, *Oh, you understand this, don't worry about it.*

Even in those few seconds of awkward silence after the professor asked if there were any questions, Miriam was able to consider these factors and realize that she needed to raise her hand. She believed something was wrong with the assignment sheet. She also saw that, even if she really was the only person in the class who was confused, which she doubted, her professor had asked if anyone had any questions—and she did.

Judgment is the critically necessary step to being purposeful. You have to understand the situation to think for yourself and be purposeful in your actions. Without that understanding, you begin to lose your personal agency.

Being Purposeful

Being "purposeful" means that you understand how you behave and why. You act deliberately and with a goal, or a purpose, in mind.

You may have had the experience of driving or walking somewhere without really thinking about what you're doing. Your mind wanders and suddenly you "wake up" to find yourself at work or school or your cousin's house with no memory of having driven or walked there. That's scary stuff. Scarier still is how easy it is to operate on autopilot for large chunks of the day. It's possible to drift from situation to situation without thinking about your actions.

Being purposeful means paying more attention to the situations you face and thinking about what you're doing. It means thinking about the purpose of your actions, what you are trying to accomplish, and then acting in whatever ways will best help you to achieve that purpose. If you sit down to study for tomorrow's psychology exam, being purposeful means looking at where and how to study best and then turning off the television so you're more effective.

To develop a sense of purposefulness, you need judgment. Judgment helps you to identify your priorities, needs, and goals so that you can act more thoughtfully. Acting purposefully, in turn, helps you to access more personal agency as you enter each new situation. When you do things to accomplish your goals, you build confidence in your abilities. In other words, you increase your self-efficacy. As you become more aware of what you are doing and why you are doing it, you also understand more clearly where you have control over the situation and where you don't. When you don't use judgment, you weaken your sense of agency and are guided by whims, habits, and the expectations of others—autopilot.

We can't always act with purpose, of course. It's demanding work, and in some situations, like the bus ride home or shopping for groceries, all you really need is to follow your habits. Sometimes it's tons of fun to follow whims, too. Let's not bad mouth whimsy. However, in the situations that count, it's important to act more intentionally, to slow down and judge the situation, and to make wise choices. That's how you access personal agency and follow your guiding purposes.

In the example of Miriam, she really does want to be responsible for her own learning. In fact, that's one of her central intentions for her time in college. That purpose is the main factor that gets her to finally raise her lonely hand in the middle of that awkward silence. To Miriam, being responsible for her learning means she needs to clear up any confusion she encounters in her courses, ask questions, and get help.

You Be the Judge 1

The following students are having difficulties with personal agency in light of an assignment in an English composition course. Determine what might be causing that difficulty. It could be due to a weak or flawed internal locus of control, a lack of judgment, or a lack of purpose. Jot down your ideas. When you finish, turn to the end of the chapter to check them.

1. Jennifer has been absorbed in a pun-generating competition on a social media site when her professor returns reviewed drafts of the assignment. She glances at the paper and notices her professor has written comments and corrections but does not study them closely. She returns to the pun competition and posts a head-smacker. The night before the paper is due, Jennifer finally looks at the comments. To earn the grade she wants, she will need to rewrite most of it. Now, she is really frustrated with herself. She stays up most of the night revising it.

2. Lucas looks at the feedback his professor has given him on his draft. The only comments he understands are the ones about missing commas, fragments, and spelling errors. He does not know how to correct paragraphs that his professor marked as "vague" or "needs development." A classmate overhears him mumble, "What am I supposed to do with this?" She suggests that he go to the writing center and talk to James, the writing specialist there. Lucas shakes his head, "Nah, it won't matter. Professor Hattman just doesn't like my ideas." Lucas corrects the mechanical mistakes and turns in the paper without any other changes.

3. Vickie receives her draft. In high school, her English teachers had built the writing process into class meetings and she didn't have to figure much of it out on her own. She didn't even need to put in a great deal of effort to produce an A paper. Now, she is staring at a draft with so many marks on it that she doesn't know how to process it. She had expected a few corrections, but not this barrage of comments that felt a bit like a personal attack. Ticked off and accustomed to putting in a low effort, she doesn't take time or energy to figure out what she could do to improve the paper. She waits until the night before it's due and attempts to revise it on her own.

Miriam also wants to be seen as a good student by her professors and other students. This makes her worry about drawing attention to how the handout appears not to convey what the professor thinks. If she's rude about that, then she risks offending her professor. If she's wrong about the handout, then she won't look good to her professor or the other students. When her professor sees her hand and calls on her, she doesn't complain about the handout. Instead, she simply asks, "Can you help me see where those instructions are found on the handout? I'm having a hard time finding them."

When six other students exhale in relief, she knows that she's not the only student who's confused. Instead of appearing dumb to others, she's just become a hero. By acting purposefully in this situation, she has built just a little more personal agency for herself so that it will be just a tiny bit easier to raise her hand the next time she faces a similar situation.

Changing Your Internal Dialogue

Exercising judgment and acting purposefully are habits that you will build over time. Each time you respond thoughtfully to a situation that calls for you to take responsibility and exercise personal agency, you'll strengthen these habits. However, there are also tools out there to help. We'll look at three of them—changing your internal dialogue, making wise choices, and analyzing fears.

The habitual thoughts that bubble up in your mind as you experience a difficulty can be useful. They uncover your beliefs about whether you feel in control of your situation, whether you have a sense of self-efficacy, and whether you have a growth mindset. These thoughts are called your internal dialogue or self-talk. Consider these thoughts swimming around Dylan's mind over a bad couple of days:

» Why am I wasting my time on this? I'm never going to figure it out.

» These professors think their class is the only thing I've got to do all day.

» I might be able to study if it weren't for my stupid roommate.

» Why didn't she say there would be a test today? How was I supposed to know about it?

» How can it be three a.m. already? I just started this game. I'm such an idiot.

Figure 4. Analyzing your actions helps you determine good steps to improve them, either right away or in the future.

This self-talk expresses how Dylan's mind is interpreting events. In some cases, he thinks badly about himself, and in other cases, he blames others for his misfortune. It seems that Dylan doesn't believe he has much control over his circumstances. He isn't really taking responsibility for his less-than-thoughtful choices, either, because he's not seeing them as choices *he* has made.

Dylan's actions follow from his thoughts. If he habitually thinks he's never going to figure out his homework, he won't put in much effort to figure it out or get help. If he habitually thinks he can't control his game-playing tendencies, he might not do anything to keep himself from losing time and energy the next time his favorite game beckons. If Dylan habitually blames others for lapses in his study habits and record keeping, he won't adopt more effective ways to study and keep track of his assignments. Assuming Dylan isn't satisfied with his current progress in college, he will need to interrupt the voices in his head and challenge them.

If your self-talk judges you harshly for mistakes you have made, you can feel helpless. If it judges other people — rightly or wrongly — for your difficulties, you may feel better, but you still have to deal with the difficulty. The kind of thoughts that help you make better choices for yourself are those that encourage you and recognize that a mistake is a single event in time and not a character flaw. Positive self-talk helps you find solutions to your difficulties. Here's what Dylan could say to himself instead:

» This is taking a while, it's tough, and I am frustrated. I need a break and maybe some help.

» I have lots on my plate this week. I need to adjust my schedule.

» My roommate has friends over and they are playing video games. I cannot study here. I'll go to a coffee shop.

» Whoops. I didn't record the test in my planner. That sucks. I won't do that again.

» You will not control me, video games. I'll see you when this homework is done.

In these examples, Dylan doesn't beat himself up or anyone else. He accepts his difficulties and thinks about ways to solve his problems instead. He exercises judgment about his situation and purposefully embraces the personal agency that he has.

Making Wise Choices

William Glasser, a renowned psychiatrist and educational theorist, developed a treatment approach called "reality therapy" that focuses on present behaviors and how to change them for the better. His approach soon moved from the clinic into the classroom, where it became a ten-step method for teachers to use in helping disruptive students modify their behavior. As a college student, two questions from this process can be useful as you judge your situation and act with purpose from an internal locus of control.

Question 1: What Are You Doing?

This is a question that a teacher might ask a disruptive student. Glasser believed that if a student simply stepped back and noticed their actions, then they could reflect on those actions, judge the situation, and act more intentionally—and with less disruption to others.

When you ask yourself this question as a college student, the purpose is not to get you to stop being so disruptive in the classroom but to simply step back from a challenging situation and judge that situation. What you are doing has many components to it, so instead of asking just one broad question, you might ask several smaller questions that get at those components.

What's Your Present Situation?

To begin, describe what is happening that is creating difficulties and do so with as much detail as possible. You want to capture the full picture, so you can work on a variety of solutions.

To illustrate, we'll look at Tamara's situation. She lives with her mom, dad, and younger brother. The family doesn't have much money. Her mom cares for a few young children in her home while her dad works long hours at the local food processing company. They have one car. Tamara's dad allows her to take the car to campus as long as she takes him to work first. That generally works. However, at least once a week, getting him to work means she doesn't get to class on time because he refuses to get to work earlier than

Figure 5. Some options—like using a bike for transportation—might become a wise choice after you thoughtfully analyze their benefits.

he needs to. She has missed twenty to thirty minutes of class each week for several weeks, and it is starting to have a real impact on her learning. However, her dad isn't willing to arrive early. He thinks he's already doing her a favor by allowing her to have the car this much.

What's Your Goal for This Situation?

With this step, you clearly state what you want to happen instead of what is happening. Tamara wants to be able to get to school on time. She wants to maintain a positive relationship with her dad. Tamara also wants to be able to drive herself to campus because it gives her control over her day. She doesn't take public transportation because she does not like being forced to follow a rigid schedule. She also does not want to spend sixty dollars per month for a bus pass.

Is There a Problem or an Obstacle?

This is important. To exercise agency over any situation, you have to be able to identify what is in your way. These can be external obstacles, such as a father who believes his work schedule is more important than his daughter's school schedule or the cost of a bus pass. Obstacles are internal as well, such as not wanting to be controlled by the bus schedule. Tamara has to figure out how to overcome these obstacles if she is going to get to school on time.

What Are You Doing to Achieve That Goal?

You are already exercising some kind of agency over the situation. You're making choices, even if you are not yet doing anything. What choices have you made? Tamara chooses to miss parts of class every week because she wants to use the family car and she can't change her father's behavior. She visits her professor during office hours to find out what she's missed. That helps, but it is not ideal.

Figure 6. Some programs give students the opportunity to study in a real-world environment. Hands-on experience is one way to determine if a career is right for you. In this example, you also get to read about bugs.

What Else Can You Do?

This is where you want to free your thinking as much as possible. You want to keep yourself from limiting your options, especially from internal obstacles. Tamara can think about ways to communicate better with her father. She can sit him down and show him all the material she's missed by being late to class. She can explain how the money he is paying towards her tuition is being wasted if she's missing class. She might even consider asking her dad to come with her to an appointment with a college counselor to help him understand her situation.

Tamara can also think about alternative ways to get to school on mornings when her dad doesn't want to leave early. She might take the bus one day a week as a compromise. She can check with student life to see if there is a ride-share or car-pooling option she could use. She could create a course schedule to avoid conflict with her dad's work schedule. She could also think about buying her own car.

What's the Likely Outcome?

With each option you identify, try to figure out what could happen as a result. Tamara's dad might change his mind, or he might not. Tamara will have to adjust her schedule to be able to take the bus once a week. She will

Time is the coin of your life. It is the only coin you have, and only you can determine how it will be spent.

— Carl Sandburg

also need to make sure she knows which day each week she'll need to take the bus.

She may find that taking the bus is not as bad as she thought or she may find it just as bothersome as she thinks. She may be able to adjust her schedule successfully next term and it all works out, or she may find trying to work around her dad's schedule more of a hassle than taking the bus. Buying her own car would certainly be liberating, but she must tally up all the expenses and decide whether she earns enough money herself to make it worth it. Working more hours to pay for a car might affect her study hours far worse than missing thirty minutes of class once a week.

Question 2: What Will You Do?

Glasser's method is designed to help people take control of situations where their actions are not effective, and this question is where you as a college student can act with purpose to achieve better results in the challenging situations that you face.

In asking yourself this question, you are choosing wisely from the different options you identified as part of answering the first question. What are the possible things you can do? What are the likely outcomes? Choose the action that best serves your purposes within the limitations of control that you have. The decision you make won't be perfect or guaranteed to produce glorious results, but it will be good enough for now.

All decisions can be modified after new information becomes available. Tamara first decides to visit a counselor for two reasons: First, she wants to see if she can coordinate her schedule with her dad's work next term. Second, she wants to get help with how to talk to her dad about the situation. She also decides that if she isn't successful changing her dad's mind, she will take the bus one day a week.

One other part of this question is planning when and how you will assess your choice to see how it's working out. Sometimes you will know quickly, and sometimes you have to allow your decision to unfold. In Tamara's case, she knew two outcomes quickly. First, she can craft a schedule next term that works around her dad's schedule. Second, he isn't going to change his schedule to accommodate hers.

However, Tamara did have a good talk with her dad and she learned why he was so resistant. He's exhausted. He needs any extra sleep he can get so that he can work safely and efficiently. Understanding that made it easier for Tamara to choose to take the bus. She didn't like it much at first, but she then grew accustomed to it. She found she could get some extra studying in, and that was an outcome she had not considered.

This is another part of decision-making—we can't always know all the outcomes. This is another reason to take the time to evaluate your choices.

> Life is the sum of all your choices.
> — Albert Camus

Analyzing Your Fears

Tim Ferriss, an entrepreneur and podcaster, is not someone with much expertise in educational psychology, and he has not lived the life of a typical college student. Instead, he has dedicated much of his privileged life to extreme learning and maximizing personal productivity. As a result, he's studied ways we can set and meet extraordinary goals.

One of the thinkers who inspires Ferriss is a Roman stoic philosopher known as Seneca. Seneca thought it was a good idea for people to experience what they fear the most so that fear no longer affects how they live their lives. Ferriss uses this notion of confronting your fears as a way to unlock your potential. Rather than focusing optimistically on goals, he encourages people to analyze their fears to ensure they are making choices for the right reasons and not because they are afraid of challenges.

To begin, think of a choice you might make if only—what? The "if only" is that hesitation you have due to fear of some challenge. To illustrate this, let's look at Max's situation. Max has always enjoyed working with kids. He was the oldest of five children in his family, and he enjoyed the responsibility of caring for his younger siblings. As a high schooler, he worked at a YMCA summer camp and loved helping kids make friendship bracelets, play Wiffle ball, and finger paint.

However, he came to college with the expectations of his parents and his culture. He was expected to follow a traditionally male occupation, such as accounting or something in the legal field, something that would make good money. Max dutifully selected an accounting major with a minor in legal studies. He wasn't happy, though, and he found himself regularly stopping by the college's laboratory preschool to see what the kids were up to. Hearing them laugh made him feel less stressed. During one visit, the professor encouraged him to consider early childhood or elementary education as a major. Max smiled at the idea and said, "If only!"

When you run into an "if only" decision, try writing down what exactly makes the choice so hard. What do you fear will happen? The early child-

Figure 7. By finding solutions to the obstacles you face, you build your personal agency.

hood professor sat Max down and had him do just that. Max was afraid of disappointing his parents. He was afraid he wouldn't make enough money to be financially secure enough to provide for his own family one day. He was afraid of being teased by his friends for pursuing a traditionally female profession. Probably worst of all, he was afraid of some comments he's heard people make about how "unnatural" it is for a man to want to teach young children.

Once you've taken an inventory of all the fears you have about your choice, see if you can imagine ways to either prevent those fears from occurring or to recover from them if they happen. This starts to remove the barriers to making a commitment.

Max first thought about disappointing his parents. Even when he had screwed up badly in the past, their anger and disappointment had never lasted. Choosing to study early childhood education wouldn't count as a screwup. His mom had actually enjoyed hearing his "kids do the craziest things" stories from the YMCA. Next, he thought about the pay. The professor was honest with him and said that early in his career, the pay will be low, but the professor also pointed to how Max can have his college tuition paid for through grants, which helps keep expenses low. Once he eventually gains seniority, the pay improves.

She also mentioned that it was common for teachers to use their off-duty time in the summer to earn income through temporary work. Max remembered that his supervisor at the YMCA summer camp was an elementary school teacher during the academic year. He also thought about his large family and how they seemed to get along okay despite his parents' modest salaries.

Then, Max had to confront his fears of how others would view him. This was hard to shake. The professor asked him if he believed that people should make choices for themselves based on what others might think. Max's gut reaction was no, but that didn't seem to help deal with the fears. The professor gave him the contact information of a man who was a first-grade teacher and encouraged Max to talk with him to learn more.

The next thing to do when analyzing your fears about a choice is to make all the benefits crystal clear. Write down specifically what would be so great if this choice became a reality. Max knew he would get to be creative and playful for a living, two things that would make him happy. He would take tremendous satisfaction from helping young children grow and learn. The professor highlighted how important it is for young boys to have male teachers as role models. More boys struggle in elementary school than girls, so having more male teachers would help. Max couldn't help but also think about the time off from teaching as a benefit, too. He might have to work over the summer, but he would start his working life with a few more weeks of vacation time than most entry-level workers.

The final step is to consider the downsides of *not* taking this course of action. This step follows from the idea that plenty of people regret *not* taking some important course of action out of fear or a lack of judgment. This often stems from identifying the rewards in the previous step. Max doubts he would be consistently happy doing something other than early childhood

You Be the Judge 2

Read the difficulties these students are having with embracing their personal agency. Then, decide whether they would most be helped by changing their internal dialogue, making wise choices, or analyzing fears. Jot down your ideas. When you finish, turn to the end of the chapter to check them.

1. Mario's best friend is getting married the weekend before midterms. There are three days of celebrations planned with one day coinciding with Mario's classes. Mario wants to celebrate *and* do well on his exams but doesn't know how. He feels like it is either one or the other.

2. It's week three and Ian has yet to turn in a single exercise journal for his health class. Ian did not want to take the health class in the first place, but it is required. Ian has joked with his classmates that if anybody ever sees him running, he's probably being chased by a bear. He is also good at coming up with reasons for not following through. For example, the exercise machine he prefers is broken, it rained a couple times last week, and, of course, exercise journals are dumb.

3. Keiko has strong feelings about caring for the environment. She's an introvert and finds group activities a bit exhausting. She also feels busy. She sees a flier calling for volunteers for her school's Earth Day celebration and thinks it would be neat to volunteer. She loves the ideas, but she hesitates. What would her friends think about her becoming an "earthy"?

If you have no confidence in self, you are twice defeated in the race of life. With confidence, you have won even before you have started.

— Marcus Garvey

education. He already knows that accounting is not his thing. He considers that if he doesn't continue with accounting, and he does not pursue education, he would then be spending time and money trying to figure out what else he might do. Switching majors to early childhood education now seemed such an obvious choice for him. He was a little shocked at his previous hesitation.

Overcoming Procrastination

A frustrating part of academic work is that even if you feel purposeful and want to be responsible, your actions don't always live up to your expectations. You want to get that chapter read, but for some reason, you chose to re-stain the deck. You want to complete that math homework, but the textbook has a picture of Angkor Wat in it, and the next thing you know, you've just spent two hours on Google Earth visiting landmarks of Southeast Asia. You plan to start the paper on Thursday, but then you push it back to Friday for no particular reason and then to Sunday and then to the night before it's due.

This is called procrastination, and it afflicts the majority of college students. It turns what could be an otherwise satisfying adventure in personal growth into something that is kind of miserable. We talked a bit about this in Chapter 3, but let's go into it in more detail.

Procrastination happens because your brain protects itself from dull or difficult work. If your brain interprets the work in front of you as dull, it will suggest something more amusing. If it interprets the work before you as difficult—so difficult that you're not sure how to even begin—your brain *really* wants to protect you from all that discomfort and the possibility of failure. The emotional center of your brain hijacks your attention and takes you someplace safer and more enjoyable, far from that paper you have to write or exam you have to study for.

For those affected by procrastination, it's a behavior pattern that is powerfully anchored by unconscious emotions. Defeating procrastination happens only after an extended time of determined effort, and it requires you to make several changes. That means you have to take it step-by-step. Each step is an exercise in personal agency, taking control over something that might first feel out of your control.

Taking Control of Your Time

As we discussed earlier in this book, to take control of your time, you need to make a weekly plan with specific times and places where you will do the work—and other activities—in your life. When you organize your week's tasks, you can balance academic work with activities that you know will be enjoyable. You want to enjoy those activities guilt-free, without the worry of a looming assignment taking away from that enjoyment.

One reason why some students procrastinate is that they have too much flexible time. This means they don't feel a sense of urgency about any particular task until the deadline is upon them. These students believe that they "work best under pressure" because their brain seems to need this activation for them to focus.

It may sound counterintuitive, but if this is your situation, you may actually need to find more useful things to do to fill up your weekly schedule. You might discover that the busier you are, the more you seem to get done. It forces you to be more mindful about time and gives you a way to manufacture urgency sooner—before the assignment is due.

Taking Control of the Learning Environment

To develop the habit of studying at a given time, you need to study in a designated place. You are attempting to create a new study habit, so it's important that your environment supports that practice and doesn't make it more difficult.

There are a few general guidelines for choosing a study space. You should have one purpose: studying. If the space you choose is associated in your mind with any other activity, like eating or sleeping, it will not work. This is why your bed is a bad place to try to study. Your bed is for sleeping. You will end up sleeping, not studying. Your home, in fact, might be a bad place to study. It's loaded with distractions like laundry, dishes, and people asking where the toilet paper is.

Your study space should be outfitted with what you need to study, too. This means good lighting, access to a power supply, a decent amount of desk-space, and a chair that is comfortable enough to sit in for a while but not so comfortable that it puts you to sleep. You might also do well standing up, so you might consider a counter-height table and a stool.

Some students need total silence with absolutely no visual distractions.

One's philosophy is not best expressed in words; it is expressed in the choices one makes. In the long run, we shape our lives and we shape ourselves. The process never ends until we die. And, the choices we make are ultimately our own responsibility.
— Eleanor Roosevelt

Figure 8. Avoid procrastination by minimizing the distractions in your study space.

They may find a perfect study carrel hidden away in the library. Other students can't concentrate for long without looking up from reading and momentarily letting their eyes move over a pleasant scene. Some students may find it easier to stay motivated when surrounded by other students who are also studying. They may find an open space in the library or a study lounge with many tables spread out over an area.

Experiment to figure out what works for you. However, if you are a procrastinator, you need to be especially intentional and honest with yourself about potential distractions. If you are easily distracted by the activity going on around you, you need to strip away access to these distractions.

Finally, modify your technology to remove distractions. If you must have your phone with you, put it on Do Not Disturb mode. Most Internet browsers allow you to create different profiles with different levels of access to the Internet. It's a great idea to create a study profile that blocks access to websites you know can distract you. Remember, the emotional part of your brain is like a toddler, easily distracted by shiny things. Treat it like one.

Taking Control of the Process

When it comes to complex assignments like a paper or a project that require a process of development, procrastination can kick in because of the challenge of managing complexity and the fear that you might not be able to handle it. You start to panic about where to even begin. The emotional center of your brain receives this information and quickly asserts its right to whisk you away to do something familiar, comfortable, and immediately satisfying.

The first step for taking control of any long-term project is to write down the steps for that process. You need a checklist, in other words, and if you have trouble making one, you may need to ask for some help. This starts to put you in control. It helps you move from anxiety to action.

The next step is to start—even for just a few minutes. Starting and working through the first two minutes of any job is the hardest part. This is when that emotional center of your brain is desperately trying to get you to leave the discomfort of the work and check your Twitter feed. Give it two minutes, though. Just two minutes. After two minutes, your brain usually relaxes and realizes that its fears were overblown and that there wasn't that much to worry about. You will likely be able to focus now and get going. With further progress into your study session, you might even start to feel the pleasure of accomplishment.

Taking Control of Your Thinking

If you find yourself already resisting the appointment you made with yourself to study or get started with a project, stop whatever it is that you *are* doing. Take a closer look at that moment of resistance and examine it. Remind yourself that you can't let the emotional center of your brain take control.

If you hear negative self-talk about how impossible the work is, replace it with positive self-talk about how you are here to meet challenges, not avoid them. If another task distracts you, write it down and make plans to do it later in the day. Remind yourself why it is important to follow through. Imagine how good it will feel to check this task off your to-do list. If thinking about positive outcomes doesn't redirect your behavior, then remind yourself of what you are losing by not following through. Help your brain recognize that the threat comes from the stress of procrastination, not the work itself.

From here, track your successes of resisting those emotional urges, staying focused on your goals, and being more disciplined. Again, you will likely take a few steps forward and then a step back. As you become a more competent student, it becomes easier and easier to resist more frivolous activities. The work becomes less scary and more interesting. It may even be a pleasure in its own right, and the bugaboo of procrastination never surfaces. The online tool kit for this book offers additional tips on overcoming procrastination.

You Be the Judge 3

The following students struggle with procrastination. What have they not taken control of that would help them follow through? Jot down your ideas. When you finish, turn to the end of the chapter to check them.

1. Cortney has a history paper on the suffragette movement due soon. She arranges her schedule to dedicate a couple of hours to it in the library. Once in the library, she reads through the assignment sheet and then finds the chapter in her textbook that discusses the movement. The chapter does not hold her attention for long, especially with her phone buzzing and vibrating. She ends up scrolling through her social media feed. She then gets a text from a friend, which gives her a reason to leave. She tries to work on the paper again, but the cycle repeats itself. After glancing at the assignment sheet, she stares out the window. Then, she looks back into the textbook, scanning the pictures and captions. Her attention drifts off to the conversation behind her. She feels a rumbling in her stomach, so she leaves to get some food and never comes back.

2. Chad sets aside the day to work on his presentation which is due in two days. He goes to the store to get duct tape and orange juice. He alphabetizes his DVD collection. Next, he cleans the toilet bowl and irons his shirts for work. He also cooks his signature lasagna. Just when he feels ready to get to work, his roommate, Paul, arrives home and suggests they play *7th Continent*. Chad pauses and thinks, *I'll get the presentation done tomorrow*, and starts setting up the game.

3. It's about six p.m. and Mayra is sitting in her study spot in the library. She has math the next day, so she looks at the course schedule. There's a test! Okay, she thinks, I can study for that now. Out of habit, she opens her laptop. She nearly clicks on the bookmark for YouTube but manages to resist just in time. It then occurs to her that she has not checked into her online psychology class in a few days. She has this sudden, vague feeling she was supposed to have done something. Sure enough, there is an announcement about an assignment that is due by midnight. *What?!?* Looking at the instructions, she discovers that she needs to read about fifteen pages of her textbook to complete it. So, she now has a bunch of reading and writing to do before midnight, plus she has a math test to study for. She packs up and drives to the coffee shop, fuming at herself.

Final Thoughts

As long as you have choices, you have agency. You exercised that agency when you chose to enroll in college. Despite all the requirements and responsibilities that are expected of you as a college student, you still have the majority of the control over the quality of your experience as you make choices about what to do, how to do it, and when to do it. The power of personal agency comes from just recognizing that you have it.

You strengthen that power when you develop judgment and do things with purpose. Judgment asks, "What is the situation? What are my choices?" It helps you to identify more options for yourself. It also directs you to consider the possible outcomes of those options so you can narrow them down to the best choice for you right now.

Your purpose is your internal compass. It asks, "What are you doing in this situation? Why are you doing it?" It helps you determine if your actions lead you towards or away from your chosen goals. By practicing judgment and purpose, the power of your personal agency becomes clear and can grow over time.

Don't put this off. If you've been feeling a little powerless while wading into all the commotion of college, exercise your personal agency. Sort things out, make your choice, and take action. You can do it, and it will make a difference.

Reflect on Your Self-Assessment

As you considered the statements in your self-assessment, you likely had to take a bit of an internal inventory. Look at the assessment again now that you know a bit more about personal agency. Did you respond to the statements honestly? Were there any that were hard to pinpoint? The higher your score, the more likely you have a sense of personal agency. No matter what your score, personal agency is something to exercise regularly to allow you to adapt to new situations and challenges. Consider some of the DIYs for this chapter to help you along.

Do It Yourself

Here are some things that you can to do on your own to learn more about building personal agency and overcoming barriers:

1. Analyze your internal dialogue. Keep track of how you talk to yourself, particularly when things are not going well. Do you beat yourself up? Do you tend to blame or complain? Or, do you tend to problem solve and not get bogged down with a lot of self-pity?

2. Rewrite your internal dialogue. Recall a recent, frustrating situation and write down how you initially reacted to it with your usual self-talk. Then, rewrite your thought process to problem-solve or reframe the situation constructively.

3. Use Glasser's decision-making process to work through a dilemma you are experiencing:

    a. What's your present situation?

    b. What's your goal for this situation?

    c. What problems or obstacles exist?

    d. What are you currently doing to achieve this goal?

    e. What are other possible actions you can take?

    f. What's the likely outcome for each those other actions?

    g. What choice(s) will you make?

4. Use Ferriss's fear analysis to examine something you would really like to do but that you hesitate doing for some reason.

    a. Identify your "if only" goal.

    b. What fears might be preventing you from achieving this goal?

    c. For each fear, what action(s) can you take to overcome or prevent this fear?

    d. If you don't take this course of action, what is the cost?

    e. If you do take this course of action, what are the rewards?

    f. Should you take this course of action? Why or why not?

5. Using the guidance in this chapter, prepare a specific action plan for tackling your procrastination and then follow through on it:

   a. Address your thinking first: what does your internal dialogue need to say to get you focused on the task?

   b. Identify the time when you will work on tasks you usually avoid.

   c. Identify the environment you will seek out to complete your work.

   d. Break down the task into smaller steps that when completed, help you build moment.

You Be the Judge 1 Ideas

1. Jennifer failed to be intentional when it mattered. She allowed herself to get distracted by something whimsical rather than focusing on important information about her assignment. Again, there is nothing wrong with enjoying a good pun battle, but it needs to be pursued at a more appropriate time.

2. Lucas has a weak locus of control. He interprets his confusion about the feedback as a pure inability to meet his professor's expectations. He does not believe that anything he could do would change his professor's opinion of his ideas. In other words, his self-efficacy is low. To defend his self-worth, he claims that the professor is just being close-minded. Getting assistance might also make him feel like he is "dumb," so he resists it.

3. Vickie failed to discern what steps to take to improve her paper. This largely came about because of the little attention she paid to her high school English courses as well as the offense she took from the feedback she received. She interpreted the feedback as a personal attack, which suggests she's got a bit of a fixed mindset. Anger will make discernment more difficult.

You Be the Judge 2 Ideas

1. Glasser's questions will help Mario figure out how to manage these two worthwhile goals. Mario thinks, *Either I choose one or the other, but I can't do both.* Either-or thinking is common when you are facing two important goals and you may need to be cued to think about other choices that might accommodate both goals. Glasser's questions can help Mario be more open-minded about the choices he has for balancing both his friend's wedding and his midterms.

2. Ian is rebelling against this insult to his sense of personal agency. This health class was foisted upon him. He did not choose it for himself, and he may have low self-efficacy about physical fitness in general. If he wants to be successful, he has to learn to accept the things that are out of his control and take control where he can. Changing his internal dialogue about the class would make a difference in how he approaches it.

3. Keiko's situation is a good one for a fear analysis. The Earth Day celebration can be a rich opportunity for her to connect with others who feel the same way as she does. She will learn more about teamwork. She will contribute to her community. By hesitating, she's allowing her fear of being overwhelmed to make this choice for her.

You Be the Judge 3 Ideas

1. Cortney is trying. She set aside time well in advance of the due date and picked a good place to begin a history paper, the library. She did not take control over her technology, though, so it distracted her easily. She also did not take control of the process. She seemed not to know how to start. A visit to the writing center or the learning assistance center would have helped Cortney figure out a checklist for her history paper.

2. Chad needed to take control of his environment. It would have helped him to get out of his apartment, so he wouldn't have been so easily distracted by all the chores. It is not clear if he is in control of the process either, because he only set aside one day, which might not be enough to prepare the presentation.

3. While Mayra appears to be able to control her environment as well as certain distractions, she has not taken control of her time. She is operating day by day rather than week by week. If she does not do an inventory of her assignments in all her classes before they are due, she can't schedule enough time to do them well.

Self-assessment

Before you begin reading the chapter, answer the following questions. Don't spend too much time on your answer. Instead, respond with your first thought. The goal is to see where you are right now. We'll return to this assessment at the end of the chapter to see if or how your thinking has changed about these topics.

	Disagree	Unsure	Somewhat agree	Agree	Strongly agree
I know what issues interfere with my learning and have strategies to manage those issues.	○	○	○	○	○
I can motivate myself to learn something even if at first, I do not see its importance or relevance to my major.	○	○	○	○	○
On a weekly basis, I take time to review old material before studying newer material.	○	○	○	○	○
I ask questions as a way of building my understanding about new concepts.	○	○	○	○	○
I can break down complex test or study questions to determine what is being asked and figure out how to answer them.	○	○	○	○	○
I consistently take notes in class.	○	○	○	○	○
I consistently take notes of material that I view and read online for my classes.	○	○	○	○	○
I consistently read assigned texts I'm given and take notes from them.	○	○	○	○	○
I take time to consolidate my notes, clean them up, and organize them so they make sense days after I first encountered the ideas.	○	○	○	○	○
I test myself, without looking back at my notes, on material I will be tested on.	○	○	○	○	○

The more you agree with the above statements, the more prepared you are for the active learning required for college success.

Chapter 6

Becoming an Active Learner

Marissa, Jack, and Oscar are friends who all enrolled in college together. Marissa wants to pursue a psychology degree to become a therapist. Jack plans to get a degree in horticulture and manage a greenhouse. Oscar needs to take prerequisites for the nursing program. They all enjoy their courses, but four weeks into the term, all three have run into problems while studying.

Marissa feels lost in her freshman writing course. For her first essay, she had to read an article about immigration policy and respond with her opinion about the policy, but she doesn't like to share opinions. She's much more comfortable reporting information than judging it. Jack's horticulture course has simple-sounding requirements. He has to learn different plants and their care needs. However, the task is time-consuming because he must learn hundreds of plants. Then there's Oscar and his chemistry course. He has to commit to memory the properties of certain classes of chemical elements, know what happens when they interact with each other, use math to balance out equations, and then predict the behavior of hypothetical elements—things that do not exist. He's comfortable with the memorization part, but that's all.

As these three are beginning to see, learning and performing in college is complicated. In college, professors expect you to do more than memorize information and recall it when tested. (And when you are expected to memorize material, it's much more than you were asked to do in high school.) Most courses expect you to think more deeply, creatively, and critically. So, your methods for studying in different courses require a variety of strategies. If you don't have a lot of experience shifting your cognitive (or thinking) gears, you can expect to be just as frustrated as these three.

"Active learning" involves metacognition, the act of shifting your cognitive gears according to the given learning task. To become a more active learner and therefore a more successful college student, you need to grow your metacognitive skills.

"Metacognition" is the act of mentally stepping back from a situation

Figure 1. Working with complexity is part of the landscape of your college career. You'll be asked to do some high-level thinking in your classes on a regular basis.

to consider what sort of thinking it requires. It also involves recognizing how hard a task is and identifying what resources might help you achieve it. Metacognition helps you identify the appropriate study strategy to make any new information and skills stick. Lastly, metacognition includes knowing how to manage your personal barriers to learning (like noticing any fixed mindset behaviors, for example).

This chapter begins with a look at some of those barriers to learning and makes suggestions for how to deal with them. Then, it explains how your professors expect you to demonstrate what you learned and describes the thinking actions required to do so. Lastly, it shows you some practical techniques for how to learn new ideas and then not immediately forget them.

Barriers to Learning

It takes effort (and good strategies and help) to acquire new knowledge. It also takes effort to then use the knowledge you've gained so that you don't lose it. You have to be engaged in the work and use the right techniques. Before we get to the right techniques, we explain some wrong techniques along with the unhelpful beliefs that usually accompany them. These include misperceptions about learning, inexperience, disengagement, and cognitive overload.

Misperceptions of Learning

Let's say your goal is to build up your bank of knowledge and skills so that you can use it later to solve problems and adjust to new situations. What you need is durable learning, in other words knowledge and skills that stick. If that is your goal, then the process you use to learn will require effort. Unfortunately, many students believe learning should feel smooth, fluid, and familiar. As a result, many students turn to the study strategy of rereading.

Rereading material over and over feels productive because it's familiar. That sensation of familiarity makes you imagine you're learning, but you

Figure 2. Make sure to pay attention to the details.

aren't. Not really. Try to recall the information from your notes a few days or even a few hours later without peeking, and see what you remember. It's unlikely you remember much. It takes more mental work to move information into your long-term memory.

Closely related to rereading is the use of highlighting. Many students use a highlighter or the highlighting function on an electronic screen to identify parts of the text they want to remember. Again, highlighting feels productive—and it's pretty—but it does not help you retain the information from the text. That's because the act of highlighting is not active (or effortful) enough to make the ideas stick.

Familiarity does not equal learning. Just because we've seen something over and over does not mean we will remember it. For example, which of the images in the figure below is the Apple logo? Researchers at UCLA decided to test this idea on college students. When asked to draw the Apple logo from memory, eighty-four out of eighty-five students couldn't do it, even though most thought they could.

Figure 3. Whatever methods you need to use to aid your memory, your reward is the satisfaction of knowing you can apply your knowledge to real situations.

Did you pick the correct one? None of the images are the actual logo. This study shows us that we tend to be overconfident about retention of familiar information. You've been learning how to write a sentence ever since you could hold a pencil, but do you always know when you're looking at the correct version of a sentence? To do so requires effort and practice.

Students also think that if they put all their efforts into one long marathon study session ("cramming"), they will learn better. Students often use this strategy for the same reason they reread. When you look at information over and over again in a single, long stretch of time, it feels productive.

To be honest, cramming can be somewhat effective for a single exam because it helps you relearn ideas that you've forgotten. Your brain, however, does not have the chance to store all that content neatly in places where it can be remembered easily. The information is dumped randomly in your brain rather than placed in labeled mental folders and filed away in a sensible place. It's like when you "clean" your room by shoving everything under the bed. How easy will it be to find your soccer cleats when you need them?

When it comes time to take the test, your brain's electrochemical messengers will have to wander around checking synapses here and there and sift through piles of unlabeled stuff to find the information. You may eventually get it done, but you're likely to feel more stress during the test. What you learned also won't stick around for long. So, if you need that information for the next course in a sequence, you are not likely to remember much of it. You may find you have more to relearn the following term.

One last misperception of learning is the belief that you have a certain learning style. When this theory about learning was first suggested, educators thought it was a neat idea that made sense to them, so they taught it. The primary "styles" that have been identified are visual (seeing), kinesthetic (hands-on), or auditory (listening). It was an interesting theory, but it needed testing to see if it held up. Once cognitive scientists got through the experimental process, they came to the conclusion that using learning styles theory did not have much value or positive effect on learners. A student who thought he was a hands-on learner did not necessarily learn better because he was given objects to manipulate. A student who thought she was a visual learner did not learn better because she viewed pictures.

Cognitive scientists will tell you that learning is better accomplished when you use as many ways of representing information as possible and concentrate on the learning task at hand. *What* you are learning also determines *how* you will learn it. If you need to roll your r's a certain way to pronounce a particular word, you practice speaking that word while listening to an example. If you need to compose an essay, you read and analyze other essays and then use a writing process that allows you to develop and organize your ideas. Ultimately, the belief that you need to access or communicate information in one particular way limits your learning potential.

Inexperience

For some, the first year of college is just a faster-paced version of their last two years of high school. If they successfully completed Algebra 1 and 2, earned solid grades in senior-year English, and managed to get through their classes, they have a good foundation in the key academic disciplines. This means that the challenges they encounter during their first terms at college are more practical than academic. They have to adjust to the faster pace of homework. They have to learn how to manage their own time without teachers or parents nagging them. They have to get comfortable with more complex ways of thinking.

What about the students who didn't enjoy or care about or do particularly well in high school? What about the students who come to college after

Figure 4. Inexperience is a temporary problem. Most foundational classes will give you the direct contact with their subject that you need to overcome feeling inexperienced in a complex environment.

many years of working or raising families or following other pursuits? They have to handle the same challenges as the recent, successful high school students. However, they may have an added challenge of courses that are wholly unfamiliar. If they don't have high school algebra in their recent history, for example, then college algebra may take more than just learning to use some new ideas about math. It might feel more like learning a foreign language.

Many colleges try to help inexperienced or returning students transition quickly into college courses by requiring writing, math, or other college preparation classes. These requirements aim to get them up to speed for college-level work. If you're advised to take any of these courses, please don't make the mistake of skipping over them to save time and money. Once in a hundred times that works, but ninety-nine times, it doesn't work, and that's more likely to be your story. Attempting courses you're not ready for then *costs* you time and money instead of saving it. These courses are not a punishment but an opportunity to catch up on skills and knowledge that are necessary to your success in college.

It's also possible to be prepared generally to take a course but still feel lost in class because of a lack of experience or background knowledge. Your professor might occasionally forget that you haven't had eight years of organic chemistry like she has. She might tell you all about the subject with the language and expectations of an expert. The textbook might also be a bewildering collection of six-syllable words that aren't in a normal dictionary because textbooks tend to be written to the faculty who order them rather than the students who read them.

This can be frustrating. It can make you want to drop out of college, in fact, because you feel like you don't belong here. If that's what you're feeling, don't go anywhere. That feeling means that you do belong. It means you have just run into something new for you to learn. Help is closer than you may think, too. You can walk right into your professor's office—knock first—and ask what she meant by riboflavosincro. This is a new word for you, and you want to understand it.

If that takes more courage than you feel like spending in one afternoon, you can take the same work—or your textbook—and go to your college's tutoring center. The tutoring center is generally staffed by compassionate students who have been where you are and have

Figure 5. If you're not sure about what's being covered in your class, you can always ask your professor to explain in more detail. Most are happy to talk with students one-on-one, especially when you are genuinely interested in learning more.

struggled with the same material. They will be happy to work with you on those new terms and any background ideas that remain puzzling, and they will admire your grit in taking on this challenge.

What if you don't have enough time for the tutoring center because you have to get to work or your babysitter has threatened to quit if you're not back on time? Happily, you live in the age of the Internet, and all those confusing terms and ideas are waiting for you there. You're not the only person who is inexperienced with those topics and ideas. Many people are struggling with the same content. You can find many nice and smart people online who do their best to help with thoughtful explanations.

Disengagement

Students can go through periods of disengagement, during which they withdraw from their roles and responsibilities as a student. This can happen for many reasons. Sometimes they find themselves in required courses that make no sense to them at all. Why, for example, would the advisory board for the welding program require you to take a course in gender studies? Why would some statewide planning group think that a brilliant writer like yourself should ever have to study math? What does that have to do with the delicate construction of a love poem?

The answer to almost all these questions is simple. There is more to life than welding or love poems or whatever else you want to focus on, and advisory and planning boards want you to be ready for it. They want you to be a successful welder or nurse or sociologist, but they also want you to be a successful citizen and human. To assist you in that process, they require you to take courses that stretch you in directions you would not choose for yourself.

Sometimes those stretches make some sense. Being a better writer *will* help you explain yourself in your science course. Being proficient at math *will* help you be a more logical thinker. Studying workplace psychology *will* help you avoid being a jerk in the workplace.

At other times, the usefulness of these courses may not make sense. What does US history have to do with anything? That was then, and this is now. How does a poetry course help? Why do you have to take economics when you have so little money at the moment? In those cases, there are two useful approaches.

One approach is to find out why this course is required. There's usually a valid reason. Manufacturing companies, which are traditionally male-dominated, may want welders who are sensitive to the dynamics of gender on the shop floor because they're hiring more female welders. Logic and reason are tools of the writer just as they are for the mathematician. Ask your professor. Ask a guidance counselor. Research it online. Find out how the knowledge and skills you're acquiring will make you more prepared for a future you can't predict.

Another approach is to simply take a leap of faith. Accept that the people on the other side of these required courses have been doing college education longer than you. They see a value in those courses that you're not yet able to see because of your inexperience. If you can jump into a course expecting to get something good out of it, you almost always *do*.

Another reason for students disengaging from some courses is that they only want to study topics that they already know and love. They're excited about robots—or wine growing or biology or math or nursing—so that's all they want to study. Anything else is automatically boring or a waste of time. This is one form that the fixed mindset takes. Students believe they are what they are, and they love what they love. They don't want to expand.

It's great to have a sense of direction about what you want to study. You're

Figure 6. Choosing an environment that is free of distractions is one way to combat cognitive overload and have more a productive study session.

right to study and work at topics that engage your imagination and that you love to learn more about. However, a clear purpose doesn't mean you should limit yourself to those topics. Life is bigger than that, and you will be enlarged by falling in love—or maybe just in *like*—with new topics that you hadn't encountered or expected to enjoy.

Cognitive Overload

We all have limits to our mental bandwidth. We can only handle so much thinking—or stress or physical activity or excitement—before we wear out and need to rest our minds, bodies, and emotions. We mentioned the concept of cognitive load briefly in Chapter 5 but let's take a closer look at it. Cognitive load is an idea from educational psychology that says people can only process so much information while learning something new or performing a skill. Once students hit that limit, they stop processing new information and learning stops.

For professors, this is an important concept because they need to design courses that challenge you to push yourself to new limits, but they don't want to wear you out with too much homework, class activities, tests, and so on. For students, this means the more you have on your mind in general, the harder it is for you to figure out what you're supposed to do or how you're supposed to do it.

Environmental distractions increase your cognitive load. If you check your social media accounts or text with friends during class, it increases your load no matter how much fun it is. It also increases the cognitive load for the students sitting on either side of you. You are distracting them with the kitten vs. snake videos that flash on your phone screen. In fact, some research shows that the mere presence of a cell phone on your desk, even if it's not being used, adds to your load and detracts from the quality of your learning because you're thinking about what might show up. So, put away your phone. When choosing a study space, be mindful about the level of distractions it presents. Why add to your cognitive load?

Students can also overtax their cognitive load when they take too many courses in a term on top of family, work, and social obligations. You may be tempted to race through college by taking six or seven courses in a term, but

You Be the Judge 1

What barriers to learning are the following students experiencing, and what could they do to deal with it? Jot down your ideas. When you finish, turn to the end of the chapter to check them.

1. Patrick's boyfriend recently broke up with him. They had been living together, and now Patrick lives with new roommates who have different standards when it comes to a clean house and quiet hours. Patrick wants to transfer to his state's flagship university, which is selective, so he feels he needs to take rigorous courses and get all As. His scholarship requires a GPA of 3.0 or better. He's been absentminded due to his general state of sadness and missed registration day. Because he registered late, he ends up with college algebra and English composition on the same days along with general biology and Spanish on the other days. He has a part-time job as a grocery store cashier and works fifteen hours per week. He needs the income to support himself.

2. Alondra has had to manage a chronic illness most of her life and misses a lot of school. She is committed to her education, but there are days when she just cannot focus and pull it together. Last year, she graduated one term after her high school class, having completed the necessary minimum requirements.

3. Jackson is enrolled in the machining program at his community college. Demand for skilled workers in manufacturing is high, and he is essentially guaranteed a good-paying position with a local company once he finishes the program (possibly even before). He is required to take a technical writing course which makes him twitch a bit. If he wanted to take writing courses, he would have been an English major. Jackson has somehow managed to avoid any serious writing responsibilities so far, and he plans to continue his streak.

that overwhelms what you can handle. You're not going to learn much, and you may risk having to retake classes that you fail.

You also have to be careful about taking too many challenging courses at once. If you know you struggle with chemistry and writing, in other words, don't take both in the same term. Struggle with chemistry one term, and then struggle with writing the next term. Be honest with yourself and your college advisor about what you can handle. Remember, plan for two hours of homework for every hour of class in your schedule. That might be more time than you end up needing, but probably not.

Finally, your cognitive load is also affected by insecurity—and not just emotional insecurity. If your money situation is shaky, or if things are tense at home, that can steal your focus away from learning and use up lots of your energy. There's no easy solution for the insecurities of life. Every situation is different and requires thoughtful navigation. Usually this means getting help from others who have the sort of experience you need. As a student, you have to remember that you have more demands on you than your courses. Keep that in mind as you plan your class schedule and study time. While you need to stay challenged and keep growing, you don't want to threaten your progress by taking on too much at one time.

Demonstrating Knowledge

To figure out your strategies to learn college content, you need to know how your professors will ask you to prove it. In other words, you need to know how your learning will be assessed and what assessments (tests, quizzes, essays, presentations, etc.) your professors have designed for their courses. You need to understand the types of questions professors will ask and the quality of answers they expect.

When you get a writing or research assignment, you need to know if your job is to report your understanding of a concept discussed in the course or if you need to pull together information from several sources, analyze it, and draw your own conclusion. When you perform a skill, such as a speech or role-play of a motivational interview, you need to know what the professor considers an acceptable performance. From there, you identify the type of thinking required by the assignment. How do you plan to answer those questions, develop those essays, and rehearse those skills? We'll examine these questions in the next section.

Figure 7. Before you can expect to perform complex analysis, you have to know the basics. It's important to have a firm grasp on the way things fit together before you can analyze how they work.

Types of Assessment

You're probably most familiar with assessments in the form of tests with a variety of multiple-choice, matching, fill-in-the-blank, or short-answer questions. A researched paper is another popular assessment, and so is a portfolio of writing or other homework that's collected throughout the term. In some cases, an assessment may take the form of a collaborative project. For professional and technical disciplines, you might have a performance evaluation and a supervised internship where you are assessed over several weeks while working at the jobsite.

Ideally, your professors will provide you with timely and sufficient information about when and how your work will be assessed in their courses. They may also direct you to resources that will help you prepare. This information is often spelled out for you in the course syllabus, an exam study guide, or an assignment sheet. However, sometimes a professor simply tells you this information during class and assumes you're taking notes.

In whatever form it comes, this information about an upcoming assessment is important. Read it carefully. Ask questions about anything you don't understand. Information about upcoming quizzes and papers is often discussed at the beginning or the end of class meetings, so you should also work hard to arrive to class on time and not leave early.

The type of assessment for any course almost always reflects the kinds of skills and knowledge that the course teaches. One thing to consider, then, is whether a course is primarily teaching you information or skills. If your course teaches you information, then the assessments will expect you to retrieve that information from your brain and sometimes to explain the relationship of different ideas or sets of information to each other. If your course focuses on skills, then the assessments will mostly ask you to demonstrate your skills by performing specific tasks.

With information-based courses, the ideas and information you are expected to store in and retrieve from your brain are known as "declarative knowledge." Examples of declarative knowledge include the location and content of different library databases, the difference between an independent and dependent variable in an equation, and the vocabulary of commands in JavaScript. It's the knowledge of facts, concepts, and theories. You know the sun is hot, a star, and at the center of our solar system. That's declarative knowledge. You could declare that knowledge along with many other facts and principles you've learned and stored in your brain.

Because Eduardo wants to become a nurse, he's had to learn information about many medical terms. He's learned that shock, for example, is an emergency condition where the organs of the body do not receive an adequate supply of blood. The first stage of shock is known as compensated or nonprogressive shock. The first symptoms of shock are clammy hands and feet, pale or blue-tinged skin, a fast but weak pulse rate, a fast breathing rate, and low blood pressure.

Professors usually evaluate the declarative knowledge in your brain through standard exams, like tests and quizzes with multiple-choice, matching, short-answer, and short essay-style questions. Well-designed tests challenge you to demonstrate your personal understanding of the course information, so they will often be written using different examples from what you have recently read in the textbook or heard in a lecture. If you find yourself frustrated that the wording and examples on the test don't seem to match the wording of the textbook or lecture, that probably means that you have focused on memorizing terms and definitions without taking that a step further and making sure you understand the ideas or facts defined by those terms.

With skill-based courses, the skills you are expected to understand and demonstrate are known as "procedural knowledge." Procedural knowledge is knowing and being able to smoothly perform a series of tasks to solve a problem or create something new. Ultimately, the purpose of *any* college program of study is to expand your range of procedural knowledge. Examples of procedural knowledge include performing a library database search to identify three reliable and relevant sources, solving a math problem that involves a dependent and independent variable, or writing computer code to create a user interface. Procedural knowledge shows that your knowledge is not just theoretical—you know *how* to do something and can perform that task.

For Eduardo, the procedural knowledge he's expected to demonstrate includes accurately evaluating a patient's condition in the first stage of shock and responding quickly. He needs to raise the patient's legs, cover them with a blanket, and provide supplemental oxygen and fluids as needed. He must then be able to determine the underlying cause of the shock and address it appropriately.

Assessments of procedural knowledge are usually student-made products like a report, sculpture, or detailed solution to a math problem. You might also be given a practical exam, such as giving a speech, performing the protocol for dental radiation infection control, or operating a brazing torch—all things you do while your professor watches. Your professor will evaluate your product or performance with a set of descriptions that define a satisfactory or less than satisfactory demonstration of skills. These descriptions are often charted in what is called a "grading rubric."

Here's an example of a grading rubric for a business plan:

	A	**B**	**C**	**D**
Organization	Information is very organized with well-constructed paragraphs and subheadings.	Information is organized with well-constructed paragraphs.	Information is organized, but paragraphs are not well constructed.	The information is disorganized.
Paragraph Construction	All paragraphs include introductory sentence, explanations or details, and concluding sentence.	Most paragraphs include introductory sentence, explanations or details, and concluding sentence.	Paragraphs included related information but were typically not constructed well.	Paragraphing structure was not clear and sentences were not typically related within the paragraphs.
Quality of Information	Information clearly relates to the main topic. It includes several supporting details and/or examples.	Information clearly relates to the main topic. It provides 1–2 supporting details and/or examples.	Information clearly relates to the main topic. No details and/or examples are given.	Information has little or nothing to do with the main topic.
Internet Use	Successfully uses suggested internet links to find information and navigates within these sites easily without assistance.	Usually able to use suggested internet links to find information and navigates within these sites easily without assistance.	Occasionally able to use suggested internet links to find information and navigates within these sites easily without assistance.	Needs assistance or supervision to use suggested internet links and/or to navigate within these sites.
Mechanics	No grammatical, spelling or punctuation errors.	1–3 grammatical, spelling or punctuation errors.	4–6 grammatical spelling, or punctuation errors.	7 or more grammatical, spelling, or punctuation errors.
Product Idea	Idea is realistic, well planned, and each part of the business plan fully developed.	Idea is realistic, mostly well planned, and 1–2 sections of the business plan are NOT fully developed.	Idea is somewhat realistic, partially well planned, and 3–4 sections of the business plan are NOT fully developed.	Idea is not realistic, is not well planned, and each part of the business plan is NOT developed.
Sources	All sources (information and graphics) are accurately documented.	All sources (information and graphics) are documented, but has 1–2 errors.	All sources (information and graphics) are documented, but has 3–4 errors.	One or more sources are not accurately documented.

In order to do well with this type of assessment, you need to understand all of the short descriptions in the rubric. If you run into any that don't quite make sense, make sure you ask your professor or other students and get some help with that.

Marissa was required to submit a rough draft of her paper on immigration. Her professor returned it with the usual comments in the margin and a rubric with boxes circled. One of the circled items was "attempted to apply academic conventions, several errors." Another item circled was "unclear or incorrect paraphrasing." Marissa knew what paraphrasing was but did not know how her paraphrasing was unclear or incorrect (she had declarative knowledge but not procedural knowledge). She did not know what an academic convention was. She thought they were big meetings people went to in Las Vegas. She made an appointment with her professor to get more guidance.

The professor directed Marissa to a handout from early in the term that outlined academic conventions (standards) for discussing someone else's ideas. It identified ways to refer to the author, how often to refer to the author, and how and when to embed direct quotations from the information source. It turned out Marissa only mentioned the author's name twice. Once in the introduction, which was appropriate, and again a few paragraphs down, but she used the author's first name rather than his last. Marissa had also chosen direct quotes that were not especially insightful or unique. There was no reason to include them and instead, she should have just paraphrased the ideas. Finally, Marissa's professor had her reread parts of the original article and restate what she understood. The two then examined how Marissa wrote the idea in the draft, and she realized how she had confused push factors with pull factors.

Finally, you should be aware that no college course is entirely information-based or skill-based. You can't develop procedural knowledge without some declarative knowledge. Even heavily skill-based courses like algebra, writing, and machining require you to learn new terms, facts, and ideas. Applied fields like medical assisting, accounting, and fire suppression are largely procedural, too, but these programs consist of lecture-based courses that deliver the important declarative knowledge you need to perform the skills of the profession.

You'll also find that some courses that are heavy on information — general psychology, biology, and history, for example — provide you with a swiftly

The greatest weapon against stress is our ability to choose one thought over another.
— William James

flowing stream of information in the form of class lectures and long textbook reading, but these professors also expect you to then use that information to accomplish tasks such as predicting, analyzing, creating, or evaluating.

Types of Thinking

Beneath these assessments lies a range of thinking actions. To develop your metacognitive skills, you can learn how to describe different kinds of thinking and recognize examples of each kind. Your ability to do that means you have a better sense of what's required of you when you read the terms on an assignment sheet or study guide. You can't read your professors' minds, but you *can* get familiar with two common classification systems they use to design assignments and assessments: Bloom's Taxonomy and Costa's Levels of Inquiry.

You Be the Judge 2

Examine these course descriptions. Identify the kinds of knowledge the course is designed to teach. Then consider how the course might assess your procedural or declarative knowledge with a test, demonstration, or product. Jot down your ideas. Your answers should show how information in the course descriptions point toward the types of knowledge and assessment you can expect. When you finish, turn to the end of the chapter to check them.

1. Basic Science for Dental Assistants presents introductory concepts of chemistry, cell biology, anatomy and physiology, microbiology, and oral histology and embryology. The course includes practical application of problem solving, scientific observation, and basic laboratory techniques.

2. JavaScript Web Programming 1 covers the fundamentals of JavaScript as a web programming language, including basic programming concepts as they apply to using and writing JavaScript. It focuses on learning to create interactivity using JavaScript with text and graphics.

The course provides the foundation for continuing with JavaScript in the Intermediate JavaScript course and features current web-standards and compliant techniques for using JavaScript.

3. Physical Geography focuses on the physical subsystems of the earth (atmosphere, biosphere, hydrosphere, and lithosphere), with emphasis on human-environment relations. It includes basic map skills, latitude/longitude, weather, climate, biogeography, volcanism, erosion, and desert landscapes.

Bloom's Taxonomy

Bloom's Taxonomy, named for educational psychologist Benjamin Bloom, identifies six different types of academic questions or thinking tasks. The word taxonomy describes to how these six types are organized from the simplest to the most complex. This is not a hierarchy, where one task is more important than another. Still, in order to accomplish the more complex skills, you must have understanding as well. You will not be able to make judgments about or evaluate information that you do not first understand. It's just a set of categories that attempt to describe the many different types of thinking that are expected of students.

Type	Description	Thinking Actions	Sample Tasks or Questions
Remember	Recall facts and basic concepts	Identify, locate, list, recall, label, name, recite, memorize	What are the basic principles of learning discussed in this chapter?
Understand	Explain concepts and give examples	Describe, explain in your own words, summarize, translate, paraphrase	Describe a technique for encoding and explain in your own words how it supports learning.
Apply	Use prior knowledge and skills to solve problems in new situations	Solve, calculate, develop your own example, dramatize, forecast, predict, repair, adjust	Predict what might occur if a student relies on memorization techniques for a math course.
Analyze	Examine information, break it down into its components, and recognize how those components relate to each other	Compare, contrast, outline, determine reasons for, find similarities, draw conclusions about, identify relationships, classify, categorize, interpret	Read this case study and determine the reasons for the student's low grade.
Evaluate	Make a judgment using a set of standards	Judge, prioritize, recommend, justify, defend, rank, discuss strengths and weaknesses	Given the difficulty of your course load this term, rank each course according to the amount of time you will need to study to earn a B or better.
Create	Develop something original using a variety of elements	Compose, invent, devise, create, hypothesize, design, build, construct	Construct a study plan for final exams.

Remembering, understanding, and applying are necessary types of thinking for almost all academic and professional work. That is what Jack's horticulture course expects from him. This expectation is typical of introductory courses designed to help students learn important terms and concepts within an academic or professional area. Jack did poorly on his first quiz

Figure 8. As you dive deeper into the complexity of each discipline you encounter in college, you will need to do more than simply remember information. Most college classes require you to process that information and apply it to new situations. That takes practice.

mostly because he hadn't given enough time to the work of remembering the names and understanding the requirements of all those plants. He reread his class notes the night before and thought it would be enough, but he was sadly mistaken.

With many courses, the thinking demands become more complex. That's why Eduardo is struggling with chemistry. He doesn't have a problem with remembering and understanding properties of various elements. Where he struggles is with predicting what could happen when elements interact, a kind of analysis that requires he recognize a chemical effect and its cause. Marissa struggles with her essay because she doesn't understand what she's supposed to do. She knows how to read, understand, and report information, but she doesn't know how to evaluate academic information and make a judgment of her own.

As you advance in an academic discipline or technical field, your courses expect more complex types of thinking from you. You might feel bewildered at first. That's to be expected, so don't worry about it. Your professor will help you with those thinking processes as long as you stay engaged. Your textbooks can also walk you through more complex thinking, if you read closely. With practice, you will add to your mental tool-kit of thinking strategies and become more comfortable with how to use them.

Costa's Levels of Inquiry

Another educational psychologist, Arthur L. Costa, proposed a similar framework to organize types of thinking. His system organizes thinking around three stages or levels of learning:

1. Gathering information

2. Processing information

3. Applying or generalizing information in new situations

Level	Description	Thinking Actions	Sample Tasks or Questions
1	Understand meaning, express understanding, and commit knowledge to memory	Describe, define, explain, identify, label, list, locate, match, name, outline, paraphrase, recognize, reconstruct, restate, sort, summarize	What are the basic principles of learning discussed in this chapter? Describe a technique for encoding and explain in your own words how it supports learning.
2	Process, gain control of, and use the knowledge learned, see how parts work within the whole, and solve concrete problems	Analyze, arrange, calculate, categorize, classify, compare, contrast, compute, determine, diagram, differentiate, distinguish, find causes, give reasons, sequence, take apart	Predict what might occur if a student relies on memorization techniques for a math course. Read this case study and determine the reasons for the student's low grade.
3	Demonstrate mastery of knowledge learned, judge the value of the content, use information in new ways, and develop new ideas based on knowledge gathered	Appraise, argue, assess, choose, conclude, critique, decide, document, design, develop, evaluate, interpret, judge, justify, prioritize, rank, rate, recommend, support, validate	Given the difficulty of your course load this term, rank each course according to the amount of time you will need to study to earn a B or better. Construct a study plan for final exams.

Because this framework is simpler than Bloom's Taxonomy, we'll use it to take a closer look at how it can be used to build your metacognitive skills across a variety of courses.

Metacognition in Action

Costa's Levels of Inquiry represents a learning process that moves you from understanding a concept to using it in a creative way. The first level is absolutely necessary. If you don't understand the properties of metals, non-metals, and metalloids, you can't contrast them with each other and differentiate them. If you can't explain what budgeted financials are or what goes in to making a marketing plan, you won't be able to prepare either. If you are struggling to process or apply information, it is probably because you didn't gather and recall all the needed information. If you are stuck, create questions that cue your brain to gather more information and then go gather it.

Marissa has to write an essay that reflects the most complex level of thinking—evaluate an immigration policy. As far as she knows, Marissa has only summarized content like this, not evaluated it. Marissa can begin by gathering information on what it means to evaluate. According to Costa's levels, it means to make a judgment based on clear criteria. Criteria refer to ways of measuring something's value, quality, or use. So, Marissa figures out that she must come up with a way to measure the quality of this policy. She can reread the article equipped with information-gathering questions like these: What makes up an immigration policy? What are the goals of an immigration policy? What criteria would make a policy "good" or "bad"? If the author of the article evaluates the policy, Marissa can ask herself why the author thinks the policy is good or bad.

You Be the Judge 3

Take a look at the following learning tasks. Which of Costa's three levels are required by that task? Here's a tip: locate the words in the statements that reflect thinking actions such as "explain" or "differentiate," and then look them up on the chart. Items C and E do not have thinking actions that you can find on the chart, so you must translate or interpret what they could mean. Jot down your ideas. When you finish, turn to the end of the chapter to check them.

1. Demonstrate the use of oxyacetylene cutting and welding equipment.

2. Explain major issues in the field of early childhood education.

3. Prepare budgeted financials for a startup business in the form of a business or marketing plan.

4. Differentiate between metals, non-metals, and metalloids.

5. Provide constructive feedback and respond effectively to peer and professor feedback.

6. Define the purpose and functions of marketing.

Marissa doesn't have a lot of knowledge about immigration policies elsewhere, so she can add to her understanding by asking this question: What other immigration policies are out there? She can even use *Wikipedia* for this part. She will naturally transition into some processing questions: How do these policies affect people trying to immigrate? How do these policies affect the citizens of the country? How do these other policies compare to the one in the article? In what ways are they similar? In what ways are they different? With questions based on Costa's Levels of Inquiry, Marissa can find ways to evaluate the policy. If Marissa figured out the answers to these questions, her essay will practically write itself.

Unlike Marissa's writing professor, Eduardo's chemistry professor doesn't leave him to fend for himself at the top level of inquiry. The professor walks Eduardo's class through just about everything, but he does this swiftly. Eduardo will need to keep up. The course involves instruction in terminology, concepts, and calculations all at the same time. In any given class meeting, Eduardo's professor explains, breaks down, and calculates a chemical process using specialized scientific language and notation. For example, the professor might assign a task for the day that looks like this:

> » Write a balanced chemical equation for the dissolution of $Ca(OH)2(s)$ in pure water.

> » Calculate the molar solubility of $Ca(OH)2$ in $0.10\ M\ Ca(NO_3)_2$.

These two processing-level questions require prior knowledge. To have any hope of understanding how to do his homework, Eduardo would already have to know what is meant by the symbols and numbers before the answers are explained.

How does Costa's Levels of Inquiry help Eduardo out? Similar to Marissa, he can start at the gathering stage and review the basic terms and concepts before attempting new content. Rather than jumping right into a problem set of balancing equations, he can study a few example problems and label them to explain each step in as much detail as possible to himself.

Then there is Jack. Remember him? How can he use Costa's Levels of Inquiry to memorize a bunch of plants along with their care needs? Interestingly, it is easier to remember information that you have processed and applied than to simply match names to pictures over and over again. He can use the thinking actions associated with processing and applying to help him draw connections between plants and their care. For example, he can put a

---

Too many students are hung up on grades and on proving their worth through grades. Grades are important, but learning is more important.
— Carol Dweck

group of plants with similar features and care needs—such as plants that prefer shade to sun—into one category and name that category something memory-catching, like the "shady ladies." This chunking of content makes recall easier.

Acquiring Knowledge

Use it or lose it. That's an important part of learning. If you don't use what you learn—and quickly—you're likely to forget it. As figure 9 illustrates, if you don't do something with new information within twenty minutes, you've already forgotten more than 40 percent of it. If your professor explains an important concept in class and you expect yourself to remember that for the midterm next week, you'll probably only remember about 25 percent.

To remember new information and skills, then, you have to actively work with that information and practice those skills. There are a few simple ways to do that, and they all fit under the broad umbrella of "studying." In the following sections, we will explore four strategies for retaining what you learn. These include read actively, write things down, revise your notes to organize information, and practice remembering in short bouts rather than cramming.

You Be the Judge 4

Which information gathering questions could you ask to help you get started on the following higher-level thinking tasks? Jot down your ideas. When you finish, turn to the end of the chapter to check them.

1. [Psychology] Based on the following sleep diary, determine what environmental and biological factors influenced the subject's sleep pattern.

2. [Sociology] A large percentage of US soldiers serving in conflict zones are teenagers from working-class families in small towns. Give sociological reasons for why this is the case.

3. [Literature] Describe how Orwell's *1984* and Atwood's *The Handmaid's Tale* explore the death of love as a major theme.

4. [Chemistry] A nuclear technician was accidentally exposed to potassium-42 while doing brain scans for possible tumors. The error was not discovered until thirty-six hours later when the activity of the potassium-42 sample was 2.0 μCi. If potassium-42 has a half-life of twelve hours, what was the activity of the sample at the time the technician was exposed?

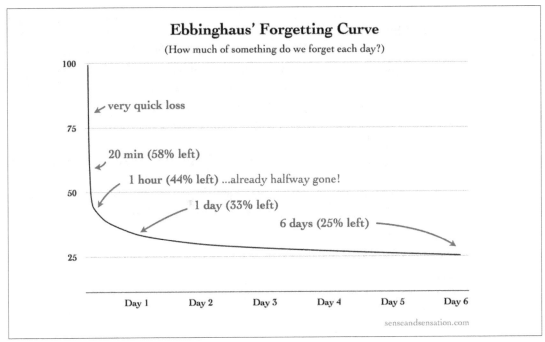

Figure 9. Ebbinghaus' Forgetting Curve.

Read Actively

In content-heavy courses, students skip reading their texts because they mistakenly believe everything they need to know is delivered through the lecture. Professors who assign reading expect you to do it, and they have no problem asking questions on their exams whose answers only appeared in the textbook. Courses where professors assign reading are likely discussion-focused, rather than lecture-focused. If you do it, you will draw more meaning from class meetings and have more confidence in your ability to contribute and perform on exams.

If you're a traditionally aged college student, many of your reading habits formed from reading on small screens. You're a professional skimmer and scanner. You can look up and locate specific pieces of information rapidly. But, if you haven't regularly sat down in a quiet, comfortable spot and read something longer and more complex than a Twitter post, your brain is not used to the type of slow, systematic, and active reading you've got to do in college.

Active, academic reading is purposeful and slow going. It's purposeful because you are working to learn something. It is slow going because you need to check methodically that you understood what the author explained, take notes along the way, and make sure you achieved your purpose for reading. There are many active reading strategies, and the type of text often determines which strategy to use.

SQ4R System

SQ4R is shorthand for several methods that can help you become a more purposeful, active, and careful reader. It stands for survey or scan, question, and the 4Rs of read, recite, record, and review. The following table breaks this method down into thinking actions and sample tasks or questions for each part of the system.

Item	Thinking Actions	Sample Tasks or Questions
S	Survey or scan	Scan through the assigned reading. If it's a textbook chapter, read the headings, check out any visuals, note any study aids like learning objectives and review questions. If it's an essay or article, note the title and any subtitles, read the first and last paragraphs, and read the first sentences of any lengthy paragraphs throughout the body of the essay.
Q	Question	Create your purpose for reading. Using cues from the text like headings and first sentences, write questions that will help you gather information (level one according to Costa's Levels of Inquiry). Put them on a separate page or write them on the text itself in a logical place.
4Rs	Read Recite Record Review	Read the text paragraph by paragraph and pause to check your understanding. Recite to yourself what you think the important information was from the paragraph. If you found an answer to one of your questions, note it. Record your thinking in the margins of the page—symbols, pictures, summary phrases, more questions. Review the content you read by looking back at your margin notes and then write a set of separate notes using any of the techniques discussed below

If you're doing it right, active reading will feel like it's taking too much time, but remind yourself that you will only read the text once. As it becomes more of a habit, you will get more efficient. You can also expect to experience a little thrill when you make deeper connections to what's going on the classroom because you read.

Figure 10. Taking notes of your own is a great memory aid. Compared to professor-supplied notes, you'll be able to quickly find what you're looking for in notes you wrote yourself.

Write It Down

If you attend all your class meetings and do the assigned reading, that's a great first step. However, it's not enough for you to just be in the classroom or to read your textbook. This is especially true if you check your phone and stare out the window during the professor's lecture or force the pages of the textbook past your weary eyes at three in the morning after work. You also have to pay attention to what you hear and see in class. You have to schedule time to do your reading when you're alert enough to think about it and take notes.

For new knowledge to become a durable memory, it needs to be encoded or entered into your brain in the same way that words are written into note-books or money is deposited into a bank account. Your brain needs to keep track of it somehow otherwise it tends to disappear.

This "encoding" begins with your senses. Whenever you enter a new situation, you hear, see, touch, taste, or smell information about the situation and encode it as a memory. That happens in the classroom, too, as you listen to lectures or participate in activities. However, if you're staring out the window or at your phone, your brain will use what you find there to create a memory. The more you can focus on the information that you paid for with

Overall Topic, Learning Objective, or Essential Question	
Cue Column	**Notes**
Jot down questions or key words that are then answered or explained by the notes.	These can be in *any* appropriate form—an outline of information, a graphic organizer, an illustration, phrases, complete sentences.
Make sure that the cues line up with the right notes.	The notes should answer the questions and define the key terms listed in the left-hand column.
	Leave plenty of white space between chunks of information.
Summary, Reflection, Application, or Evaluation	
Depending on the kind of information you noted above, record something that ties it all together for you.	

Figure 11. The Cornell Notes framework.

your tuition—that is, the information that is coming from your professor or your professor's instructions—the more valuable your memories will be.

College courses rely heavily on words, spoken or written, to provide new information. One of the best ways to encode words is by taking written notes whenever you need to listen, watch, discuss, or read. Mental notes, by the way, are not *notes*. They are memories, and as you saw in figure 9, those memories don't last long on their own.

When you write something down on paper, however, you are taking action. Because you are doing something with what you heard or read, you're more likely to hang onto it. Even if your sociology professor is one of those extremely helpful yet slightly misguided professors who hands out detailed lecture notes at the end of every class, you should still take notes of your own. His carefully written notes won't encode the lecture in your brain. Your written notes will.

The Cornell Note-taking System from Cornell University is one popular and easy method that helps you to not just capture the information you read or hear but also to organize it. Figure 11 presents the Cornell Notes template

Figure 12. Revising your notes reorganizes the information you encoded in your brain. This can result in a more effective study session later on, or even create new connections between separate ideas as you recode them.

for encoding information. This functions as a framework for encoding and organizing new information, and it also works as an easy way to review that information later.

To enhance your encoding of new information when you're working outside the classroom, you can help the encoding process by reducing distractions during your study times. Turn your phone off. Turn the television off. Turn your children or roommates off by finding a quiet place where they won't bother you. The more you can focus on your new information, the more your brain can encode that information and not what happens this week on *Portlandia* or *Ice Road Truckers*.

Revise Your Notes

Once you've taken notes, it's a good idea to revise and manipulate those notes as a way to further embed this new information in your thinking. Here, you can use highlighters, for example, to color-code related information in your notes. Reorganizing your notes into a format that will help you study for exams is another great way to capture new information and prepare yourself to retrieve and use that information in exams or with projects. Let's take a look at how that works with different disciplines.

Learning Objective	Problem	Solution	Explanation
Write down the learning objective from the textbook. Record terminology, too.	Copy the example problem here.	Write down the step-by-step solution process. Leave plenty of space between each step.	Explain each step using your own words. Do not copy the language of the textbook.
Learn the algebraic concept of converting units of measurement to similar units. Examples of units of measurement: Distance Foot = ft Centimeter = cm Weight Pound = lb Kilogram = kg	1 ft = 30.48 cm How many 33 cm tiles can fit end-to-end along the length of the wall of a room 11 feet long? Note: You want to convert the feet into centimeters here because the tiles are measured in cm and you need to know how many tiles you need.	Step 1: convert units 1 ft = 30.48 cm 11 (1 ft) = (30.48 cm)11 Step 2: set up the ratio 335.28 cm 33 cm Step 3: divide 335.28 ÷ 33 = 10.16 You need 10.16 tiles	There are 30.48 centimeters in one foot. I have 11 feet, so I can multiply 11 by 30.48 to figure out how many cm there are in 11 feet. A ratio is a way to show how two quantities relate to each other. The top of the ratio is the whole amount and the bottom is the part. I divide the whole by the part to get the number of parts I need.

Figure 13. Charting notes from a prealgebra class.

Charting for Math-Based Courses

In math and math-based courses like physics and chemistry, you learn how to apply rules and formulas to solve problems. You are simultaneously learning the language of mathematics, chemistry, or physics. Your notes should capture the problem-solving process and reinforce in helpful language what the terms mean. Charting those notes can help you to put all the pieces together. Figure 13 illustrates how this works when you're reading from a math textbook and includes an example from a pre-algebra course.

You can make the chart more effective by using highlighting to draw your attention to steps in the process that you tend to forget or make errors on. Taking the time to explain things in your own words may feel like a waste of time, but it's actually the most effective part of the chart. This is where you really make this process your own.

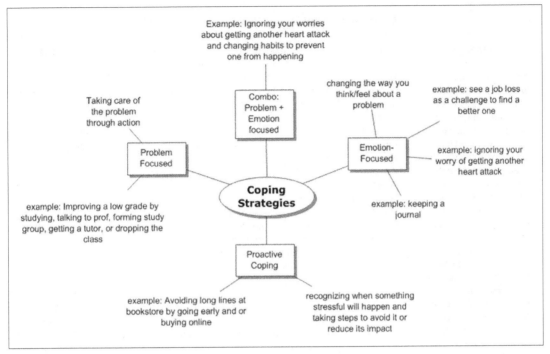

Figure 14. A content map for the topic of coping strategies.

Concept Mapping for the Sciences

Explaining human behavior from a biological, psychological, or sociological perspective gets complicated. Many different causes might lead to a single result, such as when your back starts to ache and you're not sure whether it's caused by stress, lousy posture, having to pick up and then immediately set down a two-year-old child six hundred times a day—or all three. Likewise, a single cause might result in many different effects, such as when the thought of taking a midterm exam causes your heart to race, your armpits to sweat, your mind to fog over, and your poor back to ache.

When the relationship between ideas and processes is complex like this, a simple, linear outline can only go so far to help you store the complexity of the information you encounter. The charting for math-based courses probably doesn't go far enough, either. However, a graphic organizer, like the concept map in figure 14, can serve as a better tool for organizing information and encoding these complex relationships.

Chapter 1: "September 2004, Al Tafar, Iraq"				
Passage	**Summary**	**Questions**	**Answers**	**Reasons**
Then, in summer, the war tried to kill us as the heat blanched all color from the plains. The sun pressed into our skin, and the war sent its citizens rustling into the shade of white buildings... The war would take what it could get. It was patient. It didn't care about objectives, or boundaries, whether you were loved by many or not at all. While I slept that summer, the war came to me in my dreams and showed me its sole purpose: to go on, only to go on. And I knew the war would have its way." (pp. 3-4)	Things changed in the summer. He started to feel like the war itself wanted to kill him. He dreamed about it. He saw that the war wanted to just keep going, and that it would.	Why does he talk about the war as a person that takes what it can get?	He might be starting to lose his mind.	The war isn't a person. The summer sun might be getting to him. The stress of fearing death might be getting to him.
		Why is summer important?	Heat causes separation?	
		Why do the soldiers stay in the sun while the citizens go to the shade? Why don't the soldiers go into the shade?		Duty? Different cultures?
		How does he know the war would have its way? What's his evidence?	I don't think he does know that.	There's no direct evidence from the real world of this. It shows up in dreams. Unless there IS evidence that he's not willing to admit consciously so he dreams it.

Figure 15. A chart of *The Yellow Birds* for a writing assignment.

Charting for a Writing Course

In a writing course, the professor often asks students to closely read, analyze, and respond to a complex piece of writing. Charting the important parts of the reading is a useful way to gather and organize information from the reading. That helps you to encode the information, of course, but it also helps you to participate in class discussions of the reading and organize the information and ideas you will need to explain yourself in an essay.

The labels for your chart will probably come from the assignment instructions for the essay. Those instructions often ask you to identify an important passage in a text, summarize the key ideas or events in that passage, and then develop your own opinion in response.

You remember how Marissa was struggling with her writing course? Her assignment after the immigration paper was to identify an important passage from the first chapter of Kevin Power's book, *The Yellow Birds*, which is the story of a soldier in Iraq who later suffers from post-traumatic stress disorder (PTSD). Her paper requires her to summarize what happens in this passage and then answer one question about the passage. Fortunately, she's made friends with questions, so she's good there. However, she's not sure how to keep everything organized, so she asks her friend Eduardo. His tutor showed him the problem/solution/explanation chart for his chemistry course, and he has become a bit of a charting fanatic. He suggests Marissa chart her way through Chapter 1.

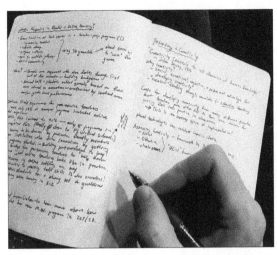

Figure 16. Your labels for your notes and charts should make sense to you, but a blur of notes like this can be recreated into a more efficient study tool with some planning.

Figure 15 on the previous page is a chart that would help her with that paper. The columns in this chart include a key passage, summary, questions, answers, and reasons. You'll also notice that the chart is incomplete at the moment. That's okay. You don't have to figure out everything at once. You can come back to a chart and keep working on it as new ideas come to you or as you continue to reread the text.

Practice Remembering over Time

You need to allow your brain to neatly organize all this new material inside its neural network. To do this, practice remembering the content in regular, periodic bouts instead of waiting a day or two before the exam and cramming it in. When you relearn material over several weeks, it makes a home in your brain. Material that's been crammed, on the other hand, behaves like a rude houseguest who visits briefly and sometimes makes a mess before heading out of town.

Self-Testing

To get better at roller-skating, basketball, welding, or any other physical activity, you can't just read about it or watch instructional videos. You have to actually put the roller skates on, shoot two hundred free throws, or fire up the welding torch. You need to do what you've been learning about. It's the

Figure 17. Creating flash cards is one method of self-testing that you can do quickly and efficiently. Use flash cards to test your memory.

same with any knowledge. If you want to keep it, you have to practice using it.

One of the best strategies for using new knowledge is to test yourself in the same way that you'll be tested in your course. If your course is like Jack's horticulture course, it will test you on how well you can remember the names and care requirements for hundreds of different plants. Flash cards are an effective and flexible tool for that kind of self-testing. Jack records the name of a plant on one side of the card. On the other side, he writes down distinguishing characteristics and care requirements. As he goes through the cards one by one, he discovers what he already knows and where he still needs to work. The cards help him to practice retrieving the plant's characteristics and care needs from his brain. That study method will be much more effective than just rereading the textbook.

If you have created concept maps or charts, you can test yourself by covering up portions of a chart and then recalling from memory the part that's covered. Eduardo needs to think about that as a way to test himself on how different chemicals interact. It will help him to visualize the nature of those interactions so that he can more easily pull that from his brain when he needs it in labs or exams or—one day—as a nurse.

For a math course, you can test yourself with corrected homework assignments. Look at the problems that were assigned from your textbook and see if you can solve them again. Then check your work against the corrected homework. If you struggle with a particular type of problem, spend more time practicing similar problems.

It's a good idea to mix up topics within a course or even test yourself on ideas from two different courses when you study. The combination forces your brain to work harder to retrieve information, and the harder your brain works, the more you remember. Brains probably can't sweat when they work hard, but if they could, that's what you would want from them.

You should also build a longer practice test when an exam approaches, one that uses the same sort of short-answer, multiple-choice, or essay-style questions that the exam will use. Your textbook should also have helpful

Figure 18. There are lots of ways you can trigger your memory to recall information, and most of them are more effective than just rereading a textbook. This student is smiling for the photograph, but she knows she needs a better system for retaining information. It's eating at her.

review questions within or at the end of each chapter, so gather test questions there. You can also find test-making software applications online and gradually build a bank of questions over the term.

If you're not sure what sort of questions the exam will use, check the course syllabus first to see if it tells you. If it doesn't, ask your professor. Your professor might even give you an actual exam from a prior year's course. You can then use it as your practice exam.

As you practice the exam, test yourself within a time limit. That will help you get used to the stress of only having so much time to retrieve and present that declarative knowledge of yours. Check your answers and review material that you had difficulty recalling.

Online, open-note, and take-home tests operate a bit differently from traditional, in-class, closed-note exams. Students who treat them as identical to traditional exams often misjudge the difficulty of the tests and assume that the extra time and the additional resources mean they don't have to prepare as much. In fact, these open exams require *more* work from you. Your professor knows you have access to notes, books, and other resources, so the types of questions on these open exams will usually require you to think more critically and use those resources effectively. You have to be able to recall all the information, but you also have to practice using it in more critical and creative ways.

I used to want the words "She tried" on my tombstone. Now I want "She did it."
— Katherine Dunham

Rehearsing for Practical Exams

To prepare for a practical exam that test your ability to perform a procedure or hands-on skill, the best way to prepare is to first ensure you understand every step of the procedure and then rehearse, rehearse, rehearse. Understanding is not the same thing as remembering each step—know why each step is needed and why it is put in the order that it is in.

The first thing to do is get familiar with the procedure by reading about it and watching any available videos. Your classwork will also help you to get familiar with the procedure, so keep doing that classwork and homework as it's assigned—that's what you're there for. Watch your professor's demonstration and make notes about how and why each step is done.

The next stage of rehearsing is to break the process down into all its steps and actually do it:

1. Break the process down into its steps mentally or on paper.

2. Visualize the procedure in your mind and mentally rehearse it.

3. Complete the process yourself, step-by-step.

When you have difficulty remembering or doing one of the steps, go back to your notes, and then keep going. If a procedure is particularly complex or if you keep getting stuck on one part of it, it's fine to practice parts of the procedure on their own, but as much as you can, try to do the whole procedure together.

As you get more comfortable with the procedure, it helps to get feedback on how well you're doing from skilled people. This includes your professor, more experienced students you know, or a professional you know who works in this field. Don't ask the people who love you how you're doing because they will lie and say you're doing great, even if you aren't. They think that's nicer (or maybe they'd rather be watching the football game). Another thing you can do to improve your skills is to teach someone else how to do it. That really forces you to not only do something but understand what and why you're doing it.

Finally, as much as possible, try to recreate some of the pressures of your testing situation, if you have one. If it is timed, set a timer. If you could be challenged with any number of interferences, practice with interferences. With enough practice, you can get to a point of unconscious competence where doing this procedure flows through you without much effort (and with less anxiety).

Memory Devices

Courses that teach medical terminology or plant identification require you to encode, store, and retrieve many terms and definitions. That's part of learning the language of those disciplines, and that's what was so hard for Jack in his horticulture course. Working with flash cards will help, but he can also learn how to group and organize those terms into patterns that he can then use to retrieve the individual terms. These techniques are sometimes called "mnemonics," which is pronounced "nuh MON iks," with the first "m" being silent.

One memory device is to use an acronym to remember the first letters of a long set of related terms. For example, the ten essential amino acids are phenylalanine, valine, threonine, tryptophan, isoleucine, methionine, histidine, arginine, leucine, and lysine. That's a lot to remember. It's easier, though, if you take the first letters of each term and arrange them into something that you can remember, such as the name of a private in the military: PVT TIM HALL.

Get it? The "P" stands for phenylalanine, the "V" stands for "valine," and so on. To remember all ten terms, you can go through the letters, one by one, which will help you retrieve all ten terms from your brain.

Another way to remember technical terms is to associate each term with words that are more familiar to you. Phenylalanine sort of sounds like "funnel all nine." Valine sort of sounds like "valiant." Threonine sounds like it begins with the number three. Tryptophan sort of sounds like "trip to fun." That may sound a little dorky at first, but those associations really do help to make the technical term easier to recall. They create silly little connections within your brain, and that helps to connect those terms to your long-term memory.

Mnemonics are only useful for memorizing terms, however, so don't invest any time in them if you need to focus on concepts or processes.

Final Thoughts

If a course is easy, that's not a good thing. Either you've already learned the material, in which case you're not getting any value from your tuition dollars. Or you're not pushing yourself to learn more than you absolutely have to, in which case, you aren't getting the full value of that course.

The study methods in this chapter will also not come easily. They require self-discipline and time-management to become useful habits for the college version of you. They also take lots of trial and error and correction because these are usually new skills that are uncomfortable at first.

As you become an active learner, what you want is a *desirable* level of difficulty, one that is just challenging enough to require effort but not so challenging that you become frustrated and give up. The growth mindset embraces these desirable difficulties. It expects them. It doesn't mind if things don't always work out perfectly because that's how learning works.

Marissa learned the value of questioning as an important strategy for developing her ideas. She still had to put in the work, but she felt more in control of her learning. Eduardo's note-taking and time-management skills leveled up. He took to heart that he would need to put in more time to process all the material for his chemistry course and made sure he spent at least an hour a day on it, revising his notes and self-testing. Similarly, Jack accepted that memorization also took time, but he needed to spread out the memorization work and not cram it together. He found a self-testing app for his phone and used short windows of time each day to practice remembering. Interestingly, when he switched to this method, it seemed like he was actually using less time than before and getting better results.

You Be the Judge 5

Given the learning goal, what study methods could the student use? Assume that these are items for a quiz or a test and the student will not have access to textbooks or notes. Jot down your ideas. When you finish, turn to the end of the chapter to check them.

1. Write a balanced chemical equation for the dissolution of $Ca(OH)_2(s)$ in pure water.

2. Use the appropriate medical term to identify parts of the musculoskeletal system.

3. Based on the given case study of a successful business, discuss the best practices the company followed.

4. Read the following observational report of a child in a preschool class. Classify the observations as either objective or subjective.

Reflect on Your Self-Assessment

By now you can see that in many ways you need to learn how to learn. Your self-assessment at the beginning of this chapter had you consider how your current ideas about learning fit in with the needs of a college environment. The higher your score, the more likely you have a good foundation for learning in an academic environment. Be prepared to adjust your methods based on trial and error and what works best for you in each course. The following DIYs can get you started.

Do It Yourself

Here are some practical things that you can do to help yourself better understand what it means to be an active learner:

1. Identify the barrier to learning that you think affects you the most and create a plan of action to cope with it.

2. Classify the questions on a recent quiz or test according to Costa's Levels of Inquiry (gathering, processing, or applying), and then make your own practice test following the same style and using the same level of inquiry.

3. Revise a set of notes you made this week. Use a format that helps you process the information best. Be sure to include at least one overarching question the material is helping you answer.

4. Create a mnemonic device for a group of related terms you must learn.

You Be the Judge 1 Ideas

1. Patrick is overloaded on many fronts: emotionally, environmentally, and academically. He is going to need help. The best person to help him is a counselor—not his friends, not a fellow classmate, not a family member. The counselor will help him make wise decisions given his plans for the future and present needs.

2. Alondra has gaps in her education, so she is likely to be inexperienced with the content of several of her courses. Given her health needs, she may also need to manage her cognitive load. She should work with her college's accessibility office and identify the best first term schedule for her as well as any accommodations she can use. She will probably need more time than the average student to learn the same content, and that's okay as long as she budgets the time.

3. Jackson has a disengagement issue. He can talk to his professors to learn more about why the writing course is required. He can also find out more about the writing course by contacting the professor. The number one skill a machinist must have is attention to detail. Machining work is highly precise and specific. He can relate these skills to those needed for technical writing. It is also possible that Jackson may have a fixed mindset about his writing skills and needs help adjusting his beliefs about it. There is also the simple logic that if he takes the writing course seriously, he will have more skills than other less prepared candidates. He will be able to use those skills to get more desirable positions. Finally, he can remind himself that he has chosen a degree program that requires more than mechanical training for a reason. If he wants to practice having integrity, he will follow through with its expectations.

You Be the Judge 2 Ideas

1. Basic Science for Dental Assistants presents introductory concepts of chemistry, cell biology, anatomy and physiology, microbiology, and oral histology and embryology. [declarative, test] It includes practical application of problem solving, scientific observation, and basic laboratory techniques. [procedural, demonstration or product]

2. JavaScript Web Programming 1 covers the fundamentals of JavaScript as a web programming language, including basic programming concepts as they apply to using and writing JavaScript. It focuses on learning to create interactivity using JavaScript with text and graphics. The course provides the foundation for continuing with JavaScript in the Intermediate JavaScript course, and features current web-standard compliant techniques for using JavaScript. [procedural, product]

3. Physical Geography focuses on the physical subsystems of the earth (atmosphere, biosphere, hydrosphere, and lithosphere) with emphasis on human–environment relations. It includes basic map skills, latitude/longitude, weather, climate, biogeography, volcanism, erosion, and desert landscapes. [declarative, test]

You Be the Judge 3 Ideas

1. Using equipment is a process, so this learning goal is at the processing level.

2. Explaining something shows that you understand it, so this is at the gathering level.

3. Preparing a plan means to construct one. For "prepare," you might have scanned the list of thinking actions and chosen one that had a similar meaning, like construct. This is at the applying level.

4. Differentiating means to see differences. This is at the processing level.

5. To give feedback is to judge or evaluate something. Responding to feedback involves thinking about it and knowing how and when to use it. This is at the applying level. As far as giving and responding to feedback, you would have to have prior experience with peer review to know what this is. This is why level 1—gathering information—is essential.

6. Defining is the beginning of understanding. This is at the gathering level.

You Be the Judge 4 Ideas

1. What are environmental factors that influence sleep patterns? What are biological factors that influence sleep patterns? What factors are present in the diary?

2. What is meant by a "working-class family"? What is a sociological reason? What kind of soldier is sent to a conflict zone? Why would a teenager go into the military?

3. What is a theme? What happens in 1984? What happens in The Handmaid's Tale? How do the characters act towards each other? Do the characters love each other? What happens to their relationships?

4. What does this symbol μCi mean? How does it measure activity of potassium-42? What is potassium-42? What is a half-life? What is the process (or formula) for calculating activity of potassium-42?

You Be the Judge 5 Ideas

1. This is similar to a math problem, so creating a problem-solution-explanation chart like those recommended for math would make the steps of the process clear. The student would first rely on notes with a full explanation of each step, and then work equation balancing problems until she could do so without looking back at the example.

2. This task would benefit from creating a mnemonic device. It would be a good use of time if the student created a silly story that she relates to the parts of the musculoskeletal system and embeds the terms she needs to remember.

3. The student needs to be able to remember and recognize best practices used in a successful business, so flash cards could work if the practice can be summed up briefly. A three-column chart that lists the name of the practice, what it is, and why it's a good idea would also be useful. The student could also ask his professor for additional case studies to analyze.

4. The student has to know the difference between objective and subjective observations. If these are key terms, flash cards could work. Still, he's being asked to look at an example of an observational report, so the flash cards would need to include example statements. A concept map that includes terms, their definitions, and a variety of examples would be helpful, especially since these are related ideas. The student would need to practice remembering by covering up parts of the chart and recalling the information.

Self-assessment

Before you begin reading the chapter, answer the following questions. Don't spend too much time on your answer. Instead, respond with your first thought. The goal is to see where you are right now. We'll return to this assessment at the end of the chapter to see if or how your thinking has changed about these topics.

	Disagree	Unsure	Somewhat agree	Agree	Strongly agree
Students should expect and accept a certain amount of stress and negative emotions while pursuing their college degree.	O	O	O	O	O
I generally get adequate sleep and do not rely on stimulants like caffeine to give me energy.	O	O	O	O	O
I generally have a healthy diet of home-cooked meals that include vegetables, fruits, and lean protein. I generally avoid processed food or junk food.	O	O	O	O	O
I exercise at least 30 minutes each day and get my breathing and heart rate up.	O	O	O	O	O
I anticipate possible hassles that can add irritation and unnecessary stress to my day and take steps to avoid them.	O	O	O	O	O
I can sense when negative emotions are impacting my thinking and behavior.	O	O	O	O	O
I can manage negative emotions so that they do not interfere with progress toward my goals or with my relationships.	O	O	O	O	O
I can turn my thinking towards positive things even in the midst of stressful situations.	O	O	O	O	O
I do not experience much test anxiety.	O	O	O	O	O
I experience test anxiety, but I have strategies for coping with it.	O	O	O	O	O

The more you agree with the above statements, the more prepared you will be to handle the emotional challenges of college life.

Chapter 7

Learning to Persist

Before he began his first term, Oscar had visions of what it meant to be a driven student. He was optimistic and excited the week before the term started. He attended the college's preview day, got all his textbooks early, scoped out the campus, and found a spot in the library he liked. He imagined himself there, surrounded by textbooks, flash cards, color-coded notes, and his graphing calculator. He also saw himself in a study group with fellow pre-nursing students, testing and retesting each other on the intricacies of the endocrine system.

What he imagined is happening—mostly—but four short weeks later, he feels like he's ready to explode. His biology midterm is just a few days away and he has hit a wall. He has an essay due in his writing course, another test in math, and to make matters worse, his boss just called him in for several evening shifts to cover for a coworker who contracted measles. He needs a good grade in biology for his application to the nursing program, yet he hasn't done as well as he'd like so far, and his confidence is shaken.

He grows irritable and unfocused. At work, Oscar snaps at a customer nervy enough to order a latte and then complain that it has milk. His boss sends him home early and not with a pat on the back. While he knows he should take advantage of this unexpected freedom to study, he can't do it. Instead, he binges on episodes of *Adventure Time* and eats some brand of cereal that claims to make you feel great.

His roommate, in an attempt to regain control of the television, asks, "Aren't midterms this week? Don't you need to study or something?" Oscar begins to fume. He glares at his roommate, makes an obscene gesture, and mouths the expression to match it. He shoves the remote under his seat and chomps on a mouthful of sugary flakes.

In spite of *Adventure Time*'s usually positive messages, Oscar questions whether he can even finish the term, let alone become a nurse. He wonders if all the stress is worth it. Oscar's situation reveals the challenges of getting a college education, which can include feelings of anxiety, anger, frustration, and sadness. Everyone, even those who seem in control, will feel stressed, inadequate, and overwhelmed at times. You *can* learn to manage these emotional upheavals and work towards your goals. In this chapter, we will talk about ways to manage stress, including test anxiety, and build the emotional intelligence you need to tackle college life.

Well-Being Basics

Stress can take its toll on your brain and body if you don't learn to handle it productively. Everyone faces it — stress is one of life's certainties — but you can manage it, even make it your friend.

Proactive Coping

Stressful situations happen. The more complicated your life is, the more likely complications will arise. If you keep this in mind and plan for hassles and headaches, you will be in better shape to manage them if and when they occur. This is proactive coping.

"Proactive coping" means you anticipate possible stressors and act in advance to prevent them or lessen their impact. For example, Oscar didn't anticipate the extra work shifts and didn't have a plan for how to negotiate the situation with his boss. If he had, he might not have felt so pressured to work when he really didn't have the time for it. Later in this chapter, you'll learn about positive emotions and how to tap into them, but proactive coping actually relies on negative emotions. The key is to think pessimistically *in moderation* and when you're in a problem-solving mood. That means early in the term or even before it starts, it's okay to worry a bit.

To practice, let's worry about a major hassle that nearly everyone in college has to manage — technology and its failure. As a student, you must use many forms of software and hardware that are not always cooperative: your college's clunky online learning system (e.g., Blackboard, Moodle, Canvas), a glitch-prone word processing program, stubborn printers, or the crashing server that takes your presentation hostage.

Think through these problems associated with technology failures as well as the answers provided:

> » What will you do if you lose your internet connection and need it to submit an assignment? *Go to the library.*

> » What will you do if you have never used your school's online learning tool before? *Go to your college's computer lab and get help from an assistant or learn the basics from online tutorials.*

> » How will you store and manage your digital work? *Use your college's cloud service, not a flash drive that is easy to lose.*

> » What if you don't know what a cloud service is? *Go to the computer lab and get help from an assistant.*

Figure 1. At an appointment with your professor, you can ask specific questions that pertain to your work. Don't hesitate to ask for help if you're not sure you understand your professor's expectations.

» What if your printer runs out of ink? *Go to the computer lab and print there or buy ink cartridges in bulk at the start of the term.*

» What if you spill your mochaccino on your laptop? *Identify a good place to get it repaired and work in the computer lab until it's fixed.*

» What if you can't afford to have your laptop fixed? *Don't drink mochaccinos around it, first. Second, plan to get your work done in the computer lab or at your local public library.*

» What if you can only do homework later at night and on the weekends? *Make connections at college with people who can help you during off hours. Go to your public library if your college's library isn't open—although most college libraries are open at night and on Saturdays, if not all weekend.*

» What if all this technology freaks you out a bit? *Remember to think with a growth mindset—get help, use good strategies, and practice often.*

Identify problems that you might have to deal with before they happen and come up with a reasonable solution for them. This includes practical matters such as transportation and child care as well as emotional matters such as a loss of motivation, performance anxiety, or family conflicts. With proactive coping, you are more likely to avoid these stressors in the first place, and if they happen, they will be less likely to derail your progress.

Take Care of Your Health

Your brain is as much a part of your body as your heart, so when you care for your physical health you also care for your mind. Try to avoid fast or frozen food, soda, and sugary or salty snacks. College students notoriously set aside their health during stressful periods of the term. They replace a healthy breakfast with a quick energy drink or triple shot of espresso and hit the drive-through in a hurry. They go for what's easy. Yet this poses other problems.

Oscar found out the hard way that too much caffeine and sugar can disrupt a person's ability to concentrate—and sleep. He stayed up late for several nights in a row, snacking on candy bars and soda. The night before his first biology exam he laid down to sleep but couldn't. His heart raced, his stomach churned, and his mind spun. He fell asleep about an hour before his alarm went off and took the exam on just a few hours of sleep. He couldn't concentrate on the questions and, at that point, didn't even care. He just wanted a nap. Artificial energy is no solution for an energy deficit.

If you do not eat at regular intervals, you're likely to feel distracted and weak, much as Oscar did. Instead, adopt a regular "brain-food" diet that emphasizes vegetables, fruits, whole grains, and low-fat dairy products. The diet might also include lean meats, poultry, fish, beans, eggs, and nuts. Limit saturated and trans fats, sodium, caffeine, and added sugars, in other words, skip processed junk food. Most importantly, keep the portion sizes modest. Let's face it—a heavy meal makes you want to take a nap, not study.

Make regular physical activity a health habit if you can. Exercise, believe it or not, helps your brain along with the rest of your body. A quick, daily walk can make a difference in your well-being, give you a burst of energy, and release stress. Many people get inspired and revitalized when oxygen hits their brain. It's okay if you don't have time for an hour-long workout. Any form of physical recreation done on a regular basis can be good for you provided it doesn't take up too much of your time. You want to be healthy, but you also need to study.

Let's return to the need for sleep. It is crucial to how you manage stress. While a couple nights of sleep loss here and there *might* impact your overall performance, it probably won't if you get seven to nine hours of sleep most of the time. One night of sleep deprivation will not ruin your mental capacity, but repeated sleep irregularity will take a toll on your health.

A few good habits will help make sure you get enough sleep on a regular basis:

» Keep a consistent sleep schedule. Get up at the same time every day, including weekends and during vacations.

» Establish a chill bedtime routine with a bedroom that's quiet, cool, and as relaxing as possible.

» Avoid using electronics or watching television while in bed.

» Eat dinner well before bedtime, and if you get hungry before bed, limit yourself to a light snack.

» Avoid caffeine in the late afternoon or evening.

» Avoid alcohol before bedtime.

» Finish your workout at least three hours before bed or exercise earlier in the day.

Finally, please remember that now is *not* the time to overhaul your exercise, sleep, and diet habits all at once. If your current routine is not a healthy one, that does need to change—over time. Your success in college and beyond depends on it. However, it's not a good idea to add a new dramatic lifestyle change in the middle of your current, dramatic lifestyle change of going to college. For now, notice how you sleep, eat, and exercise affects your mood, energy, and ability to think. The more you choose healthier options, the easier it will be to build a habit of healthy choices.

Adopt a Routine

An important form of proactive coping is to establish a routine. In previous chapters, you learned to manage your responsibilities with a daily or weekly plan. If you haven't gotten around to that, now is a good time. Set aside consistent, weekly study sessions within a schedule that also allows you to get enough sleep, eat well, exercise, and do meaningful activities other than study. A good, weekly routine becomes a source of stability and comfort for you when the inevitable stress and anxiety of tests, papers, projects, and lab reports start to bubble up as the term builds.

The difference between a weekly plan and a weekly routine is persistence. Recruit your friends and family to help you stick with it. Be ready to forgive yourself if you do not magically become as disciplined as an Army Ranger. If you believe that a study schedule is necessary—and you do, right?—and if you believe it is within your power to change your habits—and it is—then with consistent, daily effort, you really will be able to establish a routine. A good schedule can help reduce the anxiety that comes with tests and set you up for success.

The foundation of anyone's ability to cope successfully is high self-esteem. If you don't already have it, you can always develop it.
— Virginia Satir

A Closer Look at Emotional Intelligence

If it is difficult to stick to a specific routine, your emotions are likely influencing your choices. Do you follow through on a study session or skip it in favor of practicing chords on your guitar? Emotions largely direct the choices you make from moment to moment, which include those that affect how you manage your responsibilities and relationships.

Oscar was overwhelmed, so he lost his patience with a customer and avoided his studies by watching too many episodes of his favorite show. An occasional break is understandable and generally good for you, but Oscar always lashes out or retreats to cope with difficult situations. As a result, he is unlikely to reach his goals. Awareness of how you manage emotions is key for both college and life success.

Emotional intelligence involves two broad components. The first is your awareness and management of your own emotions. The second is your awareness and positive response to the emotions of other people. It requires an ability to recognize emotions, understand where they come from, and manage them helpfully. There are four key factors to emotional intelligence: self-awareness, self-management, social awareness, and relationship management.

Self-Awareness

With "self-awareness," you can accurately identify your own emotions and what triggered them. Seems simple, right? You cry when sad, eat when "hangry," and smile when happy. Yet, is it that easy? You often don't notice your emotions until you reach maximum density. When you plan to study in the library but instead choose the social scene in the student center or escape campus as soon as class ends, it's likely your emotions steer your behavior.

You might not realize it in the moment, though. If your follow through is poor, if you struggle to focus, or if you rationalize unproductive or destructive behavior (such as skipped assignments or blowups with your boss), it's time to raise your emotional self-awareness. You can't take steps to fix the problem if you don't understand how a specific negative emotion propels you into a self-sabotaging habit.

Self-Management

Once you identify your emotional state, you can take steps to manage it. "Self-management" involves knowing how your emotions influence thoughts and behaviors. The next step is to take an appropriate strategy to mute, override, or transform the emotion when necessary. At Oscar's work, he failed to self-manage when he snapped rudely at his customer. Instead, he needed to pause, smile (it *was* a little funny, after all), respectfully verify what his customer wanted, and deliver it. Oscar may have felt a release in the moment when he snapped at the customer, but he ultimately caused more problems later.

Social Awareness

"Social awareness" is the ability to recognize the emotions of others in a social situation, usually by studying facial expressions, body language, and the quality of a person's voice. It also involves awareness of the social rules of the situation itself — is it a team huddle at the start of a work shift or is it the after-work happy hour?

Sometimes, it's easier to identify the emotions of others than your own. Oscar knew, for example, that his boss was crazy busy when he asked for time off to see Wax Accident in concert. He could read his boss's emotions in his furrowed brow, his strained voice, and his fast pace as he shuttled from one task to the next. Yet, Oscar still asked. And his boss, of course, said no.

Relationship Management

"Relationship management" is the ability to respond helpfully to others' emotional states in order to create positive relationships. Relationship management is the ability to predict how a person might react in a given situation. Often, your satisfaction at work, school, or home can hinge on how well a relationship functions. You generally avoid stirring up anger, frustration, and irritability in other people. Instead, you try to inspire trust, cooperation, and friendliness. Had Oscar chosen to help his manager out by picking up an extra task and later, during some downtime, ask about the night off, he might have been more successful.

You Be the Judge 1

Take a look at how these students manage their college work. Given the advice on well-being basics, how successful will they likely be? How do you anticipate they will be doing by the end of the term? Jot down your ideas. When you finish, turn to the end of the chapter to check them.

1. Brandon's full-time student schedule totals sixteen credits. He does not work, but he does take his intramural soccer team seriously and never misses a practice or a game. He also takes his diet and exercise habits seriously, which means he plans regular workouts and avoids junk food. One major assignment is a research paper for his US history course. He must use a citation style called Chicago and at least one primary source. It is due two weeks before final exams. His attendance is consistent, and his class materials are well organized. He receives the assignment during the second week of the term, reads it carefully, and studies the rubric. It seems to make sense, so he files it away and plans to start the assignment a week before it is due. Brandon assumes he can clear out a day or two to concentrate on the assignment.

2. Ricky decides to take ten credits rather than a full-time load of courses because he hasn't been in school for over twenty years. He struggles with just about every aspect of the college culture, but especially the online learning and email systems. Still, he's motivated by the challenge. He's also outgoing and easily connects with people. He creates a weekly study plan, but he rarely follows through. Every time he attempts to focus and get schoolwork done, he gets caught in the middle of some family drama. Ricky offers to deliver a short oral presentation as his role in a group project. Everyone else contributes a piece of the presentation, and it is Ricky's job to learn the entire content and deliver it clearly, maintain eye contact with the audience, and finish within five minutes. His group members email him the slide presenta-tion days before the presentation date. On the day of the presentation, he tells his classmates that he couldn't find the slides and isn't prepared.

3. Zoë is a full-time student in a college algebra course. It is midterm. She's missed four of seventeen classes so far because she oversleeps after late nights out with her non-college friends. She tries to complete all her homework as it is assigned, but she skips problems that give her too much trouble because the professor goes over them in class. During the last class meeting, the professor hands out a practice test for a midterm exam two days later. Zoë is caught off guard. She starts to feel sick. After class, she goes to the food court and orders her usual lunch of chicken tenders and Mountain Dew. Her phone buzzes with a text from a friend who wants her to see a movie with him that night.

4. Edwin, also a full-time student, sits two rows back from Zoë in the same college algebra course. He studies every opportunity he can—on the bus to and from campus, between classes, during lunch, during downtime at his job, and late into the evening. His notes are detailed, color-coded, and labeled. If a problem gives him trouble, he sticks with it until he gets it. He uses the college's eTutoring service because he often works on his algebra homework late at night. Edwin has not slept well since the term began, however, and he basically lives on Red Bull. He gets winded when he climbs stairs. When he glances at the algebra practice test, it all looks familiar, but for reasons he cannot explain, the thought of that test makes his stomach flip. He's convinced he's already forgotten how to do most of the problems.

Develop Emotional Intelligence

The process of living
is the process of
reacting to stress.
— Stanley J. Sarnoff

People with high emotional intelligence can recognize and manage their emotions, recognize other people's emotions, and relate to others effectively. The more skilled you become in emotional intelligence the more it can contribute to your long-term well-being.

Research shows that emotionally intelligent people are more likely to engage in positive behaviors. They adapt to new situations more readily and maintain better family and peer relationships. They develop better support systems with friends and colleagues. In school, emotionally intelligent people are more satisfied, and at work they perform better, which often results in higher pay. As a result, they have better overall job satisfaction and suffer from burnout less frequently. Again, emotional intelligence doesn't mean you never experience sadness, stress, and anger. It means that, most of the time, you manage those feelings in a way that limits their negative impact. It means you don't allow your emotions to sabotage your efforts in college, work, or relationships.

The good news is that you can improve your emotional intelligence, just like other skills. You can apply a growth mindset to emotional intelligence, too.

Recognize Emotion

You can raise your awareness of emotion (yours and others) as expressed in faces, postures, gestures, voices, and behaviors with a few simple techniques. Try these tips a few times a day for an emotion check. You can set a timer or do it at set intervals, such as at meals. Certainly, do this any time the little alarm in your head signals that your emotions are affecting you in a bad way.

Try these questions to help you recognize your emotions:

» **Check in with your physical sensations:** Is your jaw clenched? Are your shoulders up by your ears? Is your gut calm or is it disgruntled? Any other signs of tension? Are you twitchy? What about that heart rate?

» **Observe your current behaviors:** Do you sigh, roll your eyes, scowl, swear (even under your breath), pace, tap your foot or pencil, snap at (or ignore) others, slouch more than usual, procrastinate? Are you respectful, helpful, on time?

We cannot change
anything unless we
accept it.
— Carl Jung

» **Observe your current thoughts:** Are you preoccupied with a particular problem or task? Do your thoughts zoom from one idea to another? Do you imagine negative experiences? Do you daydream about positive experiences?

This information will help you take stock of your emotional situation and decide whether you are angry, impatient, sad, stressed, worried, happy, anxious, or excited.

Label Emotion

Develop a broader vocabulary to describe the range of emotions you and others feel. Sometimes, you just know that you feel bad or good or maybe nothing at all. It can help to differentiate between levels of "badness," "goodness," or even "nothingness." That specificity can help you pinpoint the problem and manage it—if you can name it, you can address it.

When it comes to "bad" emotions or behaviors, use labels in a narrow way. Instead of saying "life sucks," find a word that more closely points to the source of that suck. For example, you might feel angry, sad, anxious, guilty, impatient, frustrated, lonely, weak, revolted, fearful, inferior, unworthy, unrecognized, unloved, disorganized, or unsuccessful. These words get beneath the surface and can help you and others understand how you really feel. Label feelings of "nothingness" if you can. This can be difficult. Usually, feeling nothing is associated with negative emotions. For example, you might feel empty, hollow, worthless, disengaged, or disinterested, like your life has little meaning. Those feelings can be problematic.

Use specific labels in the same way for "good" emotions. For example, you might feel happy, euphoric, elated, hopeful, strong, smart, loving, joyful, confident, in control, amused, organized, engaged, relaxed, patient, worthy, successful, and so on. Often, however, people are just in a state of balance—and balance is good. There is nothing wrong with being content. You've likely heard the phrase "no news is good news." If your needs are met and your life is on track, that's a real positive. You may not be crying tears of joy at every beautiful sunset, but it doesn't mean you don't appreciate it. It's important to determine when the nothingness feeling is positive or negative.

Understand Emotion

Once you identify your emotional state, consider the causes and consequences of these emotions, such as how they influence your attention, thoughts, decisions, and behavior. This is especially important to do when you're overwhelmed and stressed out.

Take a minute to ask yourself what the root cause of this feeling is and how it impacts your life. For example, if your schedule is particularly hectic, ask yourself why. Did you get stuck in traffic? Did you have a disagreement with someone? Perhaps you procrastinated and now need to catch up? Are you avoiding something? Are you in a situation that you don't know how to handle?

Now ask yourself how this situation impacts your life. Do you make good, reasonable choices? Do you perform as well as you can at work or school? Do you get along with others? Do you think that others are satisfied with how you interact with them? Do you get negative or positive feedback?

Express Emotion

People need to know how and when to express emotions appropriately with different people and in different situations. It can be quite healthy to express emotions. However, if you express them at the wrong time or in the wrong place, you can cause friction and derail your plans.

When Oscar snapped at his customer, he expressed emotion at a time that simply wasn't okay. His boss wasn't happy, his customer wasn't happy (he had to give her the coffee for free and lost a tip), and he didn't feel any better. In fact, he made the situation worse. He could have waited until his break and chuckled at the customer's silly complaint (seriously, café latte literally means *milk* coffee) and likely would have had a more sympathetic audience who shared his experiences.

You learn to express emotion largely through imitation of the people who raised you, your peers, and your teachers. If those people were emotionally intelligent and modeled how to express emotions positively, you probably know how to do it. If, on the other hand, they never learned to manage their emotions either, you may be in for challenges (and opportunities to grow).

Emotional intelligence is also culturally regulated. For example, in the dominant American culture, males are socially permitted to express anger in certain public situations, but they are expected to suppress sadness. Women are often allowed or even encouraged to express sadness, yet they are often expected to suppress anger. This is changing, but the impact of these cultural expectations and how they affect men and women's communication styles can't be overlooked. Also, Americans, in general, are viewed as "smiley" by other cultures. Americans tend to smile more to express friendliness, while other cultures are more reserved.

Generally, negative emotions should be expressed openly with those who trust and understand you. They can often help you to solve a problem or to feel better in a safe, trusted space. This does not apply to casual acquaintances (with the exception of a professional paid to help you). If you experience strong negative emotions such as frustration, anger, envy, or irritation, it's best to give yourself a time-out before you do or say anything in a group of casual acquaintances or strangers.

Positive emotions are often welcomed in most situations. Still, you might not want to dance on top of a table to express your happiness at earning an A on your chemistry test, as much as that might be an entirely understandable reaction. It often comes back to what persona is acceptable and productive for you at the moment.

Regulate Emotion

Take time to build a tool kit of effective strategies to use when you need to prevent, reduce, initiate, maintain, and enhance emotions. Self-regulation limits the negative consequences of negative emotions and makes good use of positive feelings. You can learn to calm yourself, control stress, and manage your emotions so that you better manage relationships, remain productive, and stay healthy. This comes down, in large part, to how you deal with negative emotions and how you cultivate positive ones.

Manage Negative Emotions

Negative emotions are a normal part of life and are oftentimes healthy responses to personal setbacks. DNA and millions of years of evolution have taught humans to recognize and react to what their brain identifies as a threat. Emotions like fear, shame, anger, and repulsion can stop you from doing something you shouldn't (or from doing it again), such as picking up a poisonous snake, reading your roommate's diary, or cheating on a test. Emotions like sadness and grief, in fact, can be common after a personal loss and can help you heal. Failure or lack of organization can sometimes drive you to manage a situation better if you have a growth mindset.

How you handle these emotions makes all the difference. The common ways people tend to deal with emotions include expressive suppression, distraction, and reappraisal, which we'll discuss in the next sections.

Expressive Suppression

When you practice "expressive suppression," you are aware of emotions, but you do not allow them to surface in the form of facial expressions, gestures, or verbal messages. This technique can be useful if you know that the emotion will pass quickly and you can easily distance yourself from whatever triggered it.

Oscar could have suppressed his impatience with his customer because he likely would have gotten over it as soon as she left. This method is not helpful for recurring or ongoing triggers. For example, if the customer came in regularly and complained in a verbally abusive way to Oscar, suppression would not be effective or could damage Oscar's well-being.

Distraction

Another way to manage emotion is to find a mental or physical activity that distracts from and soothes your discomfort, such as a sketching, playing Tetris, or jogging around the park. This technique works well if you are then able to refocus attention to more goal-oriented activities once the storm has passed. Distraction doesn't work well if it means you avoid difficult but meaningful activities.

Oscar, for example, indulged in *Adventure Time.* A single episode makes sense because he was really in a bad mental space and the show puts him in a better mood. He still needs to be able to pass the remote over to his roommate, however, and head to his room to distract himself with a few flash cards for his biology midterm.

Reappraisal

To apply the strategy of "reappraisal," rethink the event that triggered the negative emotion in a more useful and positive way or downplay the negative impact. Here are three ways to reappraise the situation.

First, identify what you learned as a result of the event. The experience

I was saying "I'm the greatest" long before I believed it.
— Muhammad Ali

may have seemed negative at the time, but it may have taught you a valuable lesson (even if the lesson was to *not* do it that way again).

Second, identify *any* positive outcomes, even if they are small. Most negative experiences do have their silver lining. You may have gotten stuck in traffic behind some pokey, smelly old garbage truck that made you late for class. However, the truck did make you slow down well before you saw the police car behind some trees on the side of the freeway. You avoided a costly speeding ticket thanks to the fine workers at your local waste management center.

Third, identify a worse outcome that could have occurred but didn't. In other words, be grateful that it wasn't worse). You didn't get the A you wanted on your essay, but you did get a B, a good enough grade to maintain your scholarship. If it had been a letter grade lower . . . well, you hate to think about that chain of events.

Reappraisal tends to be the most effective and healthy approach for long-term management of negative emotions. Reappraisal might work well for Oscar if the milk-avoidant customer is a chronic whiner. He might learn what *her* triggers are and find ways to work around them. He might even take pride in his ability to win her over. He could view it as a challenge and look forward to her visits as an opportunity to show his boss how it's done.

Access Positive Emotions

Negative emotions will have less of an impact if you learn to rely on positive emotions more often. In the midst of stress and discomfort, a positive attitude helps you bounce back.

The following strategies can help you access positive emotions:

» **Focus on what matters:** Live by your values and work towards your personal goals rather than by other's expectations. When you experience rough patches, remind yourself of the bigger picture.

» **Perform acts of kindness:** Do something nice for someone else. It really does make you feel good. Sometimes that small dose of "feel good" is enough to tip you in the right direction.

» **Be mindful:** Mindfulness means you focus intently on the here and now rather than on a negative past or an anxious future. On a daily basis, bring your thoughts to the present moment: focus on your immediate environment's sights, sounds, and smells. Your mind may try to pull away from the present. Gently coax it back.

» **Savor:** Think about a positive event from your past, such as a fun daytrip, a restful snooze in your backyard hammock, a win in a soccer game, or a simple walk on a bright, crisp autumn day. Again, this works as "mood medication." It changes your state of mind.

» **Acknowledge the good:** Notice even the small things that are good in your day, like the fact that the rain stopped (or started), that you had enough gas in your tank, or that the cafeteria now serves street tacos.

» **Honor yourself:** Identify and remind yourself of your strengths and accomplishments. You *do* have them—lots of them. If you can't think of them, ask a friend to remind you.

» **Show gratitude:** Find experiences for which you are thankful throughout your day and express that gratitude. If your street taco is as good as you expected it to be, thank the cook.

Grow Your Support Network

Everyone has a support network, though certainly some are larger than others. The people you surround yourself will strongly influence your resilience and persistence when you face a challenge. Some can help you directly on your task while others can help with your practical needs. Others help through emotional support. You learned earlier in the book how important support networks can be to your success. They help you to cope with the inevitable challenges you will face.

If you haven't already done so, identify and develop a network that supports you in these ways:

» **Academically:** These individuals or support services on campus can keep you focused on studies and work with you to learn.

» **Emotionally:** People or groups that give you emotional support will encourage you, listen to you, and acknowledge your feelings. They will also be honest in how they help you. This may be your close friends and family, student club or organization, student health center or campus counselor, or medical professional.

» **Practically:** Sometimes you need a ride to campus, someone to babysit, or a hot meal. Take your mom up on her offer to do your laundry (once in a while). Negotiate some household chores with your little brother so you can get more study time in. Join a carpool to get to and from campus.

You Be the Judge 2

Read about the following students' negative emotions. Identify what technique they use and whether or not they are learning to persist. For students who do not manage their negative emotions well, think about methods they could use to turn themselves around. Jot down your ideas. When you finish, turn to the end of the chapter to check them.

1. Sonia feels sick to her stomach when she thinks about her required public speaking course. She has successfully completed her general education requirements for her dental hygienist program with an A average. She "saved" public speaking for last. During the first class, she learns she needs to deliver three separate speeches. She holds it together long enough to get to the bathroom before she breaks into tears. Once she dries her eyes, she heads to advising convinced she has to give up on her goal and find a different program of study.

2. Morris has little experience with writing, so his editing skills are weak. As a construction worker for many years, he never worried about the clarity of his text messages (the only form of job-related writing he ever had to do). He's now enrolled in the building inspection program and it requires two writing courses. He takes the first right away. Every writing assignment frustrates Morris. He has a powerful desire to flip his desk or toss the keyboard out the window. He does not do this. Instead, he reminds himself of his work ethic on a job site. He is proud of his attention to detail and his well-honed construction skills. He also reminds himself to edit his paper with the same attention that an inspector would use to ensure the safety and soundness of a building.

3. Zander is excited to follow his grandfather's footsteps and become a fire chief. He enrolls in the fire science program. In his first term, however, he's required to take college algebra. Zander never felt successful in math. Three weeks into the term, he receives his first exam with a D grade. Worse yet, his professor compliments the class for doing "so well" on their first exam. He's bitter. He wasn't expecting an A, but he feels he put in the work needed to do well enough. When his dad asks about the test, he lies and says he got a B-. After the disappointment of that first exam, he decides to not waste any more time and energy caring. He continues to earn poor grades. His other courses begin to suffer as bitterness seeps into his attitude towards college.

Keep in mind that support doesn't mean they enable bad habits. Friends who don't appreciate the sacrifices you make while going to college may enable you to skip a class or ignore a homework assignment. They might think you'll feel better if you take a break. Classmates who suggest the professor is to blame for your poor performance enable an irresponsible mindset. Family members who don't understand the difference between high school and college expectations may convince you that you can always ask for extra credit. Someone who enables you to repeat the same mistakes over and over, or ignore the root of a problem, isn't supportive (even though they may think they are).

Figure 2. Preparing for a test can take many forms. Some students like to study as a small group to compare notes and practice answering questions. Do what works for you.

Fortunately, Oscar has a good support system. Oscar does have study partners to help him prepare for his biology exam. He can get advice on how to approach his boss from his older brother. He can ask his roommate to do some of his grocery shopping for him when he's really pressed for time. Oscar's roommate ignored his mini-tantrum, smiled, and said, "Responsibility demands sacrifice." Oscar recognized the effort to encourage him. He sighed and handed over the remote. Then, he got up from the couch, rolled his shoulders, and strode to his room with determination.

Manage Performance Anxiety

Performance anxiety is the nervousness, dread, and fear of failure that surfaces just before and during quizzes, exams, or presentations. It troubles many students throughout their college careers. This anxiety can disturb your eating and sleeping patterns and stir up plenty of negative thoughts before the test. During a test, the anxiety can disrupt your memory, your ability to understand the questions, and your ability to stay focused. Unless you act, this anxiety may help create the thing that it fears—a poor performance.

Performance anxiety doesn't just happen, though. It's an emotional pattern that develops over many years. It takes some serious effort to manage it, but it can be done.

Figure 3. During a test, try to relax. Being prepared will help you relax some, but focusing on being calm and confident can improve your test scores and lessen your test anxiety. This guy is going to do very well.

Find Perspective

Performance anxiety requires self-awareness of any harmful core beliefs you may have about evaluation. If you experience performance anxiety, likely one of these beliefs lurks in the back of your mind. One belief that generates anxiety is that any kind of failure on a test reveals shameful, personal flaws. Perfectionism, the belief that you are only acceptable as a student or person if you do everything perfectly, also contributes to performance anxiety. Catastrophizing is another belief that feeds performance anxiety — the thought that failure on any single test will automatically result in a cascade of failures and personal harm.

These beliefs don't come out of nowhere. Students with high levels of performance anxiety have often acquired these beliefs from others (such as parents or coaches) in an honest attempt to help them succeed. Anxiety can also occur as a result of negative social comparisons to other students or siblings who do well on tests.

However, even if real experiences are at the heart of these beliefs, the reality is that a low score on a test usually means that you didn't prepare for that particular test as carefully as you could have for any number of reasons. It might be a lack of prior experience with the subject matter — you didn't prepare more because you didn't know you needed to. Maybe no one's ever shown you how to prepare or you didn't understand your professor's expectations. She wanted analysis, perhaps, and you studied definitions.

Certainly, it's important to understand why your test preparation wasn't good enough. However, when it comes to test anxiety, it's more important that you have the right perspective on the test. Remember that it's just an evaluation of your skills and understanding in one class —it's only a snapshot of where you are on that particular day. It's not a personal grade of your life and potential. If you didn't do well, that's okay. Improve your preparation for the next test, and you will do better.

Figure 4. You can find practice tests online for just about any subject. If you can get one from your professor, that's even better.

Carlie offers a good example of someone who suffers from test anxiety. She's the first one in her family to seek a degree after high school, and no one in her family has ever had much academic success. She once brought home an F on an elementary school test, and her uncle joked how she was following in her mom's footsteps, who had to repeat the fifth grade and dropped out as a high-school sophomore. Even though her uncle was trying to be funny, Carlie has lived in fear of that comment ever since.

All the way through high school, Carlie never had much help with what and how to study, so she typically did not do well on tests. Her low-to-average scores made her worry that she wasn't smart enough to succeed in school. She gradually became more and more anxious that the next failed test would be the beginning of the end for her school career.

Carlie needs to break this self-defeating cycle by learning how to better prepare for any given test. We'll take a look at that in the next section. However, she also needs to look at tests differently and reframe her thoughts about them. "Reframing" means when you look for any negative core beliefs in your mind and counteract them with more positive alternatives, positive self-talk, and tangible strategies, such as study schedules and tutoring.

Similarly, if you are a perfectionist, you can remind yourself that no one does anything perfectly without first doing it poorly. In fact, inquiry and the growth mindset expect and embrace struggles and errors and all the lessons those imperfect results will teach you. You can reframe your goal of perfectionism with the goal of mastery. You develop mastery over time with practice, trial, error, and more practice.

Manage Stress before the Test

Most students, especially those with performance anxiety, feel their level of nervousness increase the night before the evaluation. You can get through that evening anxiety, and make the morning less stressful, by getting organized.

Get Organized

Organize your notes and any other materials you need and have them ready to go in your backpack. Figure out your transportation for the next day so

You Be the Judge 3

Below are stories from the lives of students who have test anxiety. What core belief might they have that feeds their anxiety? Jot down your ideas. When you finish, turn to the end of the chapter to check them.

1. Dawn Sutherland's older sister, Delia, was the high-school valedictorian and received scholarships to top-notch universities. Delia was renowned for seemingly flawless performances across all kinds of academic tasks. It did not matter if it was English or math or science, Delia shined. When teachers discover Dawn is Delia's younger sister, they act giddy. Dawn hears too frequently how excited they are to have a Sutherland in their course and how they expect "great things" from her.

2. Ricardo's much beloved mother believes in fear as a tool to get children to behave. She is an expert in worst-case scenarios. Children are regularly kidnapped because they don't follow their parents' rules. Lives are ruined because of one fateful decision to follow a friend's bad example rather than remember a mother's wise guidance. She also makes it clear that the only acceptable professions for Ricardo is a medical doctor or a lawyer. Anything else might leave Ricardo unemployable. Yes, unemployable.

3. Autumn always starts on academic tasks right before the due date. She does not study for tests until the night before and crams whatever she can into her head. Sometimes it works. Sometimes it doesn't. She forgets the times it does not work and only remembers the times it does. Her study habits "work" for her. She has not stopped to wonder why she has test anxiety. She thinks it's just the way she operates.

that you will arrive to class with enough time to settle in. Lay out the clothes you will wear and get your breakfast and snacks prepared ahead of time. Be sure to drink plenty of water throughout the day to keep your hydration level at its prime (again, brain food).

Sleep

Once you are organized, go to bed. Go. To. Bed. Get as much sleep as possible. Set two alarms if you're one of those people who worries one might not go off (and set it away from your bed so that you *have* to get up to turn it off). If you get into bed and can't fall asleep after twenty minutes, leave your bed and try a relaxing activity, such as listening to calming music or reading something soothing and slightly boring—on paper, too, not on an electronic device. Return to bed when you start to drift off.

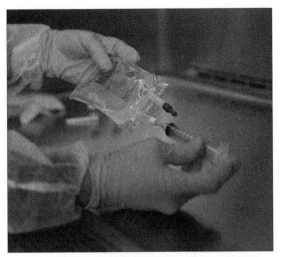

Figure 5. It's important to practice any technical skills you're expected to do in a practical exam. This pharmacy technician student practices filling IV bags in full clean room apparel, recreating the circumstances of a future test.

Set Yourself Up for Success

On the day of the test, as much as possible, follow your regular daily routine and prep your mind and body to limit distractions and anxiety. If a little bit of physical activity before the test helps work out some of your nerves, arrive to campus early enough to take a short stroll before heading to class. Bring some bottled water with you and sip lightly before the exam. Have a light, healthy snack beforehand if you know you may get hungry before the exam is done. In other words, try to avoid going into the room thirsty, hungry, or with a full bladder because these can cause unnecessary distractions.

You can try to manage distractions in the classroom as well. Some students grow stressed when they see people turn in their exams before them. Sit where your view of the door and the growing stack of exams is limited. Also, politely avoid discussing the test with others waiting with you before you begin the exam. These conversations tend to make people feel more anxious rather than less anxious. Don't let a last-minute conversation confuse you about the material. Finally, check with your professor to see if you can take short breaks if needed.

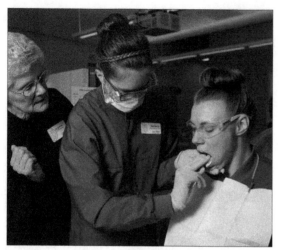

Figure 6. Practicing a skill while your professor watches is one way to get feedback on your skills. This way, even if it's graded later, you get their assessment right away and sometimes while you're still performing the action being assessed.

Manage Self-Talk

Deal with negative thoughts directly. After her lackluster math exam, Carlie adjusted her plan. The week before her chemistry midterm, she ate well, studied strategically, and got enough sleep. She did become anxious as soon as she sat down in her chair for the test, but this time she knew she was prepared and replaced the negative voice with positive encouragement. She wrote her last-minute worries down on paper. Then, she crossed them out and wrote down her strengths and why she expected to do well. She visualized herself successfully answering questions, solving problems, and responding without hesitation to the material.

Carlie focused on her inner dialogue and used her emotional intelligence. Remember, this includes a focus on the physical issues, as well. As we've discussed, physical symptoms often relate to emotions. Pay attention to your breath. If it is short and shallow, resist taking a deep breath and instead slow your breathing down. Breathe in for a few beats, pause, then slowly breathe out. Pause again, then slowly inhale. Look for any tension in your neck, shoulders, and jaw. Raise and lower your shoulders to your ears to relax them. Wiggle your jaw side to side. Yes, people may look at you, but then they'll see how it relaxes you, and they'll do the same.

As you experience these telltale signs of stress, remind yourself that stress is your body's natural preparation for a challenge. Rapid breathing and tense muscles are not symptoms of a harmful disorder. Your mind needs oxygen to think more clearly, so it signals your lungs to take in more oxygen. Your muscles tense as a way to further engage for the work ahead. Your body prepares for the coming evaluation.

Manage Stress during the Test

The test is handed out and you're anxious to get started. Hold off a second. *Listen closely* to any comments your professor makes before you look at the exam. You'd be surprised how many times students do poorly because they don't listen to instructions.

Figure 7. When you take a test, build up your confidence by doing the easy questions first. For all the questions, however, read carefully to understand what the question asks you to explain and how it wants you to organize your answer. Have a plan.

To begin, read through the entire exam carefully and circle or underline key words that describe the actions you need to take for each problem or question. Pay attention to how the exam is organized and which questions have the highest point values. Next, make a quick plan for how you will budget your time. Finally, either on the back of a page or on a piece of scratch paper, jot down the important facts, ideas, principles, or memory cues to help you with the exam.

It's not a bad idea to build up your confidence by doing the easy questions on the exam first. Be careful, though, to read each question carefully to understand what it asks you to explain and how it wants you to organize your answer. Have a plan.

A few test-taking strategies will help you keep your stress lower. They won't help much if you didn't study in the first place. However, if you did study, the strategies can provide concrete steps to handle different types of questions, which can relieve some anxiety.

Multiple-Choice Questions

Multiple-choice questions always seem like they will be the easiest—they ask you to select the correct answer from a given set of answers (somewhere in that list, the correct answer is staring right at you). However, it's never that simple. Your professors do different things to force you to think about

Figure 8. Use a to-do list to break down large projects into manageable chunks. This tool works great for keeping track of lots of different tasks, too.

the questions and answers and not just pick a phrase that you vaguely recall from the textbook.

Here are some strategies for how to answer these questions:

» **Underline important words:** Look for words such as "best," "least," "especially," "usually," "first" and "last" in the question to help you determine the right answer.

» **Be alert:** Some questions ask for a *non*-example. If the word "not" or "false" appears in the question, circle it. Make sure you look for the negative.

» **Answer the question in your mind first:** Do this before you read the answer choices.

» **Consider each option:** Read the choices as "true/false" statements. Cross out false answers.

» **Watch out for absolutes:** Words such as "never," "always," "every," and "none" are absolutes and are not usually found in correct answers.

Once you take these steps compare the answers that remain with your initial answer before you make your final choice.

True-or-False Questions

Be alert for absolute statements in seemingly binary questions—questions that require an either/or answer. Statements that use "never," "always," "every," and "none," are rarely true. Another strategy is to think about a positive statement in the negative. If the statement reads "Procrastination is a helpful response to deadlines" think of it as "Procrastination is an unhelpful response to deadlines." Then compare the positive and negative statements. If the negative statement sounds correct, the original statement is probably false, as in the example. If the positive sounds correct, the original statement is probably true.

Matching Columns

You may be asked to match questions or terms from one column with answers or definitions from a second column. Read the instructions carefully to understand how to match the items. What sort of relationship connects them?

Once you have that figured out, these other techniques come into play:

» Read all the phrases first when you are asked to match single words to phrases.

» Make the obvious matches and then work on the ones that require more thought.

» Mark items off as you use them so you can see which items remain.

» Remember that there may be items that go unmatched or one item may have two matches.

Short Answer

Again, read the question carefully and circle words that say exactly what information is requested. You need to understand the actual question in its entirety. If the question has more than one part, number each to make sure

Figure 9. Different types of test questions will need different types of answers. It's important to use the right strategies for answering the different types of questions on your test.

you answer all parts of the question. You can number the parts of your answer, too. That will impress your professor.

When you're asked to give a *short* answer, make every word count. Don't write stuff that is kind of about the question. You won't improve your answer by adding "fluff." Focus on the quality of the content with direct and specific answers.

Essay Questions

Essay questions almost always expect two things from you. First, they want you to clearly and briefly state your answer to the question at hand—usually in just a sentence or two. Second, they expect you to explain why your answer makes sense in a paragraph or more. To do that, you have to include relevant evidence.

These techniques will help you do well with essay questions:

» Read the question carefully and circle keywords and number the parts. Pay attention to any words that describe your professor's expectations.

» Create a quick outline for your essay before you write it—just a line for each future paragraph. Make brief notes about important terms, names, and dates you will mention in each paragraph.

» Introduce your essay by identifying the question and presenting your main answer in the first paragraph.

» Avoid spending time on a catchy introduction. You don't have time for that, and anyway, your professor has to read it whether it's catchy or not.

» Check again to make sure you answered all parts of the question.

» Write neatly, skipping every other line, so that you can later go back, correct errors, and possibly add things you forgot in the blank lines.

Don't be startled or discouraged by another person handing in an exam early in the class period. Tests are not foot races. The fastest test-taker does not always win. More often than not, students who turn tests in early have actually given up. They didn't know the answers, so they did what they could and didn't want to spend any more time on it. If the voice of self-doubt starts to yammer at you about being slow, tell it to shut up. It's often the slowest test-takers who do the best. They work methodically and review their answers before turning the test in, and by doing so they give themselves the best chances of success. You do you.

You Be the Judge 4

How well do you think these students manage the stress of testing? Jot down your ideas. When you finish, turn to the end of the chapter to check them.

1. It is José's turn to give his speech. He has about five minutes to wait. He quietly lists all the worries he has and then crosses each out. Next to each line he writes, "I practiced this speech fifteen times over three days. I made good eye contact. I never went over ten minutes and I never went under nine minutes and forty-two seconds. Megan, someone I barely know, laughed at my introduction, which is good. I wanted her to laugh. She also recognized my thesis and thought my summary was clear."

2. Rex arrives early to class as usual. The first thing he does is ask the professor if he can retake the test if he fails. The professor refers him to the syllabus. He then asks if there is any extra credit. The professor refers him to the syllabus. A few students walk in. He strikes up a conversation with them, asking how much they studied. He asks which topic gave them the most trouble. He asks if they think the test will be hard. He asks if they think the professor will grade it easy. He says he hopes all the questions are "multiple guess." His classmates roll their eyes and take their seats at a distance.

3. Sydney has her exam and finds the blank side of a page. She writes down some of the mnemonic devices she created for several key terms and concepts. She then studies the exam in front of her. She scans each section and notes what kind of questions are asked, what topics they cover, and how many points each is worth. She sees a short essay question at the end and reads it. Ugh, she thinks. Still, it's not worth *that many* points. She decides to work on the other questions for sixty minutes and then give herself thirty minutes for the essay question. That will leave ten minutes to review her answers. She notices her jaw is clenched hard and wiggles it. She notices her face feels warm and her breathing is a bit quick. She moves her attention to her breath and starts slowing it down. She says to herself, "Let's find the easy ones first."

Figure 10. Tests are a normal part of being in college. If you can master your feelings about tests, you'll be that much closer to mastering the test itself.

Last, and this applies to practical tests as well, if your brain freezes up on you during the exam, don't run screaming from the room. Instead, take a quick rest. Close your eyes and say something encouraging to yourself. Open your eyes and scan the room for three physical objects you hadn't noticed before. This temporary distraction releases your brain from its frozen state. Sip some water. You brought water, right? Practice slow, intentional breathing and muscle relaxation techniques. Then return to the test and expect your mind to reset. It will.

Respond to the Results

If you prepare well for an evaluation, chances are your grade will reflect that preparation. A good grade isn't luck. It means you successfully learned the ideas and skills that your professor has been teaching and you were able to control any anxiety that surfaced. A low grade means that somewhere your preparation took a wrong turn or, possibly, that anxiety got the better of you.

You will naturally feel disappointment with a low grade and satisfaction with a high grade, but try to prevent those emotions from feeding any lingering, unhelpful beliefs. It's better to reflect on what the test shows you about your current strengths and weaknesses. That means you need to pay attention to what your professor writes on your evaluation and what he or she explains to the class.

When tests or papers are first returned in class, resist the urge to check your grade right away, which can distract you from class discussion. Instead, listen to your professor's general feedback to the class and take notes. Something that everyone generally did well on is less likely to be used on another test. Something that gave many students trouble will likely return, so you'll need to review it.

Strategically review your test or paper by identifying each error you made and making a note to yourself about why you made the error. Look for a pattern in those errors. You might have missed several questions that asked for non-examples, for example, because you missed that "non" part of the question. Or, you might not have recognized that the question asked you to explain how two different ideas connect. You

Figure 11. When you get your test results back, do your best to stay positive. Remember that the sting of a low grade is offset by the benefit of knowing exactly how to do better on your next test.

still don't see the connection, so you make a note to check in with a tutor or someone else in class to figure it out. If a question asked about unfamiliar material, talk with the professor to figure out how you missed it in the first place.

Don't forget to give yourself a mental high five for those questions you answered correctly. Confirm that the correct answer was the result of good preparation and not just a lucky guess. Think about how you successfully made that information stick—it helps to solidify good habits. If it was just a lucky guess, add that item to the material you need to review.

So, you analyzed your errors, now what? Don't file that test away just yet, especially if you never want to see it again. It helps to make corrections to the test. That may seem like a waste of time—it's not going to change the grade, after all—but it actually helps you avoid making the same error twice. When you wrote the wrong answer, you reinforced some faulty information in your memory. You can reverse that process by writing down the correct answer. Your corrected quizzes and midterm exams are an important study tool for final exams. Make sure you file them with your notes.

Some professors choose not to return tests, so make appointments to see them soon after the test to review it and your performance. Take notes on what you had trouble with.

Final Thoughts

You can build your emotional intelligence just like any other skill—with focus, practice, and a desire to achieve. In doing so, you'll find yourself able to maintain a clearer perspective, at least most of the time, and better able to persist through difficult challenges.

College certainly comes with challenges. Carlie's ability to improve did not appear magically. When she learned that entering the EMT program meant passing numerous tests with a B or better, she didn't feel confident that she could perform consistently at that level. She drifted into the advising center, wondering if she could be successful in *any* program.

Her counselor listened to her worries about test anxiety and gently challenged her beliefs about it. She gave Carlie some anxiety reduction techniques and referred her to the learning assistance center. There she developed a study plan for her most challenging course, chemistry, and learned how to take more effective notes and create practice tests. She found a phone app that she uses to review key terms. She returned to the center with each graded test to discover ways to prepare for the next one and celebrate her successes along the way. She has also learned more about what works for her through trial and error, which is part of being human.

Carlie and Oscar both rose to their challenges by improving their emotional intelligence. They increased their self-awareness and learned to manage their own thoughts, feelings, and behaviors to their advantage. This is something we can all do, and it will benefit ourselves and those around us. Most importantly, emotional intelligence sets each individual up to make the most of life and appreciate those challenges that make it both worthwhile and beautiful.

Reflect on Your Self-Assessment

You may have noticed that many statements in your self-assessment focused on self-awareness and relationship management. It probably seemed odd when you looked at this at the beginning of the chapter. You may have wondered what relationships have to do with your success in college. Now, though, you should have a better understanding of how important emotional intelligence is to your academic career and life in general.

The higher your score on the assessment, the more emotionally intelligent you are. Keep in mind that as new challenges arise, it's normal to have to exercise your emotional intelligence—and everyone likely has a few problem areas. Consider what you learned in this chapter and hit the emotional gym. Give some of the following DIYs a try.

Do It Yourself

Here are some practical things that you can do to boost your emotional intelligence and manage how you handle and respond to the rigors of college life:

1. Create a proactive coping plan. List as many potential stressors you can think of and then identify something you can do to either avoid them or lessen their impact. Any time you can responsibly avoid a stressor, do so.

2. To being the process of reappraisal, check your beliefs about stress: Watch "How to Make Stress Your Friend" by Kelly McGonigal (www.ted.com/talks/kelly_mcgonigal_how_to_make_stress_your_friend).

3. Visit the website *Greater Good in Action (*https://ggia.berkeley.edu), a project of the Greater Good Science Center out of the University of California, Berkeley. Experiment with a few of the resiliency practices listed.

4. Prepare for your next exam by rehearsing the stress management techniques listed in the chapter.

5. Analyze a test you recently completed for your errors and prepare study materials to help you better prepare for the next test.

You Be the Judge 1 Ideas

1. Brandon will likely pull something off because he's organized and in good physical health, but it will not be high quality. He is not allowing enough time to grasp everything he needs. He (and the reference librarians) will be stressed once he starts the work and realizes everything he has to do.

2. Ricky has some things going for him, but he's got adjustments to make. On the plus side, he's motivated, easily connects with others, and he has made a weekly plan. He's also being realistic about how many credits he should attempt. On the minus side, he didn't spend enough time learning how to use necessary technology. He also is unable to balance the needs of his family with

his college responsibilities and he's not following through. He needs to be proactive with both. If he doesn't learn to manage the family drama in particular, he's not likely to sustain his energy over the long haul.

3. Zoë is going to have a hard time preparing for the test in just two days. She hasn't followed any kind of weekly routine and allows her friends to interfere with her studies. Her diet isn't great either. Given the anxiety she feels when she learns about the midterm, she's likely to give in to the impulse to see the movie. In that case, she might even give up studying . . . and not even show up for the exam.

4. Edwin is likely to perform well enough on the test, but he won't live up to his potential because he's not sleeping enough or taking care of his body. That lack of self-care also affects his stress levels, which is likely to affect his performance, too.

You Be the Judge 2 Ideas

1. Sonia is able to manage her emotions and does not burst into tears during class. That is a win. However, she's allowing her fear to derail her plans. At least she's seeking out an advisor who hopefully refers her to a counselor for emotional support.

2. Morris honors himself by recognizing his strengths and connecting them to the challenge before him. He's thoughtful about finding the relevance between editing a paper and his chosen profession as a building inspector. He's reappraising the situation in a positive way.

3. Zander is poorly managing his bitterness by trying not to care. He does care though, and the bitterness keeps expressing itself. Zander needs to reckon with his math anxiety if he ever hopes to become a firefighter, let alone a chief. He can do this by talking his problems out with trusted friends or family. He could do some reappraisal of his situation and work on finding the positive. He needs some perspective as well. He might not be successful at his first attempt at math, but with help and effective strategies, he can succeed in his next attempt.

You Be the Judge 3 Ideas

1. Dawn has been compared to her sister throughout her life and has not been given the opportunity to be her own person. These expectations from others create a belief that she must live up to her sister's example and if she doesn't, she will be a disappointment. That's her worst fear.

2. Ricardo has probably picked up his mother's catastrophic mindset, also known as slippery-slope thinking. One mistake leads to a series of unavoidable problems. It also does not help that he fears becoming a disappointment to someone he loves if he does not succeed in either the medical or legal field.

3. Autumn believes she has good study habits. She probably tells people that she works best under pressure. She seems unaware of other study methods that would allow her to perform more consistently on tests and with less anxiety.

You Be the Judge 4

1. José has prepared well for his speech. He has practiced enough and kept the assignment's expectations in mind. He unloads his worries on paper and reminds himself of the good work he has done. He will still be nervous, but he is doing all he can to perform well. It is unlikely he will choke during the speech.

2. Rex does not seem prepared for this exam in a way that gives him any confidence in himself. He's also making sure his professor has a low expectation of him as well. He is not doing himself a favor by discussing the test with his fellow classmates. Whatever they say will likely make him feel worse.

3. Sydney takes as much control over the testing situation as possible. She creates a plan of attack. She notices her stress reaction and intervenes. Good job, Sydney.

Self-assessment

Before you begin reading the chapter, answer the following questions. Don't spend too much time on your answer. Instead, respond with your first thought. The goal is to see where you are right now. We'll return to this assessment at the end of the chapter to see if or how your thinking has changed about these topics.

	Disagree	Unsure	Somewhat agree	Agree	Strongly agree
I have a set of goals that give my work in college purpose and direction.	O	O	O	O	O
My goals are specific, so that I can figure out what actions to take to achieve them.	O	O	O	O	O
My goals are measurable, so I can see myself making progress towards them.	O	O	O	O	O
My goals are challenging, but realistic. I am confident that with my present skills and mindset, I can achieve them.	O	O	O	O	O
My goals are meaningful to me. They are based on my personal interests and needs and not based on others' expectations.	O	O	O	O	O
My goals have a time frame. I identify a specific time when I want to have accomplished them.	O	O	O	O	O
I generally focus on how I can increase my skills and knowledge rather than earn a specific grade.	O	O	O	O	O
I expect to have setbacks as I work towards my goals, so I plan for them.	O	O	O	O	O
If I am disengaged in a required course, I can find beneficial ways to motivate myself anyway.	O	O	O	O	O
If I am disengaged in a required activity, I identify a beneficial reward that will motivate me to do it.	O	O	O	O	O

The more you agree with the above statements, the more you are able to sustain your motivation for college work.

Chapter 8

Developing Healthy Motivation and Goals

You have your reasons for making college yours. They are probably long-term reasons that have to do with changes you want to see in your life as you move towards a career or towards further studies and then a career. Those long-term goals are great, but it's also important to have short-term goals along the way and to be thoughtful about why you are doing what you're doing.

Alexei has his reasons for being in college. His long-term goal is to become an engineer. He wants to do that because he loves solving problems and because it pays well. To work towards that goal, he's taking his general education courses at a community college and then plans to transfer to a four-year engineering program in two years. That's the long term. In the short term, he has to decide on his class schedule for the coming term.

Three of his courses are required by his pre-engineering plan, but he needs to take one more. He narrows his choices down to two different courses. Basic Photography should be an easy course because Alexei's already an experienced photographer, and he took two photography classes in high school. He's unlikely to learn much more than he already knows, but he is sure he can earn a high grade. The higher grade will help keep his GPA up, which is the reason for taking the course.

However, Alexei also wants to learn as much as he can while at school. There is a sociology course on the environment and sustainability that he's curious about. He is interested in environmental engineering, so this course seems like a good fit. However, he knows it will require more effort and time from him and could result in a slightly lower grade.

So, what should Alexei do? Should he go for the easier high grade in a course he isn't as excited about, or should he go for the more challenging course that he's really interested in? What would you do?

This chapter will take a closer look at extrinsic motivation, such as earning high grades, and how it helps us achieve short-term goals. We'll also look at intrinsic motivation, such as personal satisfaction, and how it helps us achieve long-term goals.

Figure 1. Many students are motivated by the reward of graduation at the end of their academic career. This is an example of external motivation.

External Motivation

Motivation is whatever causes you to do something. External motivations are those things in the world, outside of yourself, that cause you to act. Whenever dangers emerge around you, for example, you act to protect yourself. You drive a longer way home to avoid a dangerous intersection. You wash your hands eight times a day to avoid illness. You might also act to pursue external rewards—being nice to your boss to get a promotion, signing up for a department store credit card to get 10 percent off a big purchase, going bowling with your great uncle so that you have a better chance of success when you ask him for a loan to help you pay for a car.

Many students rely on external rewards for motivation. They want high grades. They want praise from their teachers. They want respect from other students. Others are driven by pressure from their parents to do well in school or by pressure from siblings or friends who have already done well and expect them to do the same. Often several external motivators operate together. Students want a high grade to look good in front of other students—and to quiet the parents who are always grumbling about how they need to stop playing video games and start living up to their potential.

External motivators can be effective for short-term goals. Wanting to earn a high grade on a test, for example, can motivate you to study hard and practice important new ideas so that they stay in your brain. Wanting to impress a new friend can be great motivation to get you to clean the kitchen.

However, not all external rewards are actually all that healthy for you over the long term. Consider social status, for example. Doing things to impress others in the short term might cause you to stray from doing the long-term goals you really want to accomplish with your life. You might also avoid doing anything challenging but worthwhile because you fear embarrassment. It might also make you kind of phony.

Focusing on getting good grades can also cause you to narrow your attention to the mechanics of getting a grade rather than on actually learning new ideas and skills. You shift your attention away from what is interesting or useful for the future and think in terms of checking off boxes. Over time, the effort to get those grades becomes more work than the grades are worth, and that's especially true when the good grades come from a longer-term project rather than a single paper or quiz.

When the external motivation comes in the form of pleasing people, the motivation usually weakens as you move forward in your life. Those relationships shift over time. People move away. They change. They die. Even if the others in your life stay more or less healthy and act the same from year to year, your own changing life means that the value of their approval or disapproval will change. Counting on those external motivators to sustain you over the long term probably won't go very well.

Consider Alexei's decision about what courses to take next term. He's identified at least one significant external reward for taking photography—a high grade. He has to decide if the grade is enough of a motivation to take a course that he may not enjoy. It might be. It's not easy to get into the engineering program he has chosen, so grades do matter. However, if this is an acceptable choice for this term, Alexei will have to be careful to not make it a habit to take easy courses or look for professors who are known to be easy. If he does that, then it won't be long before earning high grades takes the place of actual learning.

> Your goals are the road maps that guide you and show you what is possible for your life.
> — Les Brown

Internal Motivation

What drives you? What do you want to accomplish for yourself? What is important to you? These questions will help you start to recognize the internal motivation in your life. While these personal rewards might be more difficult to notice at first, they actually provide greater and more enduring motivation than external motivators. These are the rewards that you choose for yourself, and because they align with your values and with what you hope for yourself, they remain important and rewarding over a much longer span of time. Three powerful sources of internal motivation are autonomy, mastery, and purpose.

Autonomy

Whenever you feel in control over your life, you're usually more committed to what you're doing and more willing to face obstacles and overcome them with hard work. In college, the learning is also more satisfying because it's something that you've chosen for yourself, not something imposed by others.

Students who are really good at following all the rules, expectations, and tasks assigned to them are considered great students by the teachers and principals in elementary and high schools. They are certainly successful there, too. However, they may only be achieving what others have set out for

You Be the Judge 1

Consider these situations where external motivators drove the students' behavior. Decide if using external motivators is appropriate. Jot down your ideas. When you finish, turn to the end of the chapter to check them.

1. Cameron needs scholarships to be able to afford attending university. He has long wanted to be a chemist and loves lab life. He does not see himself as a "navel-gazing diarist" and dreads the idea of writing personal statements for his scholarship applications. He turns his phone and car keys over to his mother and tells her not to give them back until his personal statement is written.

2. Preethi posts pictures of herself to her social media site at least once a day. It can sometimes take her more than an hour to plan her getup and location. The steady stream of reactions keeps her preoccupied and giddy.

3. Kailao's goal is to win the powerlifting com-

petition that his older brother won a few years before. On his bathroom mirror he's taped a photoshopped picture of himself holding up his brother who is holding up the trophy. He trains until he lifts more than his brother did for the competition. When he competes, he comes in second.

4. Simone likes to read, but the book she's been assigned is a real dud. It's the first book she's met that has made her fall asleep reading it. Most of the people in her discussion group are bizarrely into it, though, and she does not want to be a drag. She bucks up and gets through it by reading it at her favorite coffee shop.

them. Eventually, the lack of autonomy can start to feel limiting—or even false when students have something else in mind for themselves. It's hard to stay excited about something that you haven't chosen for yourself. When you have autonomy, you're able to map out a path that makes sense for you, and that remains something to be excited about.

Mastery

Whenever you get better at something you value, your motivation to work harder and longer increases. Students notice that they have increased competence, skill, and knowledge, and they find added inspiration to work even harder to achieve more improvement.

Figure 2. A sense of autonomy leads to pride and fulfillment in your work.

You've seen that already outside of school. Think about anything that you are good at and that you enjoy doing. There was a time when you didn't know how to do it. There was also a time when you were learning how to do it, and you weren't excellent. That was frustrating. As you began to become competent, it got less frustrating and more satisfying. The better you got, the more satisfying it became. That's how mastery provides motivation for continued improvement. Because you're working on this for your own satisfaction at becoming better, the reward is deeper, personal, and lasting.

Purpose

When your reasons for going to school are directly connected to your ideas about contributing to a cause higher than yourself and serving your community, you have purpose. Purpose adds a sense of meaning to your life. If you're deeply concerned with the condition of the environment, like Alexei, you may be driven to seek solutions as an engineer. This is purpose. You may be inspired by a teacher who made a difference in your life and eager for the opportunity to do the same for someone else. This is purpose. You may be worried about the lack of empathy you see in the world and decide you want to become a storyteller and use your love of language to craft tales that

Figure 3. Working with close attention to detail reflects a mastery of your chosen skill. The desire to master your discipline is an example of internal motivation.

change hearts and minds. This is purpose.

When you choose to pursue a career that has good opportunities, earning potential, and working conditions, these may seem like external motivators at first glance. But, if you are doing it for the satisfaction of providing a secure and stable homelife for your kids, this is purpose, too. The satisfaction you get from your studies might include external rewards in the form of grades or praise. However, the real engine with this type of internal motivation is the drive to make a difference in the lives of others in a positive way. That's what powers your commitment to gain the ideas and skills you need to accomplish this long-term goal.

Risks and Rewards of Internal Motivation

To achieve long-term goals, students must have levels of determination and inspiration. External rewards might help along the way with part of the long-term plan, but to maintain the vision and passion for long-term achievement, internal motivation provides much greater drive. However, there are some consequences to consider when it comes to internal motivation.

First, with autonomy comes responsibility. Once you find yourself free from external control and able to follow your own chosen path, you are now responsible for the results, for better or worse. When you do well, you can take pride in the dedication, focus, and shockingly wise decisions you made. If you come up short with your goals, then that's on you, too. You can't blame your professors for expecting more from you than you were able to deliver. Instead, you need to examine what you did poorly or failed to do at all and then correct those errors. You have to ask for help. You have to try again. That's going to be more satisfying in the long run than blaming others or retreating from challenges, but it does require work.

Second, remember that developing mastery is a slow process. It takes time to work your way through the stages of conscious incompetence to unconscious competence. It's not usually a straight line of improvement, either, which can

Figure 4. Most people who successfully pursue their career find a sense of purpose in their work. Many people who work in public and emergency service gain purpose from helping others.

be especially discouraging when these are goals that matter to you personally. To improve, you have to step beyond your comfort zone and take risks. You must continually challenge yourself. You must be patient, too, because you will understand what mastery looks like long before you're able to produce it yourself. That's hard when you're doing something for external reasons.

Third, when you pursue goals that are shaped by a deep-seated purpose, your drive is powerful but the stakes are higher. Purpose makes you tough and able to perform under stressful conditions. Your purpose might twist your sense of what is realistic and risk-worthy, though. You might sacrifice some well-being in pursuit of a daring, purpose-driven goal that requires maximum effort, focus, and discipline. Also, a purpose that convinces you to take on audacious goals puts pressure on the ultimate outcome. Success brings a magnificent sense of accomplishment, but failing to achieve a high-flying goal can bring you low. Purpose is best balanced with judgment about what makes the most sense, given your current circumstances.

It's common for students to internalize external rewards, to think that pleasing others or earning grades has great internal value. In fact, if you've been good at pleasing others in elementary and high school, it's hard not to think that this kind of success is a part of who you are. However, it's not. You may be so used to the feelings that come with pleasing others that you think that's who you are, but those feelings still depend on external sources. Meanwhile, purpose, mastery, and autonomy truly are built into you as a person. They exist even when no one is watching. There is nothing wrong with pleasing others or choosing to pursue outcomes that others have chosen for you, but those external motivators may ultimately prove too weak to

You Be the Judge 2

Determine which internal motivator is mostly spurring the student on—autonomy, mastery, or purpose. They can overlap a bit. Jot down your ideas. When you finish, turn to the end of the chapter to check them.

1. Yuuto's trips to art museums with his grandfather gave him an appreciation for art. Throughout school, he participated in as many art courses as he could. Later, he learned about artists helping refugee children cope with their distress through art therapy and art education. He plans to equip himself to become an art educator and therapist.

2. Ekaterina begins work on her paper within a day of receiving the assignment. The first thing she does is make two appointments at the writing center—one to review her first draft and the second to review her almost-final version. She studies the rubric and the examples her professor provided. She writes. She has questions. She gets help from a tutor. She writes some more. She goes to her writing center appointment, asks more questions, and gets helpful feedback. She revises. She goes to her second writing center appointment and gets encouraging feedback. She makes minor edits and submits her assignment. When it's returned, she earned an A and there are glowing comments from her professor. That makes her feel good. Still, she notes a few corrections and sticks around after class to make sure she understands the errors she made.

3. Oliver scans the list of topics for his assignment. None of them appeal to him. He visits his professor during her office hours and brings a list of three different topics that he would like to explore. He and the professor work out an agreement so that Oliver still meets the expectations of the assignment exploring one of the topics he chose.

sustain motivation for long-term goals.

You remember Alexei and his choice about which course to take. That isn't a big decision with lifelong implications. However, once you start to put a few decisions together, it starts to become a habit, and habits do have long-term impact. In choosing which course to take, Alexei must decide if the internal rewards he might have in learning more about sociology are a more important motivation than the external rewards of an easy, high grade that he expects to get from taking photography. The possibly easier, higher grade is a more practical goal for him to consider than the personal satisfaction of learning something new and challenging himself.

Alexei understands the course's potential impact on his GPA. However, he also knows that he likes new challenges and understanding what sociologists have to say about environmental problems serves his bigger purpose for his life. In general, it's more important to his success to choose internally rewarding courses. If Alexei makes this kind of decision-making a habit, he will build more lasting motivation to help him work towards his long-term goals.

Setting Appropriate Goals

A goal is a result we intend to reach mostly through our own actions. Our motivation is intertwined with the goals we set for ourselves. Students who set appropriate goals and have a realistic understanding of how to reach them are more successful than students who do not. They know what to do and why they are doing it. Having specific, realistic, and meaningful goals can help you manage the growing pains of a college education.

Identifying your goals is the first step, and prioritizing them is the second. Your education is one important area of your life, but you have other needs connected to friendship, family, health, and, for many, spirituality. Create goals for these areas and rank them. They are all important, to be sure, but to determine how to coordinate your energy, time, and support, you want to know which is the most important right now. The rest will need to be organized around that.

A long-term goal is built from a series of mid-term and short-term goals. Short-term goals focus on today and the next few days and perhaps weeks. Mid-term goals involve plans for this school year and the time you plan to remain in college. Long-term goals may begin with graduating college and everything you want to happen after that.

Figure 5. Facing challenges on the path to your long-term goal is normal. Improving your skills in an area where you struggle is a matter of gradual improvement.

Let's say you have a long-term goal to become a juvenile corrections counselor. You can build mid-term goals to complete the necessary courses for the degree and short-term goals of mastering the knowledge and skills you need to pass each course within the program. If you think about your goals in this way, you realize how even the little things you do every day can keep you moving towards your most important long-term goals, like a job in juvenile corrections.

Effective goals need to be clear and oriented towards action so you have some idea of the practical steps to take to achieve them. They need to have deadlines to help you manage your time. Most importantly, though, they must reflect the three internal motivators of autonomy, mastery, and purpose. Set goals that you have chosen for yourself, that will give you a proper sense of challenge, and that connect to the larger purpose you hope for in your life.

Writing out your goals is important. It starts building the reality you wish to create for yourself. We'll take a look at two possible structures for doing that, WOOP and SMART goals.

WOOP

The first structure for setting appropriate goals is called **WOOP**. It stands for **W**ish, **O**utcome, **O**bstacle, and **P**lan. This method is a way to exert self-control. It helps you think about and find long-term goals and then determine the short-term steps towards those goals. More importantly, it helps you identify likely challenges you may encounter. Goal-setters who don't anticipate problems are usually sidelined by them. It is also a test to see if you understand how to achieve your goal and if you are choosing a goal that is realistic for your current situation.

Wish: Imagine something important you want to accomplish. It should be challenging but feasible. For example, you might say, "I wish to be an athletic trainer for a college sports program."

Outcome: Focus on what you think will be the best result from accomplishing this wish. How will you feel? In this step, pause and really imagine the outcome. For example, you might say, "I will be happy doing work that I enjoy and feel proud when I help athletes perform at their best."

Goals are dreams with a deadline.
—Napoleon Hill

Obstacle: Attempt to bring to mind the main obstacles to this wish, such as the external difficulties that might slow your progress and the internal, personal issues that might get in your way. This is where you discover whether or not you fully grasp what it means to achieve this goal. If you struggle identifying obstacles, you probably haven't done enough investigation into it. Go do that. Here's an example of an obstacle statement:

> An external threat is the time and money needed to complete a master's degree, which is strongly preferred or required by college sports programs. It is a science degree, so the curriculum includes time-intensive science courses that require math. An internal threat is my tendency to lose focus in class and take poor notes. I also do not have confidence in my math skills.

Plan: Figure out actions that will effectively deal with the obstacles. So, you might respond to the obstacle statement with something like this:

> Because the goal takes time and money, I will break it up into shorter goals. I will first earn an associate's degree and get a personal training certificate. I can then find work as a personal trainer. If possible, I will find an employer that offers tuition assistance to get a bachelor's degree. With a bachelor's degree, I'll get a position with more responsibility and higher pay. I will find a master's degree program that fits my needs at that time. Because I have several learning concerns, I will meet with a learning specialist and get help. I will make getting more confident at math one of my first goals for the term.

From here, you can transition into using a SMART goal structure to help you formulate short-term and mid-term goals.

SMART Goals

The letters in **SMART** stand for goals that are **S**pecific, **M**easurable, **A**chievable, **R**elevant to you and your internal motivation, and **T**ime-based.

Specific: Choose goals that target particular actions or behavior. For example, if you want to change your relationship with math, select a specific

Setting specific goals helps learners in at least three ways: the goals focus attention on important aspects of the task; they help motivate and sustain task mastery efforts; and they serve an information function by arming learners with criteria that they can use to assess and if necessary adjust their strategies as they work.

— Jere Brophy

goal related to math homework habits. "Study math" is too vague. Instead, you might create a goal to follow a specific routine for studying math that includes reviewing an earlier problem, relearning new material, completing the homework problems using a problem-solution-explanation chart, and doing a mini self-test.

Measurable: Be sure you can measure your completion and your progress along the way. Decide *how* you will measure your goal. If a routine is what you want, create a tracking chart. Every time you complete the routine, give yourself a gold star. How will you decide if you're on track? Will you measure by grades? Completion of assignments or tasks? If you want to be a trainer, maybe one of your goals is to show your experience by running a marathon, for example. In training for it, you might track your distance and speed, how long it took you to run two miles the first week, and then the next, and then maybe how long it took you to run three miles, and so on. It will depend on the goal you've set. Measuring helps you evaluate how well you are reaching your goal. It can also help you set up intermediate rewards.

Achievable: Set goals that you can actually complete. Your study routine is four hours long because when it comes to math you think that you will need it. Being inexperienced in math does mean you need time to practice, but most brains can't sustain four solid hours of active learning before they fizzle out. You *might* pull it off once, but it's not likely you can do it again. Start with a ninety-minute routine punctuated with a five-minute stretch break in the middle. Add more time as you go and as you need, but don't go much more than two hours without a bigger break in between.

Relevant: Set goals that are relevant to the purpose you are charting for your life. If your ultimate long-term dream is to be an athletic trainer for a college sports program, then your goals should keep you on a path towards it. You know from your WOOP work that math poses an internal obstacle, so a routine that helps you learn math better and therefore builds your confidence is directly related to your ultimate goal.

Time-based: Your goals should have a limit and be based on some kind of deadline system. Without deadlines, goals can go on forever—or be put off forever. The short-term SMART goal for studying math might read like this:

> In order to increase my math skills as well as my math communication skills, I will follow the following ninety-minute math routine:

Figure 6. Lots of hands-on work goes into a long-term goal of becoming a corrections officer. With WOOP and SMART goals, you can set goals along the way that put your long-term work in perspective.

» Review material from the previous class and work a math problem using a problem-solution-explanation chart.

» Relearn material for the most recent class by rereading my math textbook and comparing it to my class notes. I will fill in any gaps in my notes based on my reading of the textbook.

» Complete the current problem set using a problem-solution-explanation chart and my notes.

» Self-test without referring to my notes.

» Follow this routine after every math class plus one extra day, or five days per week. Aim for a routine of four days a week by midterm.

Goal-setting should be one of the first things you do as you begin a program of study in college. You probably envisioned a lovely dream for yourself before taking steps to enroll in college. The humble tools of goal setting—being realistic, measurable, and specific—will bring shape to that dream. You will see it becoming a reality.

Managing Discomfort

To achieve long-term goals, you have to expect and work through discomfort. You *will* have difficulties, and that's a good thing, too. Difficulty is a sign that you're getting somewhere. You've come against the boundary of your existing competence and have found new ground where you're not yet competent.

Long-term goals require you to keep going through setbacks or times when nothing seems to be happening. You need to move forward with a growth mindset and understand that learning is a process of trial, error, and correction — not one victory after another. It also means you might need to give up some short-term and more amusing activities in order to work on your long-term goals.

Discomfort is also a good indicator that it's time for you to examine what you're doing and check to make sure the goal itself is worth pursuing. Does what you are doing help you to become more autonomous? Are you increasing your mastery over something that matters? Are you serving the bigger purpose you have for yourself? As long as your learning is providing internal rewards, the discomfort is worth the effort. In fact, those internal rewards give you the motivation you'll need to keep going. We'll take a look at two types of discomfort in the next section, including optimism bias and self-doubt.

You Be the Judge 3

Decide if the following goals are SMART goals. Jot down your ideas. When you finish, turn to the end of the chapter to check them.

1. Cory, an eighteen-year-old welding student, wrote: "My goal is to own my own auto body repair shop by the time I am twenty-two."

2. Kendra, a math major, wrote: "My father expects me to graduate magna cum laude, so I am doing whatever I can to earn a 4.0 GPA every term."

3. James, a business management major, wrote: "Since accounting is my weakest subject and I want to be much more confident with it, my goal this term is to dedicate an extra hour per week working with a tutor to go over anything that I do not understand."

4. Inna, an undecided student, wrote: "I will take a career exploration course and meet with a career counselor at least twice this term to identify an educational plan that will give me direction but some flexibility, too."

Optimism Bias

Most people pursue long-term goals with a little too much optimism. This psychological quirk is called the "optimism bias." It works in your favor, but it also works against you. Optimism gives you the initial push you need to launch into a long-term goal, and that push brings with it a little burst of joy. However, optimism also can blind you to seeing the obstacles that you will most certainly meet.

Students with an optimism bias don't fully consider the amount of work required to complete tasks, so they're underprepared when the challenge becomes greater than expected. They overestimate their ability to resist temptation and don't take steps to limit distractions and diversions. Some don't consider the possibilities of certain external challenges, either, even though they know that cars can break down, work hours can increase or decrease, and relationships can suddenly explode and demand much more of their time than they had budgeted.

When challenges arise, these overly optimistic students often become overly pessimistic about their goals. This swing from optimism to pessimism creates a real risk that they will give up completely. If students get familiar with this psychological quirk, they can learn to avoid its harmful side effects. If this is something you struggle with, the WOOP technique can help you counter the optimism bias by anticipating obstacles. Now when you find yourself confronted with a broken-down car, extra shifts at work, or a disastrous breakup, you can make a plan for how to deal while still pursuing your goal.

> Many people fail in life, not for lack of ability or brains or even courage but simply because they have never organized their energies around a goal.
> — Elbert Hubbard

Self-Doubt

Other students struggle with anxiety and other negative feelings about themselves or their abilities. Maybe they are among the group of people who don't have to worry about the optimism bias because they are actually a bit more pessimistic by nature. They may feel like imposters who don't belong. They may feel isolated, especially if they are the only one in their family or social circle to give college a try, and have doubts about choices they made. They might even struggle with full-blown regret. They may simply feel overwhelmed with seemingly competing, important goals.

These are all normal feelings, and they come to anyone who is pursuing goals that have great meaning. While discomfort is, well, uncomfortable, students must remember that they shouldn't feel bad about feeling bad. They just need to stop, take another look at the internal motivators that got them here in the first place, and find the motivation to keep on going—just a little—in spite of those bad feelings. They can remind themselves that the stress is just one more sign that they are on the right path. Of course, if it's a little much to cope with on your own, you can find help from your peers in the student life area of your college or more professional guidance from a counselor.

Meeting the Right Challenge

To achieve any kind of goal, and especially important long-term goals, people are most motivated when their goals are appropriately challenging. The goals should not be so easy that they hardly feel worth the effort, and they shouldn't be so hard that making progress is next to impossible. All students have a zone of development, and it's that sweet spot where the challenges are real but not too much to bear.

If the goal is too easy, the discomfort is boredom. You're not learning anything you didn't already know, so why bother? The answer in this situation is to look for ways to make the goal more challenging. If you're assigned to write a paper about something you already know all about, for example, you can ask your professor for an alternative assignment about some new topic. Or you might ask your professor how you could make this a more challenging assignment. Your professor will be stunned by your initiative, which is good for your college persona, but more importantly, you'll have more engaging and challenging work to do.

If the goal is too difficult for your skills at the moment, however, you may need to back up and review your plan for achieving the long-term goals. Consider that you may have been operating under unrealistic expectations about how long this process will be. Reset those expectations and extend the deadline for your goals rather than give up entirely. If your program of study requires success in several writing intensive courses, for example, and if your writing skills are not well-developed yet, then focus on short-term goals that will help you achieve competency in writing.

It may be that your circumstances won't allow you to achieve the original goal you set. You want to be a nurse, for example, but even after much effort and help from others, you may not be able to achieve the necessary grade point average to gain admission into the nursing program. You don't have to give up on a career in the healthcare field. You can visit with a counselor to learn about other ways you can fulfill your purpose as you see it. You may be able to try nursing again in the future. It is important to not give up at this point, but adjust your expectations.

You Be the Judge 4

Determine what kind of discomfort this student could experience and what his or her plan could be to cope Jot down your ideas. When you finish, turn to the end of the chapter to check them.

1. Avram has worked as a professional automobile mechanic for over ten years in his home country. After immigrating to the United States, he hopes to reestablish himself in the same profession, but needs several certifications to qualify for the most desirable positions. He also needs to develop his English skills. The program he enrolled in starts with the basics for the first two terms before getting to more advanced content.

2. Karen was homeschooled by an admittedly math-phobic parent. While she received a creative and diverse education in literature, history, art, and some of the social sciences, her math education stopped after basic geometry and pre-algebra. It has now been over three years since Karen has spent any serious time with math. Karen wants to be a biologist who works in forestry restoration. She must complete three college level courses in math up through calculus. The generic plan she was given schedules all three during her freshman year.

3. Reyna read the college catalogue with gusto. She located the pages for her program of study—computer science—and flagged the course descriptions of all the courses she needed to take. She highlighted each according to what term she would take them: orange for fall, blue for winter, and green for spring. She got her books early and started previewing them. She set up her weekly study schedule two weeks before the start of the term. She excelled in high school, so had little concerns about college. She had also been on an all-girls robotics team from middle school on and imagined that she would have similar opportunities in college. She looks forward to transferring from her community college to a selective four-year university program in two years' time.

4. Reyna is also one of a handful of women in her computer science courses. She is also the only one who identifies as Latina. While her classmates are generally polite, they are not social and do not include her casual conversations. She has made a few efforts to generate connections, but they have not worked so far.

Final Thoughts

Because Alexei values internal rewards, he decides to take sociology over photography. He chooses it as a more rewarding and challenging course. He knows that it will make him uncomfortable, that it will demand more of his time, and that from time to time, it will make his brain hurt. He may not have the skill or ability—yet—that he will need to succeed. However, he also knows that he's going to get more out of this challenge than he would from a course that teaches things he already mostly knows.

As you face your own questions about what comes next and how best to move forward in short-term goals towards the mid- and long-term goals, it's important mostly to be thoughtful about what you are doing. You don't have to always take on the most challenging goals. You just need to do your best to set short-term goals that will move you towards your long-term goals.

The SMART and WOOP methods will both help you to be realistic about how much you can actually do with the time and energy that's available. They will also help you set goals that come with their own motivation to build autonomy, mastery, and purpose in your life.

Reflect on Your Self-Assessment

Most of us are great at having goals, visions for ourselves and how we see ourselves in the future. Despite this, we often fail to plan adequately for these goals, so they fail to become a reality. The self-assessment you completed earlier in the chapter helped you establish a baseline for if and how you set goals. The higher your score, the more effective you are at setting goals. Now that you know more about the importance of planning, spend some time on it. The following DIYs can help get you started.

Do It Yourself

Here are some practical things that you can do to help yourself better understand what it means to have healthy motivation and goals:

1. Identify what motivates you to persist in college. For each motivator, determine if it is primarily external, given to you by an outside entity, or internal and coming from your own personal interests and purpose.

2. Complete a WOOP for one of your longer-term goals. You may need to investigate by talking to an advisor, a counselor, or a professor to learn more about any potential obstacles for which you will plan.

3. Identify a course that feels like a slog and you struggle to engage with it. Identify some short-term external motivators that could help you complete it. If you achieve your study goals this week, for example, you get to go on a hike, guilt-free.

4. Create a SMART goal for your most challenging course this term. Then create a SMART goal for your next term, based on what you have noticed about your behaviors this term.

5. Identify any discomfort you are feeling as you progress through this first year in college. Write about that discomfort and consider why you think you are feeling that discomfort. Identify resources to help you cope with it.

6. Check out this TED talk: "The Optimism Bias: A Tour of the Irrationally Positive Brain," by Tali Sharot (https://www.ted.com/talks/tali_sharot_the_optimism_bias).

You Be the Judge 1 Ideas

1. This is a smart use of an external motivator. Cameron is using access to his phone and car to motivate him to do something unpleasant but important. He is also avoiding having his mom bug him over and over by using her in his scheme.

2. Preethi enjoys entertaining people. There is nothing wrong with that. The issue here is that she's using up a bunch of her mental bandwidth on something that is not important to her goals — "likes" and reactions on social media.

3. When first place is your only goal, second place hurts badly. His brother having bragging rights now is probably making Kailao frustrated or angry. This may fuel an even more concerted effort to win the next time around. The bitter taste can also cause Kailao to give up strength training entirely. Champion athletes do set high expectations for themselves, but typically, they are thinking about improving their personal performance day after day, taking satisfaction from their growing skills, rather than on narrowing their attention to a particular rival.

4. Simone is avoiding the punishment of looking bad in front of her peers which is an external motivator. It works to help her get something important done. Still, if others in her group also did not like the book, she would be vulnerable to negative peer pressure. Simone is blending motivators here, though. She decides to read at her favorite coffee shop. It is a personal pleasure for her to be there and she's choosing this for herself. This is a form of autonomy, which will be discussed shortly.

You Be the Judge 2 Ideas

1. Yuuto has found a purpose to fulfill. It also happens to be tied in with autonomy in that he personally enjoys art.

2. Ekaterina seems to have mastered the writing process and is a skilled time manager. All that revising and help-seeking suggests she is driven to make her paper better. Even though she earned an A, she still wants to know what she can do to improve. She's driven by a mastery goal.

3. Oliver is using autonomy as a motivator. He also has a strong sense of personal agency. These two can make for a highly satisfying college experience.

You Be the Judge 3 Ideas

1. Cory's goal is a long-term goal, so it does not quite fit the SMART structure. It's a good start, though. It seems relevant, given he's preparing to be a welder and that is needed to do auto body repair work. It is time-based, but it does not seem realistic without knowing anything more about Cory's situation. Four years does not seem like enough time to gain the experience, knowledge, and financing to successfully run a business.

2. Kendra's goal is not her own. It's her father's. "Doing everything she can" is not specific either.

3. James' goal is a SMART goal. It is specific and behavior-based since he will work with a tutor. It is measurable since he can track how many times he meets with the tutor. It is achievable since it is not a big stretch. It is relevant, since it relates to his field of study, business. It is also time bound, since he will execute it over the course of the term.

4. Inna's goal is a SMART goal. It is specific and behavior-based since she will meet with a counselor and take a course. It is measurable since she can track her attendance and participation in the course as well as whether or not she meets the counselor. It is achievable since it is structured. It is relevant since it will help her arrive at her own decision about what kind of profession she wants to pursue. It is also time-based since it is limited to the term.

You Be the Judge 4 Ideas

1. Avram is going to be bored. He will need to find ways to make the introductory courses more engaging. He could use these introductory courses as essentially English courses and focus on his communication skills. He could help struggling students. Or, he could spice up his first two terms' schedule with more interesting electives that will keep him engaged until his primary program speeds up. He could take advantage of the lighter demands to prioritize any of his other important goals.

2. It is unlikely that Karen will qualify for college algebra during her first term. She will of course be upset by this, especially since she had so much autonomy as a homeschooled student. She will most likley have to take preparation courses and adjust her expectations as far as her timeline is concerned. She could work with an advisor to make sure she is taking other courses that are moving her towards her goals and which she enjoys.

3. Reyna is excited. She's optimistic. Reyna's optimism may bottom out around midterms when the work piles up. She will be grouchy, but as long as she understands that this is a normal response to the heightened workload and the stress of evaluation, she will get through it. She can also frequently remind herself about her goal to be a robotics engineer and why that matters.

4. Reyna is now feeling the discomfort of isolation and possibly stereotype threat (the fear of confirming low expectations of your social group). She had found robotics fun and being in an all-girl team made it even more comfortable. Now, she is feeling alone. She can reframe how she views her male peers' reactions to her. She can see them as just being focused, serious students and maybe shy rather than dismissive of her. Chances are, they are just as uncomfortable as she is, after all. Reyna might want to visit the student life center to learn about any clubs she could join. She could also make more efforts to befriend the other women in her courses. It's possible they are feeling similarly.

Self-assessment

Before you begin reading the chapter, answer the following questions. Don't spend too much time on your answer. Instead, respond with your first thought. The goal is to see where you are right now. We'll return to this assessment at the end of the chapter to see if or how your thinking has changed about these topics.

	Disagree	Unsure	Somewhat agree	Agree	Strongly agree
Working effectively with others to accomplish a goal is highly valued in both college and the workplace.	O	O	O	O	O
I am comfortable teaming up with others in learning situations.	O	O	O	O	O
My learning is enhanced from interactions with my fellow students.	O	O	O	O	O
I know how to listen actively and I do so when working with others.	O	O	O	O	O
I prepare as required for small group discussions so that I can contribute effectively.	O	O	O	O	O
When a fellow student shares an idea with which I disagree, I am able to express my response respectfully.	O	O	O	O	O
I understand the role of peer review. I give and accept helpful feedback.	O	O	O	O	O
I cooperate, communicate, and complete my tasks on time when working on a group project.	O	O	O	O	O
I know what elements are needed to make a group project more effective. I can find remedies for when a group lacks them.	O	O	O	O	O
I know who to team up with to form an effective study group. I also know how to go about studying together.	O	O	O	O	O

The more you agree with the above statements, the more you will benefit from learning with others.

Chapter 9

Learning with Others

You walk into class and take a seat, expecting to listen and take notes without having to contribute much. Your professor keeps you interested when she lectures, the information usually makes sense, so things seem like they will be fine. Then things go horribly wrong. You're asked to count off by six and get into groups. You're going to have to work a bit harder.

That, in fact, is the point of groups. When you work with your class-mates, you activate your brain in ways that listening to a lecture does not. The more that you get actively involved in a given class, the more you will get out of it—even if that's not something you'd choose for yourself. Pro-fessors who periodically interrupt their lectures with group interactions are following good instructional practice. They're supporting your intellectual engagement. They are also preparing you for the workplace.

Many companies use a teamwork approach to serve their clients. While individuals on a team each have specific roles based on their job descrip-tion, they will still participate in planning and problem-solving. Teamwork is valued in the workplace because it promotes creativity, one of the most prized assets a company can have. Teamwork brings together diverse talents and perspectives in a productive way that expands knowledge and creates workable tools and solutions. Managed well, a teamwork approach makes for happier, more loyal employees, something that also strengthens the company.

Being able to learn with others in a group thus brings all kinds of bene-fits, including better learning, more enjoyment, and highly prized workplace skills. Frequently, though, working in a group can feel risky. It is an exercise in trusting others to do their part and to treat you with respect.

In this chapter, we take a look at how groups work in college and how you can develop a collaborative persona so that your participation in those groups becomes less risky and more rewarding.

Developing a Collaborative Persona

As you learned in Chapter 3, a persona is a version of you that you present to others in different situations. It is what you say and how you act in relationship to others. In college, your persona needs to build trust and good will with your teammates. A collaborative persona is one that does not make others feel intimidated or angry by being bossy. On the other hand, it doesn't make others worry that you can't be depended upon by being too passive or disengaged.

Guidelines for Group Work

A few basic guidelines will help you to develop an effective, collaborative persona. As you read through these guidelines, think about the groups you've been in and how following them — or not following them — has affected the group dynamics.

1. Show Up on Time and Don't Leave Early

Regularly arriving late to or leaving early from group meetings sends the message that you do not care much for the work or the individuals on the team. If you have an occasional scheduling conflict, then let your team know, but do not make it a habit.

And speaking of time, stay on topic during group work. Time is valuable, especially when you're juggling multiple courses, work, and other obligations. Spending time on personal stories, complaining about the assignment (you know you have to do it anyway), or disengaging from the group slows everyone down. Value the time you have.

2. Complete Your Work as Promised

Your teammates may not say it, especially in the early part of a term, but they will be irritated with you if you don't follow through on your commitments, even if it is simply coming to class having completed a reading assignment. Some will be downright angry if they believe you are risking their grade. If you are struggling to meet a deadline, show them what you have done and tell them what you are going to do. Make sure the team will not be penalized for your difficulties.

Figure 1. Working with others can be difficult, but it's also the cornerstone of most careers. Group work in college gives you an opportunity to learn to collaborate and practice being an effective group member.

3. Take Turns

Some people like to talk because it feels good to hold people's attention. They have confidence in their point of view and have no trouble coming up with something to say. These people tend to control conversations. They often silence others, either by intimidating them or by annoying them. While it can be entertaining at a party, dominating the discussion is not helpful when the goal of a group is to learn together and consider a variety of options. If you tend to be a talker like this, keep in mind that talking could block your access to good ideas from your teammates. Go ahead and start the conversation, but then sit back and allow others to contribute before jumping back in. Actually, it's not all that entertaining at a party, either.

On the other side of the conversational spectrum are those who are too uncomfortable to speak up. It may be harder for a quiet type to say something than for a talker to hold off. It helps when your teammates give everyone time to speak. Everyone can contribute one way or another. Consider this: if everyone in the group is the silent type, things may not get done. If you are a quiet type, stretch yourself and drop in a comment or two to show your partners that you are engaged or to encourage productivity.

Figure 2. When you're working with a group, you should expect to have different opinions and levels of engagement. Focus on what the assignment requires of each person and how to avoid giving any one person too much or too little responsibility.

4. Don't Make It Personal

While it's important to get to know each other a bit before launching into a project, be respectful of each other's boundaries and differences. Maintain a judgment-free attitude towards your partners' appearances and personas. Acknowledge everyone in a friendly way.

Your group needs ideas as it begins wrestling with a topic, a problem, or sorting out how to accomplish a task. The more ideas a group can generate, the better. A common pitfall when discussing ideas is when the rejection of an idea feels like a personal rejection. If you don't agree with an idea, express your doubts carefully. Ask clarifying questions to make sure you understand the idea before dismissing it. It's safer and politer to say something like "I'm not sure I see how that will work" or "Tell me more about why you think that is." Saying "What a dumb idea" is rude and will shut others down. If there really is a problem, explain specifically why it doesn't work for the situation without suggesting the team member who offered the idea was weak-minded.

If you are hurt when your ideas are not accepted by others, remember that your ideas are not you. You come up with many ideas every day, and even *you* reject many of them. If you offer an idea to the group, it belongs to the group to consider. It's no longer yours. Don't be offended if the group decides to pass on the idea. If you believe that your idea is more valuable than your teammates recognize, it's okay to try again and explain the idea more carefully. However, if that doesn't work out, then don't worry about it. Don't let this spoil your group's forward progress.

5. Listen Actively

Unnecessary misunderstandings and conflict can be avoided with active listening. "Active listening" means that you focus on what others are saying and work hard to understand them clearly. This involves both nonverbal and verbal messages. Put your cell phone away. Make eye contact, nod your head, or lean forward to signal that you are paying attention. Take notes if it helps you stay focused on the speaker's message.

Try not to interrupt. Give speakers time to fully express themselves. Listen to understand, not respond. If you are preoccupied with how you are going to respond, you are not really paying attention. Once the speaker is finished, restate what you heard to make sure you understood and show the speaker that you were really listening. Ask clarifying questions if you aren't sure.

Group Work in Action

What follows is an example of group work in action. Watch for all five of the collaborative persona guidelines in action—or *not*—and how that affects the others in the group and the effectiveness of the group over all.

During the second week of their business class, six students were randomly assigned to a team for a group project due after the midterm. Their professor handed out the project guidelines, but she asked the class to first visit a bit and get to know each other.

Instead, Mark began to rapidly read the guidelines out loud. Then he said, "Okay, this seems easy enough. I'll handle the presentation. You guys just need to show up for a rehearsal before we present."

Sabrina smiled inwardly and thanked her higher power for getting her out of work.

Andrew and Elijah glanced at each other, and then Andrew raised his eyebrow and shook his head.

Caitlyn typed in a text message on her phone.

Clara, a former president of her high school's Future Business Leaders of America chapter, was taken aback. She paused to collect her thoughts. Then she said, "I'm glad you feel really confident about this project, Mark. If I understand you correctly, you're offering to basically do most of the work and we just need to read from a script that you'll write?"

"Yeah," said Mark. "Basically." His jaw tightened.

"That's generous," said Clara, "but the rubric has a section on collaboration. We have to show how we worked together. There are three parts to the presentation, and six of us in the group. It looks like we are supposed to divide it up."

Sabrina looked at her hands and shook her head sadly.

"Don't worry," said Mark. "I've been running my own business for over four years. I've already got a real-life product to pitch, and I've done it before. I've made actual pitches to actual buyers, so this is kindergarten stuff for me. Besides, I don't accept anything less than A-level work. As long as you guys show up to practice, I'll give everyone credit."

Figure 3. Working with difficult people is part of life. Group assignments often force students to confront their own insecurities about working together. A growth mindset lets you see these struggles as opportunities to learn how to deal with difficult situations.

Elijah stared at the ceiling and sighed.

"I guess that means we're a bunch of kindergartners," he said. "If you want to do it all yourself, be my guest. It's nap time for me anyway." Elijah grabbed his phone, got up, told the professor he needed to take an important call, and stepped out.

While Mark thought he was doing everyone a favor, and while Sabrina agreed that he was, he was actually being rude to the group. He was claiming to be an expert in an arrogant way, and he dismissed the point Clara made about collaboration. By referring to the assignment as "kindergarten stuff," he criticized anyone who doesn't see the assignment that way. He didn't know anything about his teammates' abilities, but he assumed they wouldn't be able to perform to his standards. He also expected his team to trust him but without offering any evidence that he was trustworthy. Finally, he set everyone up for a potential violation of the student code of conduct because his teammates couldn't honestly claim to have collaborated if he did all the work.

Fortunately, Clara's four years of experience with the Future Business Leaders of America helped to sort things out. Clara, first of all, demonstrated her skill at relationship management through active listening. She confirmed what she heard by restating Mark's offer. She also showed restraint in not coming out and telling Mark that he had insulted her. Instead, she complimented him for his confidence and generosity before challenging his idea. While she was gathering her thoughts, she put herself in Mark's position and empathized with him. She too wanted a strong performance from her team and was nervous about working with people she doesn't know well. She understood why he would want to take over the project because her initial feelings were to do the same.

After the awkward silence that followed Elijah's departure, Clara cleared her throat.

"You've got a lot of experience," she said, "and I feel like we are lucky to have that, but to be honest, I can't go along with your plan. I want an A, too, but I want to earn it. What can we do so everyone feels like they can trust each other to hold up their end of the project?"

Mark sighed and shook his head.

Sabrina wasn't terribly happy, either, because she could see where this was heading, and it was clear that she would now have to do more work. However, she had to agree with Clara that it will be better if they follow the assignment instructions.

Andrew was grateful that Clara was able to confront Mark because the idea of objecting to such a strong personality made him sick to his stomach. He always thought the project would be kind of fun. He went out to the hallway to get Elijah, and then the group got to work.

You Be the Judge 1

Here are some scenarios from collaborative learning groups. See how you would answer the questions. Jot down your ideas. When you finish, turn to the end of the chapter to check them.

1. Chris is excited to share his thoughts about the assigned essay, "Self-Reliance." As soon as the professor turns the class over to the groups to converse, Chris launches into a monologue on the brilliance of Emerson's insight that "the nonchalance of boys . . . is the healthy attitude of human nature." What should his partners do?

2. Lori came down with the flu right after her group delegated tasks on a project. She could not get out of bed for three days. What should she do?

3. Tasha and Joe are working together on a presentation for their sociology class. They have to gather people's opinions on a current event. Joe suggests posting an online survey to a popular social media site he uses. Tasha responds, "That place is a cesspool. We'll just get a bunch of losers with no life skewing the data." Joe is insulted. What should he do?

Getting the Most out of Groups

As you move from class to class, you'll find yourself in several different types of groups. They will all work better when you bring your collaborative college persona to the task at hand. However, the different types of groups also expect different types of collaboration from you. The better you understand those expectations, the more you will get out of each type of learning group.

Discussion Groups

The most common form of collaborative learning in a college classroom is the discussion group. In many courses, your professor presents new ideas in a lecture, video, or assigned reading, and then you are put in a group to discuss that new material. You may be asked to answer specific questions, or your group may need to develop its own questions and then answer them. This conversation with other students can help you understand complex concepts more clearly, solve problems that puzzled you, and see things from different points of view.

Struggling to answer a question with a couple of partners requires you to be metacognitive—to think about what you are thinking about. As you work together on a question, you explain your thoughts to your partner. In writing-intensive courses like English or philosophy, discussion groups are important for helping you understand assigned texts and then developing your ideas about them. Those ideas will eventually make their way into your papers.

To get the most out of a discussion group, come prepared to talk. That means do the assigned reading before class and give it enough time and attention that you're able to start forming some ideas and questions of your own about the reading. Discussion groups thrive on good questions and informed participants.

Getting the most out of a discussion group also requires you to be gentle with others when the subject matter is controversial or connects to deeply held values, beliefs, and identities. Topics such as immigration, transgender rights, and the legalization of drugs can stimulate strong emotions. Viewpoints that are different from yours can feel personally threatening when how you see yourself is closely connected to your beliefs and values about those topics. If a topic isn't personally important to you, your comments might feel threatening to others, and if they respond defensively, that defensiveness can feel threatening to you.

Figure 4. Peer review is one of the hardest and best things about college work. By getting honest feedback on your work, your performance will improve. By giving honest feedback on others' work, you show respect for their process and validate their work as worthy of close review.

For students who identify as immigrants, transgendered, or recreational drug supporters, it's almost impossible to *not* feel threatened if other students express positions that question immigration, transgender rights, and legalized drug use. The brain processes this kind of intellectual threat in the same place where it processes physical threats—the amygdala—and it activates the emotions. It's not really possible to prevent this from happening, but being aware of it allows you to think about how you might cope when it does happen.

The majority of the time, professors use challenging topics like these because they get students' attention and because they help students to start looking at these issues from other perspectives and building a more complex understanding. Professors expect you to discuss these issues, however, not debate them. A discussion is an exchange of information whose purpose is to widen everyone's understanding of an issue. Ideally, participants in a discussion find as much common ground between different perspectives as possible.

In a debate, the goal is to focus on all the weaknesses in your opponent's position and on all the strengths of yours. In other words, nothing changes in a debate. Everyone gets more entrenched in whatever ideas they started with. The culture of mainstream television and social media encourages debate rather than discussion, and you can see where that goes—nowhere. So be careful to avoid debate in your discussion groups, especially when the topic is emotionally charged.

When your professor introduces a controversial subject to discuss, these guidelines will help you to keep the discussion rewarding:

» Respect your discussion partners as intelligent human beings with concerns and questions that are equal to your own.

» Expect to have your understanding of an issue grow as a result of the conversation.

» Ask questions that help you understand the challenging ideas from your partner's perspective.

» Challenge yourself to find common ground between differing views.

» If you feel your emotions boiling over, take a break.

Peer Review and Critiques

Professors often use students to read and respond to each other's work-in-progress. These groups are sometimes called critique groups and sometimes called peer reviews, but the task is the same with both. For students new to this kind of review, these groups provide some of the most uncomfortable experiences they have in college.

In spite of that initial discomfort, however, learning how to give and receive feedback is one of the most valuable skills you can learn in college. Using honest, practical feedback from another person is a tool for self-improvement. Giving feedback effectively is a communication skill that helps relationships in all areas of your life. Peer review is a regular part of the creative process and popular in most writing and art classes. It's also used extensively in career fields that focus on developing skills. While that is important in itself, the abilities you develop through peer review transfer to many other situations—explaining frustrations to your child or partner, reviewing the employees you manage, or listening to customer complaints.

As you develop a paper or practice a procedure, you can be blind to small errors or unintentional messages within your work. Your reviewers are there to point out inconsistencies between what you meant to communicate and what they actually understood. They can also highlight the strengths of your work so that you know what to keep as you revise.

As a reviewer, you have an opportunity to see what you are doing or creating through the eyes of an audience. This can clear up misunderstandings you may have had and create a kind of helpful confusion that pushes you to clear things up for yourself in order to make them clear to others. It can also inspire new ideas for your own work.

To get the most out of a peer review, charge up your growth mindset thinking. Remind yourself that the purpose is to take an early trial and get ideas for improving it. Yes, it's common to feel a bit vulnerable when other people look at your work, especially if it is in the early stages of development. Your goal is not to impress people right out of the gate. If you're inexperienced with the given task, remind yourself that you need the benefit of more experienced reviewers to increase your knowledge and skills. If you tend to have a competitive frame of mind, remind yourself that academic achievement is not an individual sport with only the champion getting a trophy.

Use your professor's expectations to guide the kind of feedback to gather and to give during peer review. More often than not, your professor will give you a handout that lists what to look for and talk about. If you have a rubric for the assignment, you can also use it to create questions for your reviewer to answer. If the rubric calls for "concrete examples to illustrate ideas," then ask your reviewer to locate where you have used examples and whether they are examples that the readers can imagine for themselves. Once you receive the feedback, don't feel like you have to incorporate it all into your revision. Use the feedback to better understand how your audience saw your paper or artwork or demonstration, but then decide for yourself how to fix the problems.

When you review other people's work, it is kind and effective for you to first identify something you appreciated as a strength. Remember that you are not an expert, either, that you are learning alongside your classmate. That means that your job is not to tell your partner what you would have done or how they can fix something. Instead, you're there to tell them about your experience in reading or viewing their work. What did you understand clearly? Where were you confused? How well did this seem to follow the assignment's instructions? Be tactful and do not use harsh, critical language. The more specific you can be with your feedback, the better.

It's also kind and effective to actually *give* feedback. Students often worry that they don't know enough to give adequate feedback or that they might hurt someone's feelings. They tell them "It's great" or "I liked it" rather than "You integrated your sources into this essay really well, but I'm not sure you have a solid thesis statement yet." Consider this—if you don't give them feedback, they may end up with a lower grade. That is more likely to impact them than constructive, polite comments on their work. And, yes, you are just as knowledgeable as they are—you are in the same class at the same point in the term. Your opinion counts.

Group Projects

As you saw earlier in this chapter, a group project can be messy at first as the team figures out how to move forward. However, with the right attitude and strategies for collaborating, a group project can quickly become fun and interesting, and what you learn in the process will stick with you for a long time.

To get the most out of a group project, be friendly, patient, and manage negative thinking. The following will also help your group to function better:

» A clear goal or set of goals so that the project is well defined.

» A clear working agreement about who will complete what part of the project and when.

» A system of communication to share progress and identify problems.

Project groups tend to go through a series of stages as they figure out how to work with each other. Bruce Tuckman, a theorist in group dynamics, formed a team development model that identifies four stages most groups typically experience—forming, storming, norming, and performing. As you approach a group project, it helps to keep these stages in mind and consider how you and your professor can support project teams.

Stage 1: Forming

Description	Conflict Level	Member Support	Professor Support
Members learn about each other. The team needs guidance from the professor. It operates on assumptions rather than knowledge. Roles are unclear but considered.	Little open conflict as most members will be polite and open. Some conflict may be triggered internally, depending on the initial conversations.	Active listening is key. Be aware that most people want to get along, so they will initially agree to minimize conflict, but expect some disagreements to arise soon.	Give clear directions in written form. Answer questions. Offer useful "icebreakers" to allow groups to learn more about each other. Be encouraging. Demonstrate respectful communication.

Stage 2: Storming

Description	Conflict Level	Member Support	Professor Support
Previous assumptions about the goal/roles surface and don't connect. Members are confused and take issue with each other's understanding of the work. Goals and roles need to be determined clearly.	Conflict will be at its highest point here and the group may not know how to handle it well. Resolving productive conflict—disagreements about what to do and how—build trust and confidence. Interpersonal conflict must be completely avoided.	Stay focused on the goals of the project. Stay focused on solving problems rather than blaming or complaining. If interpersonal conflict arises, use active listening to defuse it as much as possible.	Help groups recognize that "storming" is a normal phase. Allow groups to work at it on their own before intervening. Check in with groups that are struggling. Get permission to help rather than take over. Give guidance to students on active listening to resolve conflicts.

Stage 3: Norming

Description	Conflict Level	Member Support	Professor Support
Members agree to and understand their roles. They agree on the work process. Communication is open and trust has been built.	Conflicts are resolved with working agreements.	Agree on roles, resources, and deadlines based on everyone's strengths. Identify how to handle missed deadlines, lack of communication, absenteeism, and work that is not up to expectations.	Give examples of working agreements. Encourage groups to focus on strengths rather than weaknesses.

Stage 4: Performing

Description	Conflict Level	Member Support	Professor Support
Members are confident, trust each other, make decisions easily and handle conflict quickly. They track their progress and complete the work assigned.	Minor issues related to project development arise, but the group handles them well.	Stick to the group's agreements. Complete your work. Ask for help if needed. Help group members appropriately.	Offer feedback on work in progress.

You Be the Judge 2

Consider the following group situations and answer each question. Jot down your ideas. When you finish, turn to the end of the chapter to check them.

1. Students are discussing government-provided universal healthcare in their economics class. One student had an uncle become gravely ill because he couldn't afford health insurance. Another student's father works for a healthcare insurance company. What could go wrong?

2. Joanna's partner gave her a draft full of spelling errors and mechanical mistakes to review. How should she respond?

3. Identify what stage of the team development process (forming, storming, norming, or performing) this group is at: Josh, Nick, Nora, and MacKenzie meet in a study room of the library to rehearse their presentation two days before it is due. They all have their own notes. Josh and Nick have printouts from the slide presentation while Nora and MacKenzie hold note cards. They invited two friends to watch and give them feedback on the presentation.

4. Identify what stage of the team development process (forming, storming, norming, or performing) this group is at: Josh and Nick are upset with their partners, MacKenzie and Nora. Neither used the cloud drive they set up for the team's work, and Nora seems to have skipped out on the meeting. Josh asks MacKenzie where she was with the project. She apologizes for not following through online, but shows them her handwritten work. She couldn't figure out how to use the cloud drive and gave up. She says that Nora had told her she didn't know what the "cloud" was. Nick apologizes for assuming that everyone knew how to use the drive. MacKenzie asks if there is a way to combine offline with online coordination. Nick and Josh think about it and agreed. Nora arrives ten minutes late. She, too, apologizes, saying her daughter had been sick all week and still couldn't go back to the childcare center. Nick sympathizes and asks Nora if she'd like help using the cloud drive.

5. Identify what stage of the team development process (forming, storming, norming, or performing) this group is at: Josh and Nick take the lead for their group and suggest using the school's cloud-computing network to house the group's work online. Nora doesn't know how to use the network or how to "collaborate online," but she nods her head. MacKenzie knows a little bit about "the cloud" and also agrees. A week later, Josh and Nick have set up the cloud drive and uploaded their work. They send messages to MacKenzie and Nora to do the same. MacKenzie responds with a smiley face. Nora does not reply. Josh and Nick send each other private messages laced with profanity. When the team meets during class, Nora is nowhere to be found and MacKenzie has a collection of handwritten notes.

Psychological Safety in Groups

Psychological safety is a key factor in everyone's ability to learn in the classroom. Psychological safety in a college classroom is the belief that you will not be punished in any way for the unavoidable errors that are part of a creative, inquiry-based process.

Professors can create a safe classroom environment with how they interact with students, direct the classroom activities, and prepare for class meetings. They can also create structure in group activities by providing clear instructions and examples. Students bear some responsibility for a safe classroom as well because the atmosphere is equally affected by their willingness to participate and ability to be courteous, positive, and focused.

When professors assign students into groups— no matter how safe the classroom has been up to this point—the level of psychological safety in the classroom changes. Some types of discussion groups are not especially risky and may even make classroom participation safer. A quick check-in with the person sitting next to you is not particularly risky and can help you feel more comfortable with your classmates in general. However, it can be risky to give a draft of your paper to someone you don't know well—or at all—and wait to hear them tell you which parts were confusing.

Psychological safety can also be threatened by unconscious forces. Egocentric bias, performance anxiety, mismanaged conflict, stereotyping, and marginalization can all interfere with productive group learning and make a classroom less safe for many students. To combat the impact of these unconscious forces, students need to become more conscious of what those forces are and then do what they can to prevent them from affecting the safety of the classroom and the effectiveness of the group.

Egocentric Bias

You know more about yourself than anyone else. You have access to your private thoughts and feelings. You remember more about what you have done than about what others have done. Because so much of your data about the world is connected to your experience, you may at times assume that what you have experienced is more or less what everyone else has experienced and that most people will agree with your point of view because it's their point of view, too. This kind of assumption is called "egocentric bias," and it almost always gets in the way of group work.

In the earlier example of a project group in action, Mark was under the influence of the egocentric bias. He assumed that the recent high school graduates in his group would slack off because *he* had been a bit of a slacker right out of high school. That's why he tried to do all the work on his own. Egocentric bias also tends to make you overestimate how much you contribute to group efforts, how well you explain yourself, and how closely people are paying attention to you.

Egocentric bias can cause intergroup conflict, as you saw, and it's especially problematic if these errors in judgment lead to blaming and complaining. To resist this problem within a group, you can pay attention to how well you are judging or misjudging the situation. You can also keep in mind that the others in the group may not agree with your thinking and certainly won't see things as you do unless you explain them carefully. If you are concerned about the fair distribution of work in a group project because you see egocentric bias in others, you can help the group by making sure everyone's roles are well defined and understood.

Performance Anxiety

Contributing an idea or suggesting a solution within a group can stir up performance anxiety for students who've had bad group experiences in the past or who are insecure in their abilities. It's hard for them to work through their fears and add to the discussion.

Students who struggle with performance anxiety within groups can help themselves by being well prepared for class and group meetings so that they know they have something to contribute. That preparation will help their confidence. It will also allow them to consider and respond to the ideas or work of others more thoughtfully.

Even so, the more extroverted members of the group can make a bigger difference by being noncompetitive and encouraging the work of others. If you're one of those more outgoing students, avoid any kind of sarcasm and be careful with humor. When people feel anxious about themselves, humor is often perceived as an attack even though it rarely is.

Never call someone's idea dumb, useless, ridiculous, or any other mean-spirited term. In the example from the business class, Mark labeled the project and course "kindergarten work." That comment shut down some members in the group and angered others. Mark might not have cared if people call his ideas dumb or ridiculous, but that's not everyone's experience.

Figure 5. Working together, even through conflict, can lead to enjoyment of projects that would otherwise be too difficult on your own. Who knows—you might even make a friend.

Everyone should have an opportunity to speak safely. You can help your teammates feel safer by holding back on negative comments, by actively listening, and by reminding quieter partners that the more ideas the group has, the better the project will be.

Conflict

Conflict and tension arise whenever people work together. When ideas are shared, some people agree and some disagree—sometimes strongly. For a group to work together effectively, it has to learn how to manage that unavoidable conflict.

Some team members have other things weighing them down from outside the classroom, too, and the emotions they carry from those other problems can sometimes supercharge the emotions that disagreement generates. If that's how you're feeling during a group meeting, it's important for you to at least try to consciously separate those external emotions from the conflict that arises within the group (use your emotional intelligence). Remember that your project is a matter of the mind, not the heart.

Other teammates may have a long, negative history with conflict in their private lives. They've gotten into the habit of avoiding conflict instead of managing it. They sit passively through discussions or agree with everything, even though they have real concerns. Worse yet, some students who lack good strategies for managing conflict may turn to passive-aggressive behaviors to express their unhappiness. They may only talk to members of the group whom they see as allies, tune out during discussions, and procrastinate or put in a minimal effort. To get the outcome they want without entering into direct conflict, they may look for ways to sabotage the work of others they disagree with.

If people in your group seem to be withdrawing or potentially sabotaging the group, you can help by giving them some attention: "I notice that you have been texting with someone on your phone for a while. When I see that, I worry that something isn't working for you. What's going on?" Then let them talk and use

Figure 6. Lab partners have to solve problems together. Lab work puts you in hands-on situations with the concepts of the week, including the material that you're not sure about. When the work becomes more challenging, rely on your parner to find solutions together.

active listening to make sure you understand what's going on. There may be an underlying need that isn't being met. They may have felt disrespected at some point or simply ignored. They may resent that the group isn't doing what they want. They may feel deeply insecure about being able to perform.

Don't argue. Just listen. It will take courage for these teammates to share what's actually going on. Once the underlying need or issue is out in the open, the group can work together to manage the conflict and make sure all its members are able to feel safe and participate effectively.

When Elijah left his group in the business example, he was angry at Mark and needed to cool off. Leaving to cool off makes sense. That helps to make sure that the conflict doesn't instantly get worse. However, the longer he stays out of the group, the more marginalized he becomes, and that will probably only make him angrier over time. To avoid the conflict entirely, he could have asked to be in a different group instead of rejoining his group. Returning to the group and working to manage the conflict and resolve his issues will be difficult for Elijah without help from others in the group.

Clara got the ball rolling when she asked, "What can we do so everyone feels like they can trust each other to hold up their end of the project?"

Andrew helped when he went to get Elijah and bring him back to the group. When Elijah returned, Clara repeated her question: "What can we do so that we can trust each other?"

Elijah lifted his hand and said, "I want to apologize for leaving. I was mad. When Mark said that he only accepts A-level work, it felt like he was doubting my intelligence. I'm glad Mark wants to work hard. I want a good grade, too. All of us need to agree that we're going to put in the effort to get an A." That was difficult for Elijah, but he did it, and he was glad to have been honest with the group. It was also good for Mark to hear this and not argue. It helped him to consider the possibility that the rest of the group may not see things exactly the way he sees them.

Stereotypes

A stereotype is the belief that certain characteristics—positive and negative—are ingrained based on a person's race, ethnicity, gender, social class, or sexual orientation. Every culture generates stereotypes about the groups within and outside of that culture. Here are some common examples:

- » Women aren't mechanically inclined, but they naturally know how to care for children.

- » Men are helpless in caring for children, but they can solve all kinds of household appliance breakdowns.

- » White, rural Americans are closed-minded, prone to violence, and ignorant, but white, urban Americans are open-minded, calm, and well-educated.

- » Asian Americans excel in school, but they are socially awkward.

Like other unconscious beliefs, stereotypes develop from years of exposure to the ideas of family, friends, television, film, and social media. More recently, the media is being more responsible in representing people as more diverse and less stereotypical, but negative stereotypes are still deeply embedded in mainstream American cultural beliefs. A single individual may seem to conform to a stereotype, especially if you do not know him or her. The more people you come to know and the better you know them, though, the more these stereotypes break down as untrue.

Within groups, stereotypical thinking can translate into marginalizing behaviors. "Marginalization" is the treatment of a person or a group as unimportant, irrelevant, or unworthy. It's also treating others as only capable of whatever behaviors are associated with that stereotype. When you view a person as a stereotype, you may act in an insensitive way, even if that is not your intention. Consider these situations:

» A transgender woman asks that people refer to her by the name Deirdre rather than Daniel, the name listed in the college's registration system. Her professor repeatedly refers to her as "Danny."

» A student in an English composition course compliments her Asian American partner for her "really good" English and asks where she's from. Her partner replies, "I'm from Seattle, Washington. English is my native language."

» Male students in the welding program roll their eyes and snicker when their female partner makes a mistake, but they take no notice of the same mistake made by a male classmate.

» At a coffee shop, a young, male political science student eavesdrops on a conversation between two women planning a class on the subject he is studying. One is a respected professor of political science, and the other is a community organizer with decades of experience working in the field. He interrupts the two women to offer them a reading list and the name and number of a professor he knows who could help them.

» A group of three young men with tan complexions and dark hair enter the campus bookstore on a quiet afternoon, joking with each other in Spanish. A clerk who was stocking shelves stops what he's doing and asks if he can help them find anything. One young man says he knows what he needs and where to get it. The group heads towards the aisle for science lab supplies. The clerk follows them and watches as they make their selections. They then wander over to the laptops and start examining them. The clerk tells the group, "If you have what you need, let me check you out. We're busy."

» A project group is figuring out who will do what. The only African American student in the group offers to prepare the annotated bibliography. One of his groupmates says, "That seems like an easy job, but it's not. Do you know what an annotated bibliography is?"

» A young man from a working-class town attends a top-notch university, Yale. He has a sticker with the Yale university logo on the back window of his Ford Fiesta hatchback. A well-dressed woman passing by strikes up a conversation with him, asking him where he lived. She then says, "I don't mean to pry, but I'm just so curious. Was that Yale sticker on the car when you bought it?"

Each of these interactions happened because of biased, stereotypical thinking. They may seem to be small and meaningless from one point of view, but they suggest that because of physical characteristics, this person does not belong, is not capable, or is a criminal.

These marginalizing incidents are called "micro-aggressions." While some people may be aware that their micro-aggressions are probably rude or unfair, it's common to excuse them by thinking "that's the way the world works" or "these people just need to have thicker skins." However, for frequently marginalized groups—people of color, people who identify as LGBTQ, women and men pursuing nontraditional careers, or people experiencing poverty—micro-aggressions happen over and over. The weight of regularly coping with these questions about their abilities, character, or sense of belonging can become a painful emotional burden. They already have thick skin. That's not the problem.

You Be the Judge 3

In the following scenarios, identify the unconscious force or forces that are threatening to derail the psychological safety in the group. Jot down your ideas. When you finish, turn to the end of the chapter to check them.

1. Zach views the discussion in his class group as a competition, where each person seems to be trying to outdo the other with a brilliant insight. He decides completing the reading assignment and participating is not worth his while.

2. Everyone in Alexandra's group lives on the south end of town, in a more affluent neighborhood. They all have their own cars. Alexandra lives on the north side and relies on public transportation. The group chooses to meet at a coffee shop on the south side. It will take Alex-

andra over an hour and several bus transfers to get there. When Alexandra explains this, a teammate says, "Can't you just get a ride from someone?"

3. Zora offers this comment in a discussion group about drug addiction: "I quit smoking three years ago and I did it going cold turkey. I'm not saying it's easy, but if I can do it, anyone can."

Figure 7. Studying in a group creates a unique dynamic for learning. Your shared goals can really improve the effectiveness of your studying.

To benefit from collaboration and learning groups, every classroom needs to be a space where all students can feel comfortable contributing and where their contributions will be respected. Actively thinking about the stereotypes you carry in your thinking is the first step in avoiding unnecessary hurt. You should also think before you speak and guard against any behaviors that can be interpreted as marginalizing. More importantly, when you realize that you *have* marginalized someone, probably without meaning to, apologize to the person. This will help to offset some of the damage you've inadvertently caused, and it will help you build better habits for yourself.

Study Groups

Most of the group work in any course is assigned to you in the form of discussion groups, peer review groups, lab partnerships, and project groups. You don't have much, or maybe any, choice about whether or not you'll work with others.

With study groups, the collaboration is voluntary. You're choosing to find others in your class and then work with them to learn and practice new, challenging, brain-expanding material. Getting together with a couple of classmates to study has consistently proven to be one of the most effective ways for you to succeed in any class. It reduces your chances of procrasti-

Figure 8. Working in groups can sometimes lead to conflicts. This is a normal part of the process. A growth mindset helps you use the conflict as a way to improve the quality of your group's work.

nating, lightens the load, and makes challenging material doable.

By committing to meet with study partners to investigate new material or complete parts of an assignment, you increase the likelihood that you will follow through because of the positive peer pressure they can apply. For example, you might agree to meet in the library to do research at a certain day and time. You might then commit to meeting in the computer lab or a coffee shop to draft your papers a few days later, and then commit to reading each other's drafts and giving each other feedback. Those small commitments help to build a habit of commitment not just in that course but the rest of your college career.

The keys to forming a successful study group are identifying compatible group members and then using your time together effectively.

The Right Partners

The ideal study group is composed of three or four students with similar aims and similar schedules. Working with a friend may seem like a better choice, but you are more likely to socialize than study with a friend. If you do work with a friend, make sure you both share the same goal of studying over socializing, and try to include others who are not friends. Look for others in your course who share your goals for learning and have the time to meet for a few hours outside of class each week and who also have a similar schedule so that it's not hard to find time to meet together.

You can find partners by speaking up in class early in the term, reaching out to specific individuals who seem engaged and focused, or posting a notice in your college's student life area or learning assistance center seeking interested partners. Typically, people who join a study group will be committed to it because it is something they are choosing for themselves.

Effective Methods

Once you have found a study partner or two or three, meet on campus in a quiet place like the library or the learning assistance center. Besides offering fewer distractions, these places also offer more resources to help when you get stuck. When you meet, organize your time according to the different tasks that are part of your class.

Learning from a Textbook Together

Courses with a heavy reading load can be managed by reading together. To learn from a text, preview the material you plan to read, locate or write a series of questions you expect to answer, and then read and take notes. You may find the answers to your questions when you read, or you may be able to locate the information you'll need to eventually figure out an answer.

If you are tackling challenging material, work together on the same chapter:

» Review any class notes related to the topic.

» Scan through the text and any supporting handouts to figure out what you are supposed to learn from it.

» Create a series of questions together.

» Read and take notes independently.

» Compare notes.

» Identify questions that could show up on a test.

» Practice remembering the answers together.

If anyone in the group is confused, work together to make sense of the material. If the person or group remains confused, then look for some extra help from a nearby tutor or reference librarian. If that doesn't help, then plan to follow up with your professor after class or during office hours.

If the material is not particularly challenging, the group can divide the reading up and then share their findings with others. In this case, after you have read your assigned section, you can explain it to your partners while they take notes. The chances are that they will have some questions that you didn't think of, so you should expect to revisit the text as needed. Make sure everyone leaves with a good set of notes for the entire reading.

Learning Math Together

Solving math problems requires knowing which procedures to use and remembering how to use them. In your group, take turns solving different homework problems aloud and making careful notes about the work to do at each step of the solution. A chart listing the problem, the solution, and explanation for each step is most useful.

Another technique involves each partner bringing a problem that has been miscalculated. The other members of the group study the incorrectly solved problem to locate the error and correct it.

Unraveling Points of Confusion

If time is short, your group can focus on specific questions or topics that the group members are struggling to understand. To prepare for the study session, each person can bring a summary of how he or she tried to sort things out—and failed. The summary should include the following:

» State the question or topic.

» List any related vocabulary associated with the question.

» List the resources available to figure it out.

» List anything that you already understood about the problem.

» Identify when the confusion set in.

You Be the Judge 4

Consider the situations these students are in and how a study group might help them be more successful. Jot down your ideas. When you finish, turn to the end of the chapter to check them.

1. Organic chemistry is a notoriously tough class. The professor presents ideas quickly and they pile up. If at any point a student hits a snag in understanding a concept, it is easy to fall behind and feel a drowning sensation come on.

2. A few students in an introductory algebra course suffer from math anxiety. This anxiety contributes to a general feeling that maybe they aren't college material, after all. There is a real risk that they might drop out if they cannot conquer this fear of math.

3. Students in a sociology course are assigned forty pages of textbook reading per week. Their professor does not lecture and uses collaborative learning almost exclusively to engage students in the ideas of the class. He also has weekly chapter quizzes to hold students accountable to the reading assignments. In other words, students cannot hope to pass the course without completing the reading assignments.

Take turns presenting these points of confusion. Ideally, your partners will not just blurt out an answer but help you solve the problem on your own. They can do this by asking you questions that direct your thinking towards the answer. For example, instead of saying, "converting your units to grams will get you the right answer," ask "what units do you need to express the answer in?"

Final Thoughts

Suddenly being tossed into a group with complete strangers and being asked to cooperate with them is stressful. The varying levels of confidence, insecurity, trust, suspicion, engagement, or disengagement make for a thick stew of uncertainty and, yes, discomfort. In addition to the responsibility of learning the course material, you are also responsible for managing yourself and the relationship you have with these strangers. If you prefer working in solitude or if you are a more competitive type, collaboration can feel like a royal pain, stifling even.

Professors are going to insist on it though because, in spite of these risks, the rewards are plentiful. Your understanding grows when you have access to the experiences of others. Your thinking is sharpened when it is tested by sincere critique. Your knowledge is more durable when it is rehearsed in front of others. Your ability to meet deadlines is strengthened when you are accountable to others. Your workload is lightened when it is shared. Your insecurity is quieted when it is met by encouragement. You become better prepared for the workplace.

The demands on your emotional intelligence—your ability to recognize and manage your emotions and do so in relationship with others—also pay dividends that go far beyond a course grade. As you practice active listening, you are demonstrating respect for and establishing confidence in your partner. A classmate expresses a hurtful idea, but you have learned how to respond without spite, preserving the unity of the group. Likewise, you learn how to express ideas without being unintentionally hurtful. Each time you collaborate with others to overcome conflict, you have gained valuable relationship skills that will serve you in many areas of your life.

Reflect on Your Self-Assessment

Your self-assessment for this chapter encouraged you to consider how you think and feel about working collaboratively. The higher your score, the more prepared you are to collaborate with others. Your answers were likely based on previous experiences, some of which may not have been great. Now you have some understanding of the importance of collaboration and some tools for working effectively with others. Consider some of those earlier experiences. Would some of the tools you've learned have helped? Hopefully so. Keep these in mind for your group assignment and give some of the following DIYs a shot.

Do It Yourself

Here are some practical things that you can do to prepare yourself for more effective group work:

1. Recall and describe a discussion group when you learned something insightful from a peer. What were you discussing? What did you already know? What did you learn?

2. Examine the expectations for a writing assignment or project you have this term. Create two or three questions for a reviewer to focus on. Ask them to review your draft. Reflect on what went well and what you would do differently.

3. Write about a situation where you felt marginalized. Then, revise the scenario so that you felt welcomed.

4. Create a "seeking study partners" posting for your campus student center. Include information about your goals, needs, and availability.

5. Form a study group and use one of the strategies for group study discussed. Reflect on what went well and what you would do differently.

6. Conduct an online search and read any of the following resources about teams:

   a. "Giving and Receiving Peer Feedback," a video from BYU-Idaho's Academic Support Centers.

  b. "What Google Learned from Its Quest to Build the Perfect Team" by Charles Duhigg, published in the *New York Times Magazine*, 25 February 2019.

  c. "The New Science of Building Great Teams" by Alex 'Sandy' Pentland, published in the *Harvard Business Review.*

You Be the Judge 1 Ideas

1. Chris's teammates should listen actively and show him respect for his enthusiasm. He will run out of steam at some point. Someone could briefly summarize what they heard Chris say, and then offer their own point of view. If Chris persists in dominating the conversation, some could smile and say, "I think we need to let someone else talk for a bit."

2. As soon as Lori realizes how sick she is, she should find a way to communicate with her professor to work out an accommodation. She could have a friend or family member make contact if necessary. When she starts to feel better, she needs to figure out what to do first. She needs to connect back with her group and renegotiate her role.

3. Even if Joe is angered, he needs to remain as calm as possible and stay focused on the goal of the assignment, collecting data. He can defend his idea simply, "I disagree. It just depends on where you post it on the site. We can get a wide variety of responses." Once they come to an agreement on how to collect data, Joe can let Tasha know that her comments were out of line by saying something like "I realize that site isn't for everyone, but I go there all the time and get a lot out of it. I think it's unfair to call anyone who uses that site a loser."

You Be the Judge 2 Ideas

1. Each of these students have deeply personal connections to the topic. If the professor does not structure the discussion carefully, it is possible that one student will say something hurtful to the other, possibly without realizing it. The discussion could turn into a heated argument.

2. Joanna should focus on the goal of the peer review session. If the point of the review is to help her partner find mechanical problems, then she can safely note them. Before doing so, she can say something encouraging about the paper's ideas. If the purpose of the review is to focus on the ideas, then Joanna needs to resist editing the paper. After identifying strengths, Joanna should be specific and tactful, not general and harsh, about its weaknesses. "Your introduction is boring and cliché" is harsh and general. "Can you think of an interesting anecdote to introduce your essay?" is specific and tactful.

3. This group is in the performing stage of the team development process.

4. This group is in the norming stage of the team development process.

5. This group is in the forming stage of the team development process.

6. This group is in the storming stage of the team development process.

You Be the Judge 3 Ideas

1. Zach is likely dealing with performance anxiety.

2. The insensitive comment made by Alexandra's classmate is an example of micro-aggression/marginalizing.

3. Zora's statement reflects an egocentric bias.

You Be the Judge 4 Ideas

1. A study group is a fail-safe for fast-paced, complex course content. If at any time a student starts to feel that drowning sensation, his study group can be a life boat and help him clear up any confusion. In fact, study groups for chemistry have been a well-studied practice and educational researchers think they are so effective that maybe chemistry professors should *require* them.

2. A study group for math-anxious students makes the stress manageable in a "we're all in this together" kind of way. Having partners to shoulder the burden makes the work lighter. The impact of a study group in this situation can't be understated. Study partners can keep you on track towards graduation.

3. Reading and taking notes on forty pages of reading will take *at least* four hours of a student's time and possibly more. If each chapter is divided up, that material can be covered in less than two hours. A study group is an excellent time management tool, too.

Glossary of Terms

Academic Discipline: a field of study.

Academic Integrity: "integrity" is the quality of being true, trustworthy and responsible. Academic integrity applies to those in an academic environment, like students and professors. Having academic integrity means avoiding plagiarism, cheating, collusion with other students or getting inappropriate assistance, fabricating or altering data, submitting the same assignment multiple times without permission, and sabotaging or tampering with the work of another student. It also means trying to do your best work rather than the bare minimum to get by and taking responsibility for your mistakes.

Active Learning: Using a variety of thinking strategies such as recalling, paraphrasing, questioning, classifying, comparing, and contrasting content from a course to learn it. Active learning usually involves trial and error, getting feedback, and making adjustments.

Active Listening: focusing on what others are saying and working to understand them clearly before responding. Techniques of active listening include devoting your attention to them without distractions, making eye contact, taking notes, using body language that shows you're paying attention, and allowing them to speak without interruption.

Amygdala: a part of the brain that plays a role in memory, emotion, and decision-making.

Analyze: to examine something closely, critically, even breaking it down into its components, in order to explain or interpret it.

Apply: to use the information you've learned to reason, solve problems, or perform a complex skill.

Auditory: the parts of the brain or body related to hearing.

Automaticity: an automatic response or habit. Automaticity means that you do something without thinking about it.

Autonomy: acting independently under your own free will, such as making your own decisions.

Boundaries: the rules, guidelines, or parameters that a person must operate within, such as following the instructions on an assignment. Boundaries can be established by anyone based on who holds the authority in the situation. A professor holds the authority in the classroom, while the student sets most of the boundaries in his or her personal life. A student may set boundaries, for example, with a person who tends to dominate his or her time.

Brain Plasticity: the brain's ability to change, for better or worse. When acquiring knowledge, the brain physically forms new neural pathways. Likewise, if the brain is sedentary, it can weaken.

Charting: a way to revise notes by organizing information into categories which requires active processing and aids later recall.

Classify: to arrange things into classes or categories based on shared characteristics.

Cognitive Load: the amount of information or stimuli a person can handle when learning something new. Many things can add to the cognitive load, such as environmental distractions, technology, and people. When there is too much new or distracting information for a learner to process, learning is weakened.

Collaborative Persona: "collaborate" means to work or willingly cooperate with others, often for intellectual gain. A "collaborative persona" is one that works well with others and avoids intimidation, passivity, or bossiness. A collaborative persona is one who is engaged, contributing to the group's work according to established guidelines, and allowing others to contribute.

College Persona: "persona" refers to the way a person presents his or her self to the world. The college persona is what a student uses on campus with other students in a learning environment, as well as what they use to approach their academic studies and goals. This persona, ideally, is learning-focused, collaborative, respectful, disciplined, and accountable for successes and mistakes.

Conflict Level: the stages of problem-solving (disagreements, differences, or interpersonal problems) a group may potentially experience. When collaborating, they may need to resolve and manage various levels of conflict before reaching a functional level.

Connections: these are the useful relationships a student forms with peers, family, and friends, as well as the campus and community resources the student may need to access in order to be successful.

Conscious Incompetence: the awareness that you are making mistakes because you have not yet fully learned how to perform a skill or explain a body of knowledge due to lack of experience or effective practice.

Conscious Competence: doing things successfully with conscious thought.

Cooperative Work Experience: when a student works alongside and learns from someone in the community, usually within the student's intended field. An internship would be an example of a cooperative work experience.

Critique: a form of peer-review or professor assessment during which the reviewer looks at the quality and accuracy of your work and offers an opinion of it, often describing what they feel works well and identifying areas that they believe do not.

Cue: a signal or sign that indicates that it's time to do or remember something or that triggers a certain behavior. Cues can be written, like key words or phrases, or can be physical, like gestures, spoken words, or sounds.

Culture Of College: the "culture" of a group is a combination of its behaviors, beliefs, symbols, and values. Members of the same culture have a shared understanding of what behaviors are considered successful and useful as well as what are considered problematic and inappropriate. The culture of college applies to a shared understanding of the purpose and function of college as well as the expectations for how people act in their particular roles (student, professor, dean, counselor, etc.).

Debate: as opposed to discussion. A debate typically involves the attempt to persuade someone that a particular viewpoint is correct, often regardless of ideas contributed by their opponent. Consider how an attorney argues in a courtroom. The goal is winning the argument as opposed to solving a problem or learning new information.

Declarative Knowledge: knowledge about facts and things, including definitions, characteristics, formulas, descriptions, and locations. This is in contrast to procedural knowledge, which focuses on understanding *how* something is done. (see also "procedural knowledge")

Dendrites: extensions of nerve cells that receive and transmit signals to the body of that cell.

Digital Persona: how you present yourself through your words, icons, and images in any electronic outlet. This includes social media, email, texting, online class discussions, etc. In a college setting, this means being aware of appropriate ways of communicating in a professional way, unlike the informal approach used in your personal life.

Discussion: as opposed to a debate. A discussion involves active listening and respectful communication. In group discussions, for example, students should offer their opinion, listen to the opinions of others, consider those opinions, and process the information. Sometimes this means responding, but not necessarily. It means thinking critically about a topic in order to solve a problem or gain knowledge. (see also "debate")

Disengagement: a loss of connection. This is considered a barrier to learning. Disengagement is when a student "checks out" of his or her studies mentally, sometimes physically as well. As students find a course too challenging or unnecessary, or as life gets more difficult to balance with school, some find themselves disengaging and no longer taking an interest in learning. They stop paying attention, stop completing assignments, and maybe stop showing up for class at all.

Egocentric Bias: one of several errors in reasoning our brains make (known as "cognitive biases"), it is the initial filter through which we interpret events. Because we only have access to our own experiences, we first think that everyone else has the same experience and interpretation of that experience when often, they do not. To collaborate effectively, remember you have an egocentric bias and do not assume others perceive circumstances the same way you do.

Emotional Intelligence: being aware of and regulating your emotions, managing them so that you're successful in social and academic situations.

Encoding: how the brain converts new information to a way that it can be stored and recalled. Your senses, study methods and techniques can help you encode information. For example, taking notes, listening to lectures, charting or mapping information, and doing self-tests are techniques that encourage encoding.

Engaged: interested, involved, occupied, and committed all relate to the concept of engagement. In college, being engaged means you pay attention in class, remain involved with your studies, discuss material with peers and, essentially, approach your courses with an interest in learning the material no matter what it may be.

Essential Question: a question that is answered by drawing together a range of information and requires critical thinking rather than a fixed answer. An essential question places that range of information into a meaningful relationship, or provides a context in which to use that information. They are used to stimulate critical thought as compared to a question with few possibilities, like "What is a stegosaurus?" which looks for a specific, scientific description.

Evaluate: to make a judgment or reach conclusions based on critical thought, following a set of standards.

External Locus Of Control: the belief that control over a situation resides externally and is not within a person's power to alter. (see also "locus of control" and "internal locus of control")

External Motivation: people are motivated to do things by both internal and external factors. External factors are those things that happen outside of the self, often things that we cannot dictate or may not be able to control. Examples of external motivators would be grades, promotions, the avoidance of illness or injury, or praise from others. (see also "internal motivation")

FAFSA: Free Application for Federal Student Aid. This is a government application all college students complete annually to determine their eligibility for student loans and grants.

Fixed Mindset: the belief that your intelligence is a fixed characteristic and cannot be changed like your height. Students who believe, for example, that they are a C student and cannot become a B student, or that they are naturally bad at math and cannot improve, may have a fixed mindset.

Formal: in a college setting, formal means professional or academic, usually as it relates to language, tone, and the quality of work. Formal language, for example, avoids slang and emojis, is well-edited and precise. (see also "informal")

Forming: one of Bruce Tuckman's stages of team development during which a group first begins to learn about each other. In this stage, members' roles and duties are unclear, as is their knowledge of one another, and they still need guidance from a professor.

Gray Matter: though technically the darker-colored portions of the brain consisting largely of nerve cells and dendrites, we commonly associate this with intellect.

Growth Mindset: the belief that knowledge and traits are not fixed but can be changed and improved upon with practice and effort, like muscle strength.

Hierarchy: a ranking system, such as best to worst, most common to least common, or most important to least important. When we say an animal is at the top of the food chain in a particular environment, for example, we are saying that there is a hierarchy of animals that illustrates which ones are strongest and weakest in their setting (and most or least likely to survive or be eaten).

Hypothetical: a theoretical situation or scenario, one that may not exist but could exist. A hypothetical is a "what if?"

Imposter Syndrome: the belief that you do not belong and will not succeed, regardless of the fact that you can, even already have. People with imposter syndrome compare themselves to others and decide they do not fit in, even if they are functioning successfully in the environment.

Informal: casual. The common, everyday language, mannerisms and dress used when around most friends and family. For example, when you attend a BBQ at your friend's home, you dress and act informally. You use the language and mannerisms that your friends are accustomed to. (see also "formal")

Inquiry: a method of learning and processing knowledge by asking questions, both of the presented material and of how you, and others, perceive it and relate to it.

Internal Dialogue: self-talk or the conversation you have within yourself. This relates to your self-efficacy and your mindset. For example, if you tell yourself that you're no good at something and can't do it, this internal dialogue may hinder you from achieving your goals.

Internal Locus Of Control: the fact or belief that the person has the power within them to control or modify a situation. (see also "locus of control" and "external locus of control")

Internal Motivation: people are motivated to do things by both internal and external factors. Internal factors are those feelings that are important to you. Examples of internal motivators are increased independence, mastery of a skill, self-confidence, a sense of purpose, and satisfaction in a job well-done. (see also "external motivation")

Learning Barriers: those situations that hinder a student's learning. These can be real or imagined. A "fixed mindset" or negative attitude can be a learning barrier. Poor support at home, financial struggles, poor language skills, or lack of transportation can also be examples of barriers.

Locus Of Control: the term "locus" means location. The concept of locus of control suggests that a person either has control over an action or situation, or the control is located elsewhere, such as with another person, organization, or some other external force. (see also "internal locus of control" and "external locus of control")

Low-Effort Syndrome: the desire to do what's easiest, requires the least amount of effort, often in order to avoid failure or appear smart.

Mapping: a note-taking method that helps students organize, analyze, and encode information. Mapping notes in a class, for example, might mean putting the main subject in the center or at the top of the page, then drawing arrows or lines to the next step or sub-category, moving from broad to more specific details about it (like streets on a map).

Marginalization: to place certain people or groups at the margin of a dominant group. Someone who is being "marginalized" is treated as insignificant or invisible, their needs or desires ignored, and their ideas not adequately considered.

Mastery: to learn a concept or skill with solid understanding, so much so that you can complete the skill with ease and confidence, even if it requires thought.

Mechanics: the rules of written language that make a sentence function clearly and correctly, such as spelling, punctuation, and capitalization.

Metacognition: awareness of one's own thought processes and the ability to adjust thinking according to the situation and the thinker's goals. Metacognition includes recognizing the difficulty of a task, knowing what resources to use, as well as knowing what can interfere with learning and taking steps to avoid those interferences.

Micro-Aggressions: the subtle, everyday slights or snubs, verbal or nonverbal, from one person to another (often directed to someone from a marginalized group) that make them feel inferior or offended. These often occur as derogatory statements or implications about a particular group. They can be intentional or unintentional. For example, if you assume that a student who is Hispanic or Asian is not American and ask them what country they are from, you could be committing a micro-aggression.

Mnemonics: techniques that help you memorize terms. For example, a student can create an acronym for a list of words he or she needs to remember. In grammar, a common mnemonic is FANBOYS (for, and, nor, but, or, yet, so), to help students remember coordinating conjunctions.

Motor: the parts of the brain and body associated with physical movement.

Neural: the parts of the brain and body that relate to the nerves or nervous system.

Neurons: nerve cells in the brain.

Norming: one of Bruce Tuckman's stages of team development during which group members agree to and understand their roles and agree on the work to be done and the steps to take to complete it.

Optimism Bias: another of several errors in reasoning our brains make (known as "cognitive biases"), it is the tendency to expect positive results and positive experiences and that negative outcomes are not likely, so the individual does not plan for them. In other words, it's the "it won't happen to me" syndrome.

Peer Review: college students are often placed in peer groups to review one another's work. During a peer review, students offer feedback to each other on ways to improve their assignment, help each other with difficult concepts, and give praise on aspects that are working well. (see also "critique")

Performance Anxiety: the stress and anxiousness that arises from the fear that you will not do well, such as on a test, during an athletic event, or while giving a presentation.

Performing: one of Bruce Tuckman's stages of team development during which group members have learned to trust each other, communicate well, make decisions easily, resolve conflict, and keep track of the work completed and the work yet to be done.

Personal Agency: the belief that you can control and affect the outcome of many of the situations you face. This involves taking responsibility for those things that can help you achieve goals, as well as the mistakes you make. It involves learning how to recognize potential obstacles and how to work around them.

Perspective: to see things in relation to other things. Each individual looks at a situation through their own lens, with their own viewpoint. This is their perspective. Many things can impact a person's perspective, such as their gender, race, age, environment, culture, economic status, education, life experiences, and so on.

Pessimistic: a negative attitude, one that looks at the "down side" or focuses primarily on reasons why failure is likely to happen or why an undesired event is likely to occur.

Poor Sport: someone who has difficulty accepting or admitting failure or defeat. Often, when people wish to appear smart and capable at a task or subject, they have difficulty accepting their own poor performance when it occurs. They may lie about the results, blame the errors on others, or even cheat to succeed.

Practical Exam: the same, or similar to, a procedural exam or skill-based exam. A practical exam involves a student physically demonstrating their knowledge of a skill.

Precise: being clear in how you complete a task in order to achieve the desired result. In written communication, it means understanding that your words alone are responsible for explanation and that their intended meaning must be understood. It also means spelling correctly.

Procedural Knowledge: knowing *how* something is done, such as the method or steps you might take to solve a math problem or conduct an experiment. (see also "declarative knowledge")

Process: as a verb, this means to deal with something according to a certain procedure, such as sorting, storing, organizing, distributing, or otherwise handling the material. When you receive new information or stimuli, your brain undergoes a processing of that material, whatever it may be. In an academic setting, you process information by seeing and hearing the information, making sense of it, encoding it in your brain, and then retrieving it as you need it.

Procrastination: putting an assignment or other task off longer than you should or longer than is beneficial, usually because you consider the job unpleasant or difficult.

Professional: a more formal approach to communication in words and self-presentation. In written communication, this means language that avoids slang and is respectful, clear, and grammatically correct. In self-presentation, it depends on the setting. In a classroom, it could mean wearing clothes that are not offensive, revealing, or distracting. At an internship or job interview, professional may mean the use of industry specific lingo and dressing for the job.

Purpose: a sense of meaning in your life.

Purposeful: deliberate; completing something with the knowledge of what job you are doing and what you hope to gain. In communication, it can also mean clearly stating your purpose for the communication (what you need from the person or your intentions for communication).

Reappraisal Or Reframing: the act of consciously trying to look at an experience from a different perspective, usually to find a positive or neutral interpretation rather than a negative one.

Reflect: to look back on something with careful consideration.

Relationship Management: using self-regulation and social awareness to maintain a good relationship with another person or group, part of emotional intelligence. It is based on the understanding that relationships are important to success in most areas of life, different ones for different reasons.

Revise: to re-envision something. Not to be confused with editing, which involves correction, revision involves making something more useful, effective, comprehendible, clear, or otherwise better for the reader or user.

Self-Efficacy: the belief that the actions you take can help you reach a particular outcome, that they'll be effective. Self-efficacy varies depending on the task. An experienced, well-practiced oboe-player will have high self-efficacy about oboe-playing, but may not have any self-efficacy when it comes to teaching first grade, especially if they have not had much interaction with children.

Self-Regulation: managing your emotions and behavior in order to present yourself in a manner that fits the social situation and helps you be successful or functional in that environment; controlling which persona you use rather than your emotions controlling you.

SMART Goals: a method of goal-setting that focuses on setting goals that are Specific (describe an action), Measurable, Achievable, Relevant, and Time-based.

Social Awareness: the ability to know or gauge how to behave in different social situations and environments.

Social Comparison: the act of comparing one's traits, skills, and abilities to another's.

Spatial: the parts of the brain or body that relate to someone's ability to perceive depth, size, distance, and location in relation to other objects.

Stereotype: a generalization made about an individual or group of people based on a history of observations that may or may not be true. For example, a common stereotype is that women are better caregivers than men, which is not always true. Stereotypes tend to lump people into categories by appearance, gender, race, or culture rather than by facts relating to the individual.

Stereotype Threat: the belief that certain stereotypes are true and that if you fall under such a stereotype that you may not be able to be successful at certain tasks. For example, if a woman believes that she is not as capable of changing the oil in a car as a man, she may experience more anxiety over the task, even make more mistakes, because of the stereotype threat.

Stoichiometry: a section of chemistry that involves using relationships between reactants and/or products in a chemical reaction to determine desired quantitative data.

Storming: one of Bruce Tuckman's stages of team development during which a group begins to establish roles and goals but with confusion and often misunderstanding.

Syllabus/Syllabi: a document provided to the class that discusses the purpose of the course, important contact and resource information, and a set of guidelines, expectations, or rules the student is expected to follow to be successful. This usually includes a discussion of how to submit assignments, how grading and late work is handled, and often the types of assignments the students will complete during the term. Syllabi is the plural form of syllabus.

Synapse: the small gap between nerve cells across which nerve impulses cannot cross. Neurotransmitters carry the information across the synapses.

Synthesize: to gather information, often from multiple sources or locations, understand it, analyze it, combine it with your prior knowledge and develop a new concept or creation with it.

Taxonomy: a classification system.

Unconscious Competence: doing things successfully without having to think about it. The skill becomes automatic.

Unconscious Incompetence: not knowing how much you don't know about a subject and having no idea how much you need to learn.

Visual: the parts of the brain or body that relate to vision and images.

WOOP: a method for setting appropriate goals. It is an acronym for Wish, Outcome, Obstacle, and Plan. The goal-setter would begin by wishing (imagining) a goal they would like to accomplish. They would then envision the outcome if it's achieved, such as how they will feel or how their life will be. The person should then determine what obstacles might hinder them from achieving their goals and whether or not the goal is achievable. The final step is to plan out the actions that will be most effective against the obstacles.